# SEEKING THE
# HEART OF WISDOM

# SEEKING THE HEART OF WISDOM

*The Path of Insight Meditation*

Joseph Goldstein & Jack Kornfield

SHAMBHALA

DEDICATED TO OUR TEACHERS,

OUR COLLEAGUES,

AND OUR STUDENTS

FOR THE DHARMA WE HAVE LEARNED

FROM ALL OF THEM

Shambhala Publications, Inc.
2129 13th Street
Boulder, Colorado 80302
www.shambhala.com

Cover art: naphoart naphoart/iStock
Cover design: Erin Seaward-Hiatt

9   8   7   6   5   4   3   2   1

*Printed in the United States of America*

Shambhala Publications makes every effort to print on acid-free, recycled paper.
Shambhala Publications is distributed worldwide by
Penguin Random House, Inc., and its subsidiaries.

THE LIBRARY OF CONGRESS CATALOGUES THE ORIGINAL EDITION
OF THIS BOOK AS FOLLOWS:
Goldstein, Joseph 1944–
Seeking the heart of wisdom.
Includes index.
1. Meditation (Buddhism)   1. Kornfield, Jack,
1945–  .  II. Title.
BQ5612.G643   1987   294.3'443   87-9710
ISBN 978-0-87773-327-0 (pbk.)
ISBN 978-1-57062-805-4 (Shambhala Classics)
ISBN 978-1-64547-291-9 (pbk.: 2024 ed.)

# CONTENTS

# PREFACE

*Seeking the Heart of Wisdom* was born out of the authors' long collaboration in teaching vipassana meditation retreats throughout the world. These intensive retreats, ranging in length from weekends to three months, provide opportunities for a simple and direct investigation of the mind and body. Through the development of concentrated awareness, insight into the changing nature of phenomena deepens in a very personal and immediate way. This, in turn, leads to an understanding of the causes of suffering in ourselves and others and to the possibility of compassion and genuine freedom.

The book offers a clear explanation of the meditation instructions and exercises that are given on retreats. While its flavor and emphasis are drawn from silent retreat practice, the teachings are also set in a broad context that makes meditation practice meaningful and relevant in our lives. These teachings are strongly rooted in the Buddhist tradition, especially as it has developed and flowered in Thailand and Burma. Two of the main lineages that have been interwoven throughout the book are the forest monastic tradition of Ven. Achaan Chaa and the practice of intensive satipathana vipassana meditation as taught by the late Ven. Mahasi Sayadaw. Together they help to provide the breadth of perspective and depth of understanding that characterize the wisdom of the Buddha.

Readers who desire information about Buddhist insight meditation retreats and teaching worldwide may contact the Insight Meditation Society, Pleasant Street, Barre, MA 01005 (*www.dharma.org*) or Spirit Rock Meditation Center, P.O. Box 909, Woodacre, CA 94973 (*www.spiritrock.org*).

# FOREWORD

We live in an era of remarkable material development, which has produced numerous benefits. However, it is clear that despite this progress human problems have not been entirely eliminated. Political and ideological conflicts prevail between nations, giving rise to war, violence, and oppression, while at the individual level people continue to experience fear, anxiety, and other forms of dissatisfaction. This indicates that material development alone is not sufficient; there is an urgent need for a corresponding inner, mental development. An excellent means for achieving this is meditation.

There are many varieties of meditation, but what they generally have in common are techniques for making the mind peaceful. Two of the features which distinguish Buddhist traditions of meditation are insight and compassion. The more we become familiar with the mind and come to realize impermanence, suffering, and selflessness in our own lives through meditation, the more we empathize with other sentient beings and the kind heart of compassion grows naturally within us. This is important both in the individual's pursuit of happiness and in his contributing to the peace of the world.

It is encouraging to find Westerners who have sufficiently assimilated traditions of the East to be able to share them with others, as the authors of this book are doing. May such efforts further the peace of all beings.

*The Dalai Lama*
McLeod Ganj
April 20, 1987

# ACKNOWLEDGMENTS

WE GRATEFULLY ACKNOWLEDGE the important assistance we received in completing this book from many good dharma friends: Andy Cooper for doing a massive editing job; Sharon Salzberg (our co-teacher and perennial inspiration in practice) for substantial editing and revision; Roger Wheeler for his initial encouragement to gather the material for this book and for his many constructive comments; Evelyn Sweeney (a most faithful dharma student) for typing and transcribing very many of our talks; Jeanne Bendik (former manager at IMS) for years of tape transcription work; Helen Parnell and Thea Snyder Lowry and Tom Lowry for the use of their homes and computer time; Timothy Sweeny, Sam Pett, and Ellen Mooney for word processing; Dan Drayson, Richard Getler, John Miller, and Wicki Sedgwick for computer assistance; Jean Conlogue and Patricia Masters for retyping much of the manuscript; Nancy Brown for her assistance; Liana and Caroline for their patient support; and Shambhala Publications, Sam, Larry, and Emily for the paramita (perfection) of ksanti (patience).

We thank the following for permission to reprint material copyrighted or controlled by them: the Kwanum Zen School for permission to quote the poem by Seung Sahn; Columbia University Press for permission to reprint "Starlight and Non-Being" from Watson, *The Basic Writings of Chuang Tzu*, © 1964 Columbia University Press; the Lama Foundation and Sasaki-roshi for Sasaki-roshi's poem from *Buddha Is the Center of Gravity*, © 1974 Lama Foundation; the Hanuman Foundation for "Please Call Me by My True Names" by Thich Nhat Hanh, © 1983 by Thich Nhat Hanh, reprinted from Thich Nhat Hanh, *Being Peace* (Berkeley, Calif.: Parallax Press, 1987); John

Weatherhill, Inc., for the four poems by Ryokan from *One Robe, One Bowl*, trans. John Stevens, © 1977 John Weatherhill, Inc.; Farrar, Straus & Giroux and Jonathan Cape Ltd. for "Keeping Quiet" by Pablo Neruda from *Extravagaria*, translation © 1969, 1970, 1972 by Alastair Reid.

# PART ONE

# Understanding Practice

# I

# Discovering the
# Heart of Meditation

IT IS SAID that soon after his enlightenment, the Buddha passed a man on the road who was struck by the extraordinary radiance and peacefulness of his presence. The man stopped and asked, "My friend, what are you? Are you a celestial being or a god?"

"No," said the Buddha.

"Well, then, are you some kind of magician or wizard?"

Again the Buddha answered, "No."

"Are you a man?"

"No."

"Well, my friend, what then are you?"

The Buddha replied, "I am awake."

The name Buddha means "one who is awake," and it is this experience that is the very heart and essence of vipassana, or insight meditation. It offers a way of practice that can open us to see clearly our bodies, our hearts, our minds, and the world around us and develop a wise and compassionate way to relate to and understand them all. This practice of insight meditation comes from the original core of the Buddha's teachings as transmitted for 2,500 years in the Theravada tradition of southern Asia. But it is not an "Asian" practice. It is a practice by which anyone can awaken to the truth of life and become free.

## RIGHT UNDERSTANDING

The path of awakening begins with a step the Buddha called right understanding. Right understanding has two parts. To start with, it asks a question of our hearts. What do we really

3

value, what do we really care about in this life? Our lives are quite short. Our childhood goes by very quickly, then adolescence and adult life go by. We can be complacent and let our lives disappear in a dream, or we can become aware. In the beginning of practice we must ask what is most important to us. When we're ready to die, what will we want to have done? What will we care about most? At the time of death, people who have tried to live consciously ask only one or two questions about their life: Did I learn to live wisely? Did I love well? We can begin by asking them now.

This is the beginning of right understanding: looking at our lives, seeing that they are impermanent and fleeting, and taking into account what matters to us most deeply. In the same way, we can look at the world around us, where there is a tremendous amount of suffering, war, poverty, and disease. Hundreds of millions of people are having a terrible, terrible time in Africa and Central America and India and Southeast Asia and even right here in North America. What does the world need to foster a safe and compassionate existence for all? Human suffering and hardship cannot be alleviated just by a simple change of government or a new monetary policy, although these things may help. On the deepest level, problems such as war and starvation are not solved by economics and politics alone. Their source is prejudice and fear in the human heart—and their solution also lies in the human heart. What the world needs most is people who are less bound by prejudice. It needs more love, more generosity, more mercy, more openness. The root of human problems is not a lack of resources but comes from the misunderstanding, fear, and separateness that can be found in the hearts of people.

Right understanding starts by acknowledging the suffering and difficulties in the world around us as well as in our own lives. Then it asks us to touch what we really value inside, to find what we really care about, and to use that as the basis of our spiritual practice. When we see that things are not quite right in the world and in ourselves, we also become aware of another possibility, of the potential for us to open to greater loving-kindness and a deep intuitive wisdom. From our heart comes inspiration for the spiritual journey. For some of us this will come as a sense of the great possibility of living in an awake and free way. Others of us are brought to practice as a way to come to terms with the power of suffering in our life. Some are inspired to seek understanding through a practice of discovery and inquiry, while some intuitively sense a connection with the divine or are inspired to practice as a way to open the heart more fully. Whatever brings us to spiritual practice can become a flame in our heart that guides and protects us and brings us to true understanding.

Right understanding also requires from us a recognition and understanding of the law of karma. Karma is not just a mystical idea about something esoteric like past lives in Tibet. The term *karma* refers to the law of cause and effect. It means that what we do and how we act create our future experiences. If we are angry at many people, we start to live in a climate of hate. People will get angry at us in return. If we cultivate love, it returns to us. It's simply how the law works in our lives.

Someone asked a vipassana teacher, Ruth Dennison, if she could explain karma very simply. She said, "Sure. Karma means you don't get away with *nothing*!" Whatever we do, however we act, creates how we become, how we will be, and how the world will be around us. To understand karma is wonderful because within this law there are possibilities of changing the direction of our lives. We can actually train ourselves and transform the climate in which we live. We can practice being more loving, more aware, more conscious, or whatever we want. We can practice in retreats or while driving or in the supermarket checkout line. If we practice kindness, then spontaneously we start to experience more and more kindness within us and from the world around us.

There's a story of the Sufi figure Mullah Nasruddin, who is both a fool and a wise man. He was out one day in his garden sprinkling bread crumbs around the flowerbeds. A neighbor came by and asked, "Mullah, why are you doing that?"

Nasruddin answered, "Oh, I do it to keep the tigers away."

The neighbor said, "But there aren't any tigers within thousands of miles of here."

Nasruddin replied, "Effective, isn't it?"

Spiritual practice is not a mindless repetition of ritual or prayer. It works through consciously realizing the law of cause and effect and aligning our lives to it. Perhaps we can sense the potential of awakening in ourselves, but we must also see that it doesn't happen by itself. There are laws that we can follow to actualize this potential. How we act, how we relate to ourselves, to our bodies, to the people around us, to our work, creates the kind of world we live in, creates our very freedom or suffering.

Over the years and throughout various cultures, many techniques and systems of Buddhist practice have been developed to bring this aspiration to fruition, but the essence of awakening is always the same: to see clearly and directly the truth of our experience in each moment, to be aware, to be mindful. This practice is a systematic development and opening of awareness called by the Buddha the four foundations of mindfulness: awareness of the body, awareness of feelings, awareness of mental phenomena, and awareness of truths, of the laws of experience.

To succeed in the cultivation of mindfulness, said the Buddha, is the highest benefit, informing all aspects of our life. "Sandalwood and tagara are delicately scented and give a little fragrance, but the fragrance of virtue and a mind well trained rises even to the gods."

How are we to begin? *The Path of Purification*, an ancient Buddhist text and guide, was written in answer to a short poem:

> The world is entangled in a knot.
> Who can untangle the tangle.

It is to untangle the tangle that we begin meditation practice. To disentangle ourselves, to be free, requires that we train our attention. We must begin to see how we get caught by fear, by attachment, by aversion—caught by suffering. This means directing attention to our everyday experience and learning to listen to our bodies, hearts, and minds. We attain wisdom not by creating ideals but by learning to see things clearly, as they are.

What is meditation? It's a good question. There is no shortage of descriptions, theories, manuals, texts, and ideas about it. There are hundreds of schools of meditation, which include prayer, reflection, devotion, visualization, and myriad ways to calm and focus the mind. Insight meditation (and other disciplines like it) is particularly directed to bringing understanding to the mind and heart. It begins with a training of awareness and a process of inquiry in ourselves. From this point of view, asking, "What is meditation?" is really the same as asking, "What is the mind?" or "Who am I?" or "What does it mean to be alive, to be free?"—questions about the fundamental nature of life and death. We must answer these questions in our own experience, through a discovery in ourselves. This is the heart of meditation.

It is a wonderful thing to discover these answers. Otherwise, much of life is spent on automatic pilot. Many people pass through years of life driven by greed, fear, aggression, or endless grasping after security, affection, power, sex, wealth, pleasure, and fame. This endless cycle of seeking is what Buddhism calls samsara. It is rare that we take time to understand this life that we are given to work with. We're born, we grow older, and eventually we die; we enjoy, we suffer, we wake, we sleep—how quickly it all slips away. Awareness of the suffering involved in this process of life, of being born, growing old, and dying, led the Buddha to question deeply how it comes about and how we can find freedom. That was the Buddha's question. That is where he began his practice. Each of us has our own way of posing this question. To understand ourselves and our life is the point of insight meditation: to understand and to be free.

There are several types of understanding. One type comes from reading the words of others. We have all read and stored away an enormous amount of information, even about spiritual matters. Although this kind of understanding is useful, it is still someone else's experience. Similarly there is the understanding that comes from being told by someone wise or experienced: "It's this way, friend." That too can be useful.

There is a deeper understanding based on our own consideration and reflection: "I've seen this through thoughtful analysis. I understand how it works." A tremendous amount can be known through thought. But is there a level deeper than that? What happens when we begin to ask the most fundamental questions about our lives? What is love? What is freedom? These questions cannot be answered by secondhand or intellectual ways of understanding. What the Buddha discovered, and what has been rediscovered by generation after generation of those who have practiced his teachings in their lives, is that there is a way to answer these difficult and wonderful questions. They are answered by an intuitive, silent knowing, by developing our own capacity to see clearly and directly.

How are we to begin? Traditionally, this understanding grows through the development of three aspects of our being: a ground of conscious conduct, a steadiness of the heart and mind, and a clarity of vision or wisdom.

### CONSCIOUS CONDUCT: THE FIVE TRAINING PRECEPTS

The first aspect, conscious conduct or virtue, means acting harmoniously and with care toward the life around us. For spiritual practice to develop, it is absolutely essential that we establish a basis of moral conduct in our lives. If we are engaged in actions that cause pain and conflict to ourselves and others, it is impossible for the mind to become settled, collected, and focused in meditation; it is impossible for the heart to open. To a mind grounded in unselfishness and truth, concentration and wisdom develop easily.

The Buddha outlined five areas of basic morality that lead to a conscious life. These training precepts are given to all students who wish to follow the path of mindfulness. They are not given as absolute commandments; rather, they are practical guidelines to help us live in a more harmonious way and develop peace and power of mind. As we work with them, we discover that they are universal precepts that apply to any culture, in any time. They are a part of basic mindfulness practice and can be cultivated in our spiritual life.

The first precept is to refrain from killing. It means honoring all life, not acting out of hatred or aversion in such a way as to cause harm to any living creature. We work to develop a reverence and caring for life in all its forms. In the Eightfold Path this is called one aspect of right action.

Even though it sounds obvious, we still manage to forget it. There was a cartoon in the *New Yorker* magazine some years ago during the hunting season. One deer turns to the other and says, "Why don't they thin their own goddamn herds?" We get into formulating excuses: "Well, there are too many deer." As we become more conscious and connected with life, it becomes clear that we shouldn't harm others, because it hurts us to kill. And they don't like it; even the tiniest creatures don't wish to die. So in practicing this precept we learn to stop creating pain for others and pain for ourselves.

The second precept asks us to refrain from stealing, meaning not to take what is not ours. Not to steal is called basic non-harming. We need to let go of being greedy and not take too much. More positively, it means to use things with sensitivity and care, to develop our sense of sharing this life, this planet. To live, we need plants, we need animals, and we need insects. This whole world has to share its resources. It is a boat of a certain size with so many beings living on it. We're connected with the bees and the insects and the earthworms. If there weren't earthworms to aerate the soil, and if there weren't any bees to pollinate the crops, we'd starve. We need bees, we need insects. We're all interwoven. If we can learn to love the earth, we can be happy whatever we do, with a happiness born of contentment. This is the source of genuine ecology. It's a source of world peace, when we see that we're not separate from the earth but that we all come out of it and are connected with one another. From this sense of connectedness we can commit ourselves to share, to live a life of helpfulness and generosity for the world. To cultivate generosity directly is another fundamental part of living a spiritual life. Like the training precepts and like our inner meditations, generosity can actually be practiced. With practice, its spirit forms our actions, and our hearts will grow stronger and lighter. It can lead us to new levels of letting go and great happiness. The Buddha emphasized the importance of generosity when he said, "If you knew what I know about the power of giving, you would not let a single meal pass without sharing it in some way."

Traditionally there are described three kinds of giving, and we are encouraged to begin developing generosity at whatever level we find it arising in our heart. At first we find tentative giving. This is where we take an object and think, "Well, I'm probably not going to use this anyway. Maybe I should give it away. No, I should save it for next year. No, I'll give it away." Even this level is positive. It creates some joy for us and it helps someone else. It's a sharing and a connecting.

The next level of generosity to discover is friendly giving. It's like relating to a brother or sister. "Please share what I have; enjoy this as I do." Sharing openly of our time, our energy, the things we have, feels even better. It's lovely to do. The fact is that we do not need a lot of possessions to be happy. It is our relationship to this changing life that determines our happiness or sorrow. Happiness comes from the heart.

The third level of giving is kingly or queenly giving. It's where we take something—our time or our energy or an object that is the best we have—and give it to someone happily and say, "Please, would you enjoy this too." We give to the other person and take our joy in that sharing. This level of giving is a beautiful thing to learn.

As we start to learn to be more generous, to give more of our time, our energy, our goods, our money, we can find a way to do it not just to fit a self-image or please an external authority, but because it is a source of genuine happiness in our lives. Of course this doesn't mean giving everything away. That would be excessive, because we have to be compassionate and care for ourselves as well. Yet to understand the power of practicing this kind of openness is very special. It is a privilege to be able to bring this generosity into our lives.

The third precept of conscious conduct is to refrain from false speech. The Eightfold Path calls this right speech. Don't lie, it says. Speak only what is true and useful; speak wisely, responsibly, and appropriately. Right speech really poses a question. It asks us to be aware of how we actually use the energy of our words. We spend so much of our lives talking and analyzing and discussing and gossiping and planning. Most of this talk is not very conscious or aware. It is possible to use speech to become awake. We can be mindful of what we are doing when we speak, of what the motivation is and how we are feeling. We can also be mindful in listening. We can align our speech to the principles of what is truthful and what is most kind or helpful. In practicing mindfulness we can begin to understand and discover the power of speech.

Once a master was called to heal a sick child with a few words of prayer. A skeptic in the crowd observed it all and expressed doubts about such a superficial way of healing. The master turned to him and said, "You know nothing of these matters; you are an ignorant fool!" The skeptic became very upset. He turned red and shook with anger. Before he could gather himself to reply, however, the master spoke again, asking, "When one word has the power to make you hot and angry, why should not another word have the power to heal?"

Our speech is powerful. It can be destructive or enlightening, idle gossip or compassionate communication. We are asked to be mindful and let our speech come from the heart. When we speak what is true and helpful, people are attracted to us. To be mindful and honest makes our minds quieter and more open, our hearts happier and more peaceful.

The fourth precept, to refrain from sexual misconduct, reminds us not to act out of sexual desire in such a way as to cause harm to another. It requires that we be responsible and honest in sexual relations. Sexual energy is very powerful. In these times of rapidly changing relationships and sexual values, we are asked to become conscious of our use of this power. If we associate this energy in our lives with grasping and greed, exploitation and compulsion, we will perform actions that bring harm to ourselves and others, such as adultery. There is great suffering consequent to these actions and great joy in the simplicity that comes in their absence.

The spirit of this precept asks us to look at the motivation behind our actions. To pay attention in this way allows us (as laypeople) to discover how sexuality can be connected to the heart and how it can be an expression of love, caring, and genuine intimacy. We have almost all been fools at some time in our sexual life, and we have also used sex to try to touch what is beautiful, to touch another person deeply. Conscious sexuality is an essential part of living a mindful life.

To refrain from the heedless use of intoxicants is the fifth precept. It means to avoid taking intoxicants to the point of making the mind cloudy and to devote our lives instead to developing clarity and alertness. We have just one mind, so we must take care of it. In our country there are millions of alcoholics and others who have abused drugs. Their unconsciousness and fearful use of intoxicants has caused great pain to themselves, their families, and all those they touch. To live consciously is not easy—it means we often must face fears and pains that challenge our heart. Abuse of intoxicants is clearly not the way.

To enter the human realm, to establish a ground for spiritual life, requires that we bring awareness to all the actions in our world, to our use of intoxicants, our speech, to all of our actions. Establishing a virtuous and harmonious relationship to the world brings ease and lightness to the heart and steadfast clarity to the mind. A foundation of virtue brings great happiness and liberation in itself and is the precondition for wise mediation. With it we can be conscious and not waste the extraordinary opportunity of a human birth, the opportunity to grow in compassion and true understanding in our life.

## CONCENTRATION OF MIND

Out of a foundation of conscious conduct, the first steps of the mindful way, grows the second aspect of the path, which is called the development of samadhi, or steadiness and concentration of mind. As we bring the grace and harmony of virtue into our outer lives, so we can begin to establish an inner order, a sense of peace and clarity. This is the domain of formal meditation, and it begins with training the heart and mind in concentration. It means collecting the mind or bringing together the mind and body, focusing one's attention on one's experience in the present moment. Skill in concentrating and steadying the mind is the basis for all types of meditation and is in truth a basic skill for any endeavor, for art or athletics, computer programming or self-knowledge. In meditation, the development of the power of concentration comes through systematic training and can be done by using a variety of objects, such as the breath, visualization, a mantra, or a particular feeling such as loving-kindness. We will speak much more fully about the art of concentrating the mind in later chapters, since it is so important. Most fundamentally it is a simple process of focusing and steadying attention on an object like the breath and bringing the mind back to that object again and again. It requires that we let go of thoughts of the past and future, of fantasies and attachment, and bring the mind back to what is actually happening; the actual moment of feeling, of touching the breath as it is. Samadhi doesn't just come of itself; it takes practice. What is wonderful is the discovery made by the Buddha and all great yogis that the mind can actually be trained.

There is a sign outside a casino in Las Vegas that says, "You must be present to win." The same is true in meditation. If we want to see the nature of our lives, we must actually be present, aware, awake. Developing samadhi is much like polishing a lens. If we are looking to see the cells and workings of the body with a lens that has not been ground sufficiently, we will not see clearly. In order to penetrate the nature of the mind and body, we must collect and concentrate our resources and observe with a steady, silent mind. This is exactly what the Buddha did: he sat, concentrated his mind, and looked within. To become a yogi, an explorer of the heart and mind, we must develop this capacity as well.

## WISDOM

Built on the foundation of concentration is the third aspect of the Buddha's path of awakening: clarity of vision and the development of wisdom. In our lives there is much we don't see. We are too busy to see, or we forget or haven't learned about our capacity to see in new ways. Our steady and careful observation of the body, heart, and mind can bring about the growth of understanding and wisdom.

Wisdom comes from directly observing the truth of our experience. We learn as we become able to live fully in the moment, rather than being lost in the dreams, plans, memories, and commentaries of the thinking mind. There is a big difference between drinking a cup of tea while being there completely, and drinking a cup of tea while thinking about five other things. There is a big difference between taking a walk in the woods and really being there, and taking a walk and spending the whole time thinking about visiting Disneyland or what you are going to cook for dinner, or imagining all the stories you can tell your friends about what a great walk in the woods you had. It is only by being fully in the moment that the fundamental questions of the heart can be answered: it is only in the timeless moment that we can come to that intuitive, silent knowing of the truth. It is the intuitive wisdom that liberates us.

## INQUIRY AND OBSERVATION

Wisdom grows out of our clear seeing in each moment. Seeing the arising and passing of our experience and how we relate to it. It arises through our gentle and careful inquiry into the workings of the body and mind and through an open inquiry into how this body and mind relate to the whole world around us. For insight to develop, this spirit of observation and deep questioning must be kept in the forefront. We can collect and quiet the mind, but then we must observe, examine, see its way and its laws.

As we meditate we can learn more about desire, see what its root is, see whether it is pleasant or painful, see how it arises and affects our life. We can equally well observe moments of stillness and contentment. We can also begin to observe the inner workings of cause and effect, the laws of karma. Similarly, the law of impermanence can reveal itself under our attention, how it operates, and whether there is anything in our experience that does not change. As things change, we can also observe how attachment works and see how tension and grasping are created in our body and mind. We can see what closes our heart, and how it can open. Over time we may discover new levels of stillness in ourselves or find lights or visions or a whole array of new inner experiences. We can also discover our shadow and bring our awareness to the fears and pains and deep feelings we have long suppressed in our lives. Insights about the psychological patterns we live by will arise, and we can see the functioning of the level we call the personality. When we bring the same spirit of inquiry and awareness to our relation with the whole world around us, our observation can also show us the illusions of our boundaries and how to truly connect the inner and the outer.

Beyond these, our inquiry can lead us to most fundamental spiritual questions, the nature of our own self. If everything we see is changing, what can we identify in this process as ourself? We can see what concepts or body image or deep sense of self we hold as "me" or "mine," as who we are, and begin to question this whole structure. And perhaps, in deep stillness, we can come to that which goes beyond our limited sense of self, that which is silent and timeless and universal.

Wisdom is not one particular experience, nor a series of ideas or knowledge to be collected. It is an ongoing process of discovery that unfolds when we live with balance and full awareness in each moment. It grows out of our sincerity and genuine openness, and it can lead us to a whole new world of freedom.

Insight meditation is a path of discovery. It is straightforward and direct, with no frills or gimmicks. It is simple, though not easy. Although the forms vary, the genuine practice of insight meditation is this single quest: to establish a foundation of harmonious action, to collect and concentrate the mind and body, and to see the laws of life by our own true, careful, and direct observation. After understanding the way of practice and realizing that meditative life involves this whole process of awakening, there is only one thing left to do. We have to undertake it ourselves.

J. K.

EXERCISE

## Learning from the Precepts

Pick and refine one or more of the five basic training precepts as a way to cultivate and strengthen mindfulness. Work with a precept meticulously for one week. Then examine the results and choose another precept for a subsequent week. Here are some sample suggested ways to work with each precept.

1. *Refraining from killing: reverence for life.* Undertake for one week to purposefully bring no harm in thought, word, or deed to any living creature. Particularly become aware of any living beings in your world (people, animals, even plants) whom you ignore, and cultivate a sense of care and reverence for them too.
2. *Refraining from stealing: care with material goods.* Undertake for one week to act on every single thought of generosity that arises spontaneously in your heart.

3. *Refraining from false speech: speech from the heart.* Undertake for one week not to gossip (positively or negatively) or speak about anyone you know who is not present with you (any third party).
4. *Refraining from sexual misconduct: conscious sexuality.* Undertake for one week to observe meticulously how often sexual feelings and thoughts arise in your consciousness. Each time, note what particular mind states you find associated with them, such as love, tension, compulsion, caring, loneliness, desire for communication, greed, pleasure, aggression, and so forth.
5. *Refraining from the heedless use of intoxicants.* Undertake for one week or one month to refrain from all intoxicants and addictive substances (such as wine, marijuana, even cigarettes and/or caffeine if you wish). Observe the impulses to use these, and become aware of what is going on in the heart and mind at the time of those impulses.

# 2

# *Why Meditate?*

A QUESTION THAT ARISES for beginners in meditation and also, at times, for people with years of experience, is "Why do we practice? Why are we doing this?" The effort and commitment needed to pursue meditation is so demanding that it is appropriate to ask what value it has and where it is leading.

Meditation has to do with opening what is closed in us, balancing what is reactive, and exploring and investigating what is hidden. That is the why of practice. We practice to open, to balance, and to explore.

### OPENING WHAT IS CLOSED

What is it that is closed in us? Our senses are closed, our bodies are closed. We spend so much of our time lost in thought, in judgment, in fantasy, and in daydreams that we do not pay careful attention to the direct experience of our senses—to sight and sound, to smell and taste, to sensations of the body. Because our attention is often scattered, perceptions through the sense doors become clouded. But as awareness and concentration become stronger through meditation, we spend less time lost in thought, and there is a much greater sensitivity and refinement in our sense impressions.

We also begin to open the body. Often there is not a free flow of energy in the body, and as we direct our awareness inward, we experience in a very clear and intimate way the accumulated tensions, knots, and holdings that are present. There are several different kinds of painful feelings that we might experience, and learning to distinguish and relate to these feelings of discomfort or pain is an important part of meditation practice, because it is one of the very first things that we open to as our practice develops.

One kind of pain that we might experience is that of a danger signal. When we put our hand in fire and it starts to hurt, there is a clear message saying, "Take your hand out." There is a story of someone who was meditating in a little hut in the countryside and was sitting watching his breath, "rising, falling, rising, falling," and he began to smell smoke. He noted "smelling, smelling." It was not until he started noting "hot, hot" that he realized that some action was needed. It's helpful to know when things are a signal and when they're not. There is a kind of pain in the body that is a signal, that's telling us something, and these sensations should be recognized and respected.

There is another kind of pain, which can be called "dharma pain." These are the painful sensations that have accumulated in the body, those tensions, knots, and holdings that we carry around all the time but are mostly unaware of because our minds are distracted. As we sit and pay attention and become more inwardly silent, there is a growing awareness of these painful feelings. This is, in fact, a sign of progress, because we are becoming aware of what is always there but usually below the threshold of our sensitivity. What we want to do in meditation is to open to this dharma pain, to experience what is actually present.

As we watch painful feelings, the question arises of how we can distinguish the pain of a danger signal from the pain that appears naturally in our dharma practice. A simple guideline can generally be applied: if the pain goes away when you stand and do some walking, then the experience is not particularly a danger signal. It may be the discomfort of sitting in an unusual posture, or it may be the pain of accumulated tension. If it disappears when the posture is changed, then it's no problem and you can stay with it. If, however, the pain persists or grows, even after some walking, then it may be a sign that there's too much straining, that the posture is being forced in some way, and it might be better to change position or relax the posture.

What's most important in terms of learning how to open is the dharma pain, those unpleasant sensations which go away when we stand or walk, but which may become very intense in the sitting. It can come as strong pain in the back, knees, or some other parts of the body. What does the mind do with this pain that starts revealing itself to us? At early stages of practice, the tendency of the mind is to resist; we don't like to feel the pain. This resistance is a pushing away or closing off to the experience, just the opposite of opening to it.

There are different forms of resistance. One form is self-pity. We're feeling the pain, sitting with it for a short while, and then we start feeling sorry for ourselves: "Poor me. Everyone else is in a wonderful blissful state and only *my* knee hurts." It is easy to get lost in a spiral of self-pitying thoughts.

Another form of resistance is fear. We've often been conditioned to be afraid of pain. We're afraid to go into it and feel it, and that fear prevents us from opening, from allowing ourselves to experience what's there. It's helpful to notice whether this kind of resistance is present, to note the fear, to see it, and then to gently soften and open to the fear itself.

Sometimes fear of unpleasantness can take the form of preventive action even before the pain gets very uncomfortable. We do things so that the pain won't come—what could be called the "just in case" syndrome. There is a story related to this tendency of mind.

Some time ago I was sitting at a retreat in England. I would come down for breakfast in the morning, and every day we were served just the same thing: porridge, toast, fruit, and tea. The first day I came to breakfast and took some porridge, two pieces of toast, a piece of fruit, and a cup of tea. I ate everything except for one piece of toast, so I put the second piece back. The second morning I came down, and there was the same breakfast. I took my porridge, two pieces of toast, fruit, and tea. I ate everything, but one piece of toast was enough, so I put the other piece of toast back. The third morning I came down, the same breakfast, and I took the porridge, two pieces of toast, fruit, and tea. It took about a week until I could stop taking that second piece of toast, even when it was very clear that I wasn't going to eat it. There was that fear in the mind: "I'd better take it, just in case this time I'm hungry."

The "just in case" syndrome arises often in the mind. "I'll move now, just in case it gets too painful and I won't be able to stay with it," or "I'll go to sleep early tonight, just in case I'll be tired tomorrow." This kind of fear functions as a barrier to being with what is actually there, out of fear of what we think might be there if we persist: it is the unwillingness to be uncomfortable and feel pain.

There's self-pity, there's fear. Another kind of resistance, which is more subtle and which can be more undermining of our efforts, is apathy, or indifference to what is happening; in this state the mind becomes very uncaring. The noting or labeling becomes very mechanical, without vitality, and is often totally unrelated to what is going on. We may be noting "out" when the breath is coming in, or "in" when the breath is going out. An apathetic mind prevents us from being fully with our experience of the moment.

In this part of our meditation practice, in opening to what is closed, we have to recognize the different forms of resistance that may arise and to understand that at some time or another they will be present for almost everyone. There is no need to judge ourselves for being resistant; rather, we should just recognize the self-pity or fear or apathy, see these states, and remember that there is another possibility, one that has to do with opening, with becoming mindful. Instead of pushing away or closing off, we can soften ourselves, soften the mind, so that it becomes receptive and allowing, more gentle and relaxed. We don't have to be in a struggle, even with things that are painful. When we allow ourselves to be more relaxed and more open, the possibility arises of seeing more clearly exactly what is going on.

For example, if there's a certain pain in the back and we are busy resisting it or pushing it away or afraid of it, then there is no possibility of understanding the nature of that pain, the truth of that experience. If we soften and open, we discover that

"My back hurts" simply means that there are certain sensations going on. There may be tightness, pulling, stabbing, searing, burning, pressure. There is a long list of possible sensations.

When the mind is open, we are able to go from the level of "My back hurts," which is a concept, to the level of what is really happening, which are certain sensations, arising and passing. They may be very intense and unpleasant, but we are experiencing what is actually true about them. And we notice not only what the sensations are, but also how they behave. Often, when we resist painful feelings, we have the idea that there is some solid mass of pain in a part of the body. When we allow ourselves to feel the sensations that are there, when we go into them, then we begin to see that pain is not a solid mass but rather a field of vibration, characterized perhaps by tightness or burning or pressure. But what we see clearly is that there is nothing solid. We begin to experience this for ourselves and dissolve the illusion of solidity. As this happens in our practice, it begins a process of untying the energy knots and blocks in our system. We begin to allow for a freer flow of energy, which is very healing.

Learning how to work with the painful sensations that arise in our practice is essential. It is a gateway to deeper levels of understanding, and the very fact that we can become aware of these painful feelings is itself a sign of stronger attention. As we approach this gateway of understanding, we don't want to turn away. We enter deeper levels by being soft and gentle and aware of what is happening. This is how we begin to fulfill the first aspect of practice: opening what is closed. And it is this openness to experience that is the foundation for the second aspect of practice—balancing what is reactive.

### BALANCING WHAT IS REACTIVE

What is it that is reactive? Our minds are reactive: liking and disliking, judging and comparing, clinging and condemning. Our minds are like a balance scale, and as long as we're identified with these judgments and preferences, likes and dislikes, wants and aversions, our minds are continually thrown out of balance, caught in a tiring whirlwind of reactivity. It is through the power of mindfulness that we can come to a place of balance and rest. Mindfulness is that quality of attention which notices without choosing, without preference; it is a choiceless awareness that, like the sun, shines on all things equally.

Can we make our awareness so inclusive that we're willing to be attentive to the whole range of our experience? It's somewhat like going on a long journey in a strange land, a journey that takes us through many different kinds of terrain—through mountains and jungle, desert and rain forest. If we have the mind of a true explorer, when we're in the mountains we're not thinking, "Oh, if only I were in the desert now." And when we're in the desert we're not daydreaming of rain forests. If there's a real sense of exploration, we're interested in every new place that we come to.

The experience of our meditation is a similar kind of journey; it's the journey into ourselves through every aspect of our experience. There are ups and downs, highs and lows, time when it's pleasant and times of pain. There is nothing at all that is outside of our practice because our practice is to explore the totality of who we are. This takes a tremendous amount of willingness. Are we willing to be with the full range of what's going on?

There is a line from a song written some years ago that relates to this: "Some people say that life is strange, but what I'd like to know is, compared to what?" It's all part of it. There is nothing that is outside of our practice. The different experiences of physical sensation, of pleasure or pain, the different emotions of happiness or sadness, depression or elation, interest or boredom, all are part of the journey. Is it possible to open to each one of these states, to become mindful of each one in a balanced way so that we can begin to understand their true nature?

Meditation practice is neither holding on nor avoiding; it is a settling back into the moment, opening to what is there. And this balance of mind, where there's no preference, no attachment, no clinging or condemning, but just being present for whatever arises, makes possible a connection with a deep rhythm. Every activity has a certain rhythm to it. There are all the rhythms of nature, of night and day, the change of seasons. There is rhythm in music, sport, poetry, and dance. Every activity has a rhythm appropriate to it, and when we find that rhythm, a sense of effortlessness, ease, and grace arises.

There is also a rhythm in our practice, an inner rhythm to the breath, sensations, thoughts, emotions, feelings, images, and sounds. When we are nonreactive, when we open and note just what's happening in each moment, without holding on, without pushing away, without struggle, then we find this inner rhythm. And when we experience this, we begin to enjoy a certain ease and effortlessness in practice.

In order to find the rhythm, however, a great effort is needed. It's the effort to pay attention, to bring the mind into each moment. In the beginning the mind is scattered, so we have to make an effort to contain and focus it. But as we do this, moment after moment, at times everything will click and we find the balance. It's like learning to ride a bicycle; we get on and pedal and at first are continually falling off one side or the other, until in one moment, the sense of balance is established, and then it's easy. Meditation develops in the same way. It takes effort to be mindful in each moment so that the rhythm can be discovered. In every moment of mindfulness, whatever the object is, whether it is the breath, sensations or sounds, thoughts or emotions, in every moment of simply noting and noticing what's there, there's no reactivity in the mind. There's no clinging and no condemning, just an accepting awareness of what's present. Every moment of mindfulness is helping to establish oneself in this inner balance and rhythm.

## EXPLORING WHAT IS HIDDEN

The third aspect of meditation is to investigate or reveal what is hidden. What is hidden is the true nature of our experience. The truth is what is hidden. One of the main ways the truth is camouflaged is through our identification with and tendency to be lost in concepts. To a large extent, we confuse our ideas about things for the experience itself. A very essential part of meditation practice is going from the level of concept to the level of direct experience.

What are some examples of this confusion between concept and reality? If someone holds up his or her hand and asks what we see, most likely we would say, "A hand." Actually, though, we don't see a hand at all. What the eye sees is color and form and light and shadow, and then the mind jumps in and quickly puts a concept on that constellation of perception. We call it "hand," and we think that this is what we are really seeing.

If a bell is rung, what do we hear? Most people hear a "bell," or if there's a noise outside, we might say that we hear a car or a truck going by. But that's not what we hear. We hear certain sounds, certain vibrations, and then immediately the mind names it as "bell," "car," "truck," or "person." We confuse the concepts of the thinking mind with the reality of direct experience.

"My knee hurts." Sit for an hour and pain arises and the knee hurts. But "knee" is a concept. There is no sensation called "knee" or "back" or "muscle." That's not what we feel. We feel tightness, pressure, hardness, softness, tingling. These sensations are what we experience. "Knee," "back," and "muscle" are all concepts.

Why is this so important? The distinction between our concepts and the reality of experience is crucial in terms of understanding where the practice is leading, because concepts cover what is true. The concepts we have of things remain the same. The names that we give to things don't change. My "knee" hurt yesterday, my "knee" hurts today, and it will probably hurt the next time I sit. Not only do we solidify the sense of "knee" through our concept, as if it were something more or less permanent, but this sense of its being static or permanent also makes it much easier for us to identify with it as being "I" or "mine." Now, not only is there a "knee" that hurts, it is "my knee."

When we come to what is truly happening, however, we see that the experience is changing every instant. Things do not stay the same even for two moments. What we are conceiving of as "my knee" is in the reality of direct experience a mass of instantaneously changing sensations, with no solidity or permanence at all. But as long as we stay on the concept level, we are unable to see or understand this momentary nature of phenomena.

Our meditation begins to investigate what is hidden. We go from the level of concept to the level of direct experience, whether it's bodily sensations or sight or sound or smell or taste; we begin to experience the nature and process of thoughts and emotions, rather than being identified with their contents. As we connect with what we are experiencing in each moment, we begin to discover some things that may have been previously hidden or obscure.

First, we discover that everything is changing, that everything we thought was solid, unchanging, or permanent is in a state of flux. People may hear this and think, "I know that everything is impermanent. It doesn't sound so startling to me." It's true that we know it intellectually, but we don't know it deeply, viscerally, we don't know it from the inside out. Meditation is a vehicle for opening to the truth of this impermanence on deeper and deeper levels. Every sensation, every thought, every feeling, every sound, every taste—*everything*, inside and outside, is in a state of continual dissolution.

When we see that, when we really know it, that understanding deconditions grasping in the mind, deconditions our attachments. Have you even gone to a stream and tried to grasp a bubble in the water with the hope of holding on to it? Probably not, because you clearly know that it's just a bubble, arising and dissolving. Everything is like that. It is possible to see this, to experience it in a deeply integrated way. When we develop this clarity of vision and understanding, then the mind is much less inclined to grasp, because we see that there is nothing to hold on to. And as we are less attached, less grasping, less clinging, there is also less suffering in our lives.

As we see the impermanence of things, we also begin to understand the truth of the basic insecurity about all phenomena. Things are insecure or unsatisfactory in the sense that something that is always changing is incapable of giving us a lasting sense of completion or fulfillment. When we see this deeply in ourselves, it also begins to decondition the strong forces of desire and grasping in the mind. We begin to let go, allowing for the inevitable flow of change, rather than trying to hold on to something, thinking that it will make us happy forever after.

We see the impermanence, we see the insecurity. And we begin to understand what is the unique jewel of the Buddha's enlightenment—insight into the selflessness of the whole process of mind and body, understanding that there is no one behind it to whom it is happening. There is no one to whom this changing process belongs, there is no owner of it. This is a subtle and radical transformation of our normal way of understanding, and it develops into a deep wisdom as we go from the level of concept to the level of direct experience. When we understand in a very intuitive and connected way the essential insubstantiality, emptiness, and selflessness of phenomena, we begin to weaken the fundamental attachment we have to the sense of "I," of "self," of "me," of "mine," those concepts around which our whole lives have revolved. We see that this "I" is an illusion, a concept that we've created, and we start the journey of integrating the possibility of greater freedom in our lives.

It's only by paying careful attention in each moment to what is true, not to our ideas about it, but to what is actually there, that we are able to know for ourselves in a deeply transforming way the impermanence, insecurity, and selflessness that characterize all our experience.

### EFFORT AND AIM

How to do all this? How to open what is closed, balance what is reactive, and investigate what is hidden? What are the tools of our practice? Two qualities are at the root of all meditation development: right effort and right aim—arousing effort to aim the mind toward the object. Effort and aim. Everything else will come. If there is the effort to aim the mind correctly, then mindfulness, concentration, calm, equanimity, wisdom, and compassion will all follow.

For example, we sit and make the effort to aim the mind toward the breath, either the in and out at the nose or the rise and fall of the abdomen. If there is enough effort and energy, and the aim is correct, then we connect with the sensations of the rise and fall or the in and out; we become mindful of the specific sensations and how they're behaving, and from this our concentration grows and our understanding deepens.

All this is best accomplished with a sense of lightness and willingness, from a place of interest in discovering what is true. If we try to practice from a feeling of obligation or duty, then the mind often becomes rebellious and grim. Mindfulness does not mean grimness, although sometimes in the beginning of meditation practice people may confuse the two.

An image which might suggest the proper quality of right aim and right effort is the Japanese tea ceremony. Every movement is done with extreme care and precision. In the folding of the napkin or the pouring of the tea, there are many separate, distinct movements, and each is done with the same care and attention. They are done with delicacy, lightness, and grace.

Can we make our day, or part of a day, a Japanese tea ceremony, so that every movement—reaching, bending, turning—becomes a ceremony? When we practice in this way, or even practice practicing like this, then it is encouraging and inspiring to see how powerfully and quickly the awareness and understanding deepen and grow.

J. G.

EXERCISE

# Concepts and Reality

One of the most important aspects of meditation practice is going from the level of concept to the level of direct experience. In order to understand this more fully, sit quietly for a few moments, letting one hand rest lightly on the other. What do you experience? Perhaps there is the thought "I experience my hands or fingers touching." There might be a mental image or picture of hands as they rest on your lap. There may also be the awareness of different sensations such as pressure, warmth, and tingling. If you can feel quite precisely and accurately the sensations that are present in this moment of awareness, what happens to the thought or image of "hand"? You might try doing this exercise with closed eyes. Please take some time to investigate and distinguish different levels of experience.

When you walk, what are you aware of in each step? Is there an image of the form of the foot or leg? Can you feel the different sensations in the movement? What are they? What happens to the image as you feel the sensations? What happens to the sensations themselves?

Both in times of formal practice and in everyday life, practice distinguishing the level of concept from the level of bare experience.

# 3
## *Meditation Instructions*

Keep your attention clearly focused on the sensations and feelings of each breath. Be with the breath at the place in the body where you feel it most clearly and distinctly—the rising and falling of the abdomen, the movement of the chest, or the in and out at the nostrils. See how carefully and continuously you can feel the sensations of the entire inhalation and exhalation, or the entire rising-and-falling movement.

Use a soft mental notation of "rise" and "fall" or "in" and "out" with each breath. If there is a pause or space between the breaths, be aware of some touch point, either the buttocks on the cushion, the knees on the floor, or the lips as they gently touch each other, feeling accurately the particular sensations at that point. If there's a long pause between breaths, you can be aware of several touch sensations in succession until the next breath begins to come by itself, without hurrying or hastening the breathing process. When the next breath arrives, return the attention to the breathing, noting and noticing as carefully as possible.

Be aware and mindful of each breath, the rising and falling movement of the chest or abdomen, or the in and out of the air at the nostrils. Let the awareness be soft and relaxed, letting the breath come and go in its own rhythm. Feel the sensations of each breath accurately, not looking for anything in particular, but simply noticing what is actually there in each moment.

Sometimes the breath will be clear and sometimes indistinct, sometimes strong, sometimes very soft; it may be long or short, rough or smooth. Be with it as it reveals itself, aware of how it goes through various changes.

When sounds become predominant and call your attention away from the breathing, make a note of "hearing, hearing," focusing the attention and the awareness on the experience of the sound, not particularly getting involved in the concept of what's causing the sound, such as "car" or "wind," but just being with the vibration of hearing. See if you can experience the difference between the concept of the sound and the direct intuitive experience of it. Make a note of "hearing," and when it's no longer predominant or calling your attention, come back to the breath.

Often sounds will arise in the background of your awareness: that is, you are aware of them, but they're not particularly calling your attention away from the breath. In that case, there's no need to particularly make a mental note of "hearing." Simply stay with the noting of the breath, allowing the background awareness of sound simply to be there.

The continuity of attention and of mental noting strengthens the mindfulness and concentration. And so, with a gentleness of mind, make the effort to be as continuous in the noting as possible. When you go off, when you forget, when the mind wanders, make a note of "wandering" as soon as you're aware of it and come back to the breathing.

When sensations in the body become predominant and call your attention away from the breathing, focus all of the mindfulness, all of the attention onto that sensation itself. See how carefully you can observe and feel the quality of the sensation: is it hardness or softness, heat or cold, vibration, tingling, burning, pulling, tightness? Feel what the sensation is and notice as accurately as possible what happens to that sensation as you observe it. Does it get stronger, does it get weaker, does it dissolve, does it enlarge in size, does it get smaller?

Sometimes it may be difficult to find an exact word to describe the sensation. Don't spend much time thinking about it. If you can't find the right word intuitively in the moment, even a mental note of "sensation" or "feeling" will serve the purpose.

The awareness is most important. The noting is simply an

aid in aiming the mind accurately toward the object in order to feel what the sensation is and to notice what happens to it as you observe it. For example, there may be a strong pain in the back or the knees. The mind attends to it, and it feels like burning. Notice that it's burning. As you watch it, you may notice that it gets stronger or weaker, expands in area or contracts. Sometimes it may disappear.

When the sensation is no longer predominant, return again to the in and out or rising and falling. Try to keep a balance in the mind of staying soft and relaxed, that quality of being settled back in the moment, and at the same time being alert and precise. Note carefully and gently moment after moment whatever object arises, coming back to the breath as the primary object when nothing else is predominant or calling the mind away.

Also notice any reactions in the mind to the different sensations. If you're observing painful feelings and you notice a reaction of aversion or restlessness or fear, make a note of those mind states, observing them carefully and seeing what happens to them as you note them. As you note "fear" or "aversion" or "restlessness," does it get stronger, does it get weaker, does it disappear? If you're observing pleasant sensations in the body and there's enjoyment or attachment, note that also.

There's no need to go looking for different objects. Keep the awareness very simple, staying grounded in the primary object of the breath, and then notice these different objects as they arise in their own time. The idea in practice is not to look for anything special and not to try to make anything special happen; rather it is to notice carefully what it is that is actually happening.

When thoughts arise in the mind, as soon as you become aware that you're thinking, make a soft mental note of "thinking" or "wandering." Sometimes you'll be aware of thoughts just in the moment of their arising, sometimes in the middle. Sometimes the mind won't be aware of the thought until it is completed. Notice when it is that you have become aware of thinking, without judgment or evaluation. At whatever point the mind becomes aware, make the note of "thinking" and then gently come back to the breathing. There need not be any struggle or conflict with the thought process; simply note it at whatever point you become aware.

Likewise, if images or pictures arise in the mind, make a note of "seeing"; if sounds become predominant, make a note of "hearing." Let the awareness come out of a receptivity of mind, settling back in a soft and open way. As different objects of experience reveal themselves, be mindful and attentive to each object, and notice what happens to it as it is observed.

Sometimes the mind may get confused by too many objects or isn't clearly aware of where to focus. At that time make a note of that kind of confusion or uncertainty and return to the breath as an anchor. The breathing is useful as the primary object because for the most part it's always present. So one can always come back to the breath, settling into it, feeling it, noticing it. When the mind feels centered with the breathing, again notice the different objects that may arise.

When different mind states and emotions become predominant, they too should be made the objects of awareness. If we're not aware of them when they arise, they become unconscious filters on our experience and we begin to view everything through the filter of a particular emotion. Sometimes they may come associated with thoughts or images or with certain sensations in the body. There may be feelings of happiness or sadness, frustration, anger, annoyance, joy, interest, excitement, restlessness, or fear. Many different kinds of mind states may arise.

As soon as you become aware that some mind state or emotion or mood is in the mind, make a specific note of that particular state of mind, so as not to get lost in it and not to be identified with it. These mind states, like all other objects, are arising and passing away. They are not "I," not self, and do not belong to anyone. Note the mind state, be open to the experience of it, and when it's no longer predominant, return to the breath or to sensations in the body.

Be particularly vigilant with respect to the arising of the five hindrances: desire, aversion, sleepiness, restlessness, and doubt. These are strongly conditioned in the mind, and it is easy to get lost in and become identified with them. Make a special effort to notice these particular mind states. The more quickly they can be observed, as close to the beginning as possible, the less their power will be.

In addition to paying attention to the breath, sensations, sounds, thoughts, images, emotions, and mind states, there is one more factor of mind that is important to single out and notice carefully in the meditation practice, because it plays a very critical role in opening the doors of deeper insight. That is becoming aware of and noting the various intentions in the mind. Intention is that mental factor or mental quality that directly precedes a bodily action or movement.

The body by itself doesn't move. It moves as the result of a certain impulse or volition. So before beginning any movement of the body, notice the intention to move, the intention to stand, the intention to shift position, the intention to turn, the intention to reach.

Before each of these movements there will be a volition in the mind. Intention or volition is quite subtle. It's not a tangible, discrete object like a thought or an image that you can see clearly having a beginning, middle, and end. At first the intention might be experienced simply as a pause before the movement begins, a moment's pause in which you know that you are about to do something. If you acknowledge the pause and make the note "intending," that will serve the purpose.

It is important to begin to be aware of these intentions, for two reasons. First, it illuminates and reveals the cause-and-effect relationship between mind and body. This is one of the fundamental laws that lead to deeper understanding. The unfolding of the process of mind and body is happening lawfully, and one of the laws that describe this process is the law of cause and effect. By noting "intention," we get a preliminary understanding of how this works. Because of an intention, the body moves. Intention is the cause; movement is the effect. As we note it in our experience, it becomes increasingly clear.

Noting "intention" also helps us to discover and understand the selfless nature of the mind-body process. Even when we are observing the breath, sensations, thoughts, images, and emotions, and we begin to see that all of these objects are simply part of a passing show, we may still be identified with the sense of a doer, the director of it all, the one who is commanding the actions.

When we note intentions and see that they are also passing mental phenomena, that they arise and pass away, that intentions themselves are not "I" and not "mine," when we see that they do not belong to anybody, we begin to loosen the sense of identification with them. We experience on deeper and deeper levels the selflessness of the whole unfolding process.

We begin with the breath, opening to the feeling or the sensation of each breath, each movement of the rise and fall or in and out, without any expectation of how any particular breath should be, not trying to force it into a particular pattern, not thinking that there should be any one kind of sensation. It is a settling back into each moment, with a great deal of care and precision, and being open to what is revealed in that particular breath. What is the sensation of this rising, or this in-breath? What is the feeling of it? Is it long or short, is it rough or smooth, is it deep or shallow, is there heaviness or pressure or tingling?

There is no need to go through a checklist. Just by our being open and paying careful attention, the characteristics of each breath will show themselves. So we settle back and stay open, with a beginner's mind for each rising, each falling, each in-breath, each out-breath.

If there is a space or a pause between the breaths, notice one or more touchpoints, making the note "touching, touching." When sensations in the body become predominant, when they're calling the attention away from the breathing, let the mind go to the sensation that is predominant; open to it, feel it. Note what kind of sensation it is. Is it heat or cold, heaviness or lightness, is it vibration or tingling, is it a painful sensation or a pleasant one?

When you open with awareness to each sensation, the characteristics of that sensation will become obvious. Let the mind stay very receptive to the sensations. Note what happens as you observe them. Do they get stronger, do they get weaker, do they disappear, do they increase? Observe what happens, without any model or expectation of what should be there; simply be with what is. When the sensations are no longer predominant, return again to the breath.

Keep a sense of alertness in the mind with respect to different mental phenomena, noting "thinking" or "seeing" as soon as you become aware that a thought or image is present. Observe what happens to that thought or image when you note it. Does it continue or does it disappear? If it disappears, does it disappear quickly or slowly? When a thought or image is no longer predominant, return to the awareness of the breath. Keep this movement from object to object fluid, rhythmic, and relaxed. There's no need to go searching for particular objects; rather, maintain a quality of openness and alertness so that whatever presents itself becomes the object of awareness, and let all objects of body and mind arise and pass away by themselves. Our practice is simply to settle back and note in each moment what is arising, without judgment, without evaluation, without interpretation. It is simple, bare attention to what is happening.

Stay mindful too of the different mind states or emotions. These states are less clearly defined as objects. They don't have such a clear beginning, middle, and end, and yet they can become very predominant objects of experience. So if a mind state or emotion or mood becomes strong—feelings such as sadness or happiness or anger or desire, restlessness or excitement, interest or rapture, joy or calm—make the mental note of that mind state, feeling it and observing how that too is a part of the passing show. It arises, it is there for some time, it passes away.

Use the breathing as a primary object, being with it if nothing else is very predominant and coming back to the breath when other objects disappear. Also, if the mind is feeling scattered or confused, without knowing exactly what to observe, center the attention on the breathing, either the rise and fall or the in and out. When the mind feels more centered and steady, again open the awareness to the entire range of changing objects—the breath, sounds, sensations, thoughts, images, intentions, emotions—noting each in turn as it arises. Keep the mind open, receptive, and alert, so that in each moment there can be an accurate awareness of what is present.

J. G.

# 4

## *Difficulties and Hindrances*

THE BUDDHIST TRADITION speaks directly about the hindrances that are encountered in the course of the spiritual journey. Buddha said that those who conquer their own minds are greater than those who defeat a thousand men a thousand times in battle. Almost every experienced yogi can describe in detail hours or years of dealing with some version of the five basic hindrances, the disruptions of mind and blocks to the heart that arise in practice. These same difficult energies are equally well described by Christian and Jewish mystics, Sufis, Hindu yogis, and American Indian shamans.

There is a story told of Mother Teresa of Calcutta. After praising her extraordinary work, an interviewer for the BBC remarked that in some ways service might be a bit easier for Mother Teresa than for us ordinary householders. After all, she has no possessions, no car, no insurance, and no husband. "This is not true," she replied at once. "I am married too." She held up the ring that nuns in her order wear to symbolize their wedding to Christ. Then she added, "And he can be very difficult sometimes!" The hindrances and difficulties in spiritual practice are universal.

When we examine our own minds we will inevitably encounter the root forces of greed, fear, prejudice, hatred, and desire, which create so much sorrow in the world. They become an opportunity for us. They raise a central question for anyone who undertakes a spiritual life. Is there some way that we can live with these forces constructively and wisely? Is there a skillful way to work with these energies? These are not just contemporary problems. In the second century Evagrios, one of the Christian mystics known as the Desert Fathers, taught his students about the hindrances by describing them in terms of demons that come to one who meditates out in the wilderness. The demons include fear, irritation, gluttony, laziness, and pride. In the Buddhist tradition, they are personified by Mara, the Tempter. They are our fear, our habits, our anger, our resistance, our unwillingness to look at what is actually happening.

As we meditate, Mara comes in many forms. First it may come as temptation and desire, as fantasy, as looking for comfort; Mara is all the things that say, "Let's do this instead." If the temptations don't work and we are still willing to continue, Mara comes to us in a more ferocious guise. It comes as an attacker, as anger, irritability, or doubt. And if we are unmoved by Mara as tempter or attacker, then Mara comes in yet a more subtle form. It comes with whispers of pride: "Oh, look how good I am! I didn't give in to the temptation" or "I've gotten rid of the anger." Things become a little clear, and we settle for that. We get caught trying to hold on to our concentration and stillness or some particular meditative state.

When the Buddha sat under the bodhi tree, he vowed not to get up until he had come to the fullest understanding and freedom possible for a human. To understand the nature of happiness and sorrow, to find freedom in our life, we have to be willing to face all the demons in our mind. Our journey—our practice through all the realms of our mind—is to learn a kind of mind control, a traveler's equilibrium. It is not the control of making something happen, but rather the ability to stay present, open, and balanced through all the experiences and realms of life. Through practice it is possible to train the heart and mind, to make them concentrated, to make them steady and luminous and free. It's possible to become balanced in the face of every kind of experience. Ultimately, it is possible to overcome and transform the forces of Mara with the sincerity of our practice, which means our love and the willingness to be truly mindful. With honesty we can learn to be unmoved. We can come to understand that which is deeper than those forces. We start to see that the worst and most difficult things also change, that they too are empty experiences, light and shadows that we all share and that arise and pass in the clear space of mind.

The beauty of these teachings is that they are not just theoretical or grandiose. There is a practical path we can follow to experience whole new levels of happiness in our lives, to learn a new relationship with ourselves and our experience. Depending on our relationship to these hindrances, they can be the cause of tremendous struggle or valuable fuel for the growth of insight. The first step necessary in working with these energies is to identify them clearly. Classically, there are said to be five primary hindrances, although you may have discovered some of your own. In fact, many yogis speak of being assailed by several of them at once—the "multiple-hindrance attack." To understand them better, let us consider them one at a time.

## THE FIVE HINDRANCES

The first hindrance is desire for sense pleasure: pleasant sights, sounds, smells, tastes, bodily sensations, and mind states. What's the problem with desire—what's wrong with it? Nothing, really. There's nothing wrong with enjoying pleasant experiences. Given the difficulties we face in life, they are nice to have. But they fool us. They trick us into adopting the "if only" mentality: "If only I could have this," or "If only I had the right job," or "If only I could find the right relationship," or "If only I had the right clothes," or "If only I had the right personality, then I would be happy." We are taught that if we can get enough pleasurable experiences, pasting them together quickly one after another, our life will be happy. A good game of tennis followed by a delicious dinner, a fine movie, then wonderful sex and sleep, a good morning jog, a fine hour of meditation, an excellent breakfast, and off to an exciting morning at work, and so on. Our society is masterful at perpetuating the ruse: "Buy this, look like that, eat that, act like this, own that . . . and you too can be happy." There is no problem with enjoying pleasant experiences, and to practice does not mean to dismiss them. But they don't really satisfy the heart, do they? For a moment we experience a pleasant thought or taste or sensation, and then it's gone, and with it the sense of happiness it brought. Then it's on to the next thing. The whole process can become very tiring and empty.

Of course, we don't always ask for a lot; sometimes we settle for very little. At the beginning of a meditation retreat people often spend a lot of time dwelling on desires they carry in with them: "If only I had that house," or "If only I had more money." But as they settle into the limits placed on them by the retreat, the desires get smaller: "If only they would put out something sweet after lunch," or "If only the sitting were five minutes shorter." In a situation like a retreat—or a prison, for that matter—where the possibilities for fulfilling desires are limited, it becomes clear that the strength of a desire is determined not by the particular object, but by the degree of attachment in the mind, and the desire for a piece of candy can be as powerful as the desire for a Mercedes Benz.

Again, the problem is not the object of desire, but the energy in the mind. The energy of desire keeps us moving, looking for that thing that is really going to do it for us. The wanting mind is itself painful. It's a self-perpetuating habit that does not allow us to be where we are because we are grasping for something somewhere else. Even when we get what we want, we then want something more or different because the habit of wanting is so strong. It is a sense that being here and now is not enough, that we are somehow incomplete, and it keeps us cut off from the joy of our own natural completeness. We are never content. It is the same force in the world at large that creates the havoc of people wanting and consuming, hoarding, and fighting wars to have more and more, for pleasure and for security that are never fulfilled.

In India they say that when a pickpocket meets a saint, the pickpocket sees only the saint's pockets. What we want will distort and limit our perception; it will determine what we see.

If we are hungry and we walk down the street, we don't see shoe stores or the weather or the clouds. We see there is a nice Greek restaurant. "I could have feta cheese and a nice salad," or "There's an Italian restaurant. Maybe I'll have pizza or manicotti," or "There's McDonald's. Maybe I'll have a burger."

People can get so lost in the imagination that meditators on retreat have often glimpsed a potential partner and gone through a whole romance (meeting, courtship, marriage, children, even divorce) without ever actually saying a word to that person. We call this the vipassana romance.

So the force of desire can cloud our minds, bringing distortion and delusion in its wake. As it says in the *Tao Te Ching*, "The secret waits for eyes unclouded by longing." We can see how desire interferes with our being able to open up to things as they are, in a freer, more joyful way. It interferes with our power to deeply open to the truth, to relate directly and wisely to what is actually here.

The second difficult energy we encounter is aversion, hatred, anger, and ill will. While desire and the wanting mind are seductive and can easily fool us, the opposite energy of anger and aversion is clearer because its unpleasantness is obvious. Anger and hatred are usually painful. We might find some enjoyment in them for a while, but they close our heart. They have a burning, tight quality that we can't get away from.

Like desire, anger is an extremely powerful force. It can be experienced toward an object that is present with us or one that is far away. We sometimes experience great anger over past events that are long gone and about which we can do nothing. Strangely enough, we can even get furious over something that has not happened, but that we only imagine might. When it is strong in the mind, anger colors our entire experience of life. When our mood is bad, then no matter who walks in the room or where we go that day, something is wrong. Anger can be a source of tremendous suffering in our own minds, in our interactions with others, and in the world at large.

Although we generally don't think of them as such, fear and judgment and boredom are all forms of aversion. When we examine them, we see that they are based on our dislike of some aspect of experience. With the mind full of dislike, full of wanting to separate or withdraw from our experience, how can we become concentrated or explore the present moment in a spirit of discovery? To practice we need to come very close to and investigate this moment, not push it away or pull away from it. So we need to learn to work with all these forms of our aversion.

The third common hindrance that arises is sloth and torpor. This includes laziness, dullness, lack of vitality, fogginess, and sleepiness. Clarity and wakefulness fade when the mind is overcome with sloth and torpor. The mind becomes unworkable and cloudy. When sloth and torpor overcome us, it is a big obstacle in practice.

Restlessness, the opposite of torpor, manifests as the fourth hindrance. With restlessness there is agitation, nervousness, anxiety, and worry. The mind spins in circles or flops around like a fish out of water. The body can be filled with restless energy, vibrating, jumpy, on edge. Or sometimes we sit down to meditate and the mind runs through the same routines over and over. Of course, no matter how much we worry and fret over something, it never helps the situation. Still the mind gets caught in reminiscences and regrets, and we spin out hours of stories. When the mind is restless, we jump from object to object. It is difficult to sit still, and our concentration becomes scattered and dispersed.

The last of the five hindrances is doubt. Doubt can be the most difficult of all to work with, because when we believe it and get caught by it, our practice just stops cold. We become paralyzed. All kinds of doubt might assail us: Doubts about ourselves and our capacities, doubts about our teachers, doubts about the dharma itself—"Does it really work? I sit here and all that happens is my knees hurt and I feel restless. Maybe the Buddha really didn't know what he was talking about." We might doubt the practice or doubt that it is the right practice for us. "It's too hard. Maybe I should try Sufi dancing." Or we think it's the right practice but the wrong time. Or it's the right practice and the right time, but our body's not yet in good enough shape. It doesn't matter what the object is; when the skeptical, doubting mind catches us, we're stuck.

### WORKING WITH THE HINDRANCES

How do these five hindrances interfere with our clarity of mind? There is a traditional analogy comparing our nature to a pond, and the point of practice is to see to the depths of the pond. Desire comes like beautifully colored dyes in the water that obstruct our vision. When we are angry it is as though the pond were on a boiling-hot spring. Again, we cannot see far. Sloth and torpor are like a thick layer of algae growing on the pond's surface. Restlessness is like a strong wind blowing on the pond's surface and creating waves. And doubt is like mud stirred up from the pond's bottom. Getting caught by any of these hindrances makes it impossible to see clearly into our heart and mind.

We are each challenged by these hindrances again and again in the course of our practice. So it is important that we learn to work with them when they arise. If we are able to work with them skillfully, we can actually use these times to strengthen, clarify, and deepen our awareness and understanding.

How do we approach them? Certainly not by judgment or suppression. Suppression doesn't work, because suppression is itself a form of aversion. It deadens our awareness and our life. On the other hand, we don't want to get involved in expressing all the hindrances and acting them all out. That simply reinforces the patterns (and might get us in other trouble as well).

If we don't suppress these energies and don't act upon all of them, then what is left? The most direct way is to be mindful of them, to transform them into the object of meditation. Through the power of mindfulness, we can make these very forces another aspect of our meditation, using awareness of them to bring the mind to greater freedom. Working with them can be the source of insight and energy. We can directly observe the nature of desire, anger, doubt, and fear and really understand how these forces operate in the mind. We can use their power to enliven and strengthen our investigation. And these very forces can teach us the truth of the dharma, for we can see in their operation the laws of kharma, or impermanence and impersonality. With mindfulness, our way of transforming Mara's army is wonderfully simple. We don't have to fight to overcome them. Instead, through awareness, we allow their energy to teach us their laws. We learn to experience even their extremes without being caught or overcome by them. Learning to work with the hindrances in this way is a particularly important part of actualizing our practice amid the stress and demands of daily life.

There is a second whole way of working with hindrances. This is recommended for use when they are particularly strong. Through cultivating their opposite states as a balance or remedy, we can help weaken the hindrances and unhook ourselves from our strong entanglement with them. When they are weaker, we are better able to observe them mindfully. A third way for more advanced students to work with these energies deserves a brief mention as well. When concentration becomes quite strong and the power of mindfulness is well developed, it becomes possible to simply *let go* of these states as soon as they arise. This letting go has no aversion in it; it is a directed choice to abandon one mind state and redirect the concentration to a more skillful object such as the breath or a state of mental calm. This ability will come spontaneously in deeper states of practice, and most students need not be concerned with it unless it arises naturally. It cannot be used in the early parts of practice because without sufficient balance and steadiness it easily becomes aversion, a movement of judgment to get rid of the hindrances instead of observing them with mindfulness.

Let us begin with our usual meditations. How do we actually apply these ways of working in practice? For example, if sense desire arises, greed arises, wanting arises, what do we do? We look directly at this mind state and include it in the field of awareness. First make a soft mental note of it: "desire, desire." We can observe sense desire just as we observe the breath or sensations in the body. When a strong desire arises, turn all the attention to it; see it clearly. What is this desire? How does it feel in the body? What parts of the body are affected by it—the gut, the breath, the eyes? What does it feel like in the heart, in the mind? When it is present, are we happy or agitated, open or closed? Note "desire, desire" and see what happens to it. Pay meticulous attention.

If we look closely, we can learn a lot about this force that so greatly affects our lives and the world around us. It can cause wars; it is the force behind all the advertising in our society, behind much of our life. Have we ever stopped to examine it, to feel it directly, to discover a wise relation to it? When we look, we see that it creates tension, that it is actually painful. We can see how it arises out of our sense of longing and incompleteness, the feeling that we are separate and not whole. We see that it is also impermanent, essenceless. As we investigate desire, it reveals itself to us. It is actually just a thought and an accompanying feeling that comes and goes from the empty mind—that is all it is. That is easy to notice when we are not caught up in it, but many other times it seems very real. As Oscar Wilde said, "I can resist anything but temptation." The wanting mind is powerful, and learning to observe it will take some practice. Much of the power of desire comes from its being a habit with us. Our habitual patterns of desire are conditioned and reinforced in many ways, and they have tremendous momentum. But being mindful of desire does not mean getting involved in aversion toward it. Rather, it means watching desire come and go without being caught by it, and seeing its nature clearly.

Still, many times as we look carefully we can also see that beneath desire there is a more neutral, universal energy with which we live, an energy called the will to do. While sometimes it is associated with greed and grasping, it can also be directed by love, by compassion, and by wisdom. With the development of awareness we can get a taste of living in states free from so much desire, of a more spontaneous and natural way of being without as much struggle or ambition. When we are no longer caught by desire, compassion and understanding will more naturally direct our life. This can be experienced and sensed directly in our practice. But it cannot be grasped by our thinking mind. It comes more clearly as we begin to recognize the moments of desirelessness and contentment that come between our desires. This is an exquisite area in which to pay attention.

When desire arises, it is a force that pulls us out of the moment into our imagination. Sometimes it becomes so strong that we are unable to watch it. One antidote is to resolve to practice moderation with regard to the object of desire. Another antidote is to reflect on impermanence, even on death. How much will fulfilling this desire mean at the end of our life? Recognize that no matter how many times we get what we want, it always passes. It's endless. It's like one of the Sufi tales about Mullah Nasruddin. After buying a basket of hot chili peppers because they were so cheap he couldn't resist, he began to eat them. Tears streamed down his cheeks, his tongue burned, and yet he continued. When one of his students asked him why, he replied, "I keep waiting for a sweet one!"

Of course, in our lives we will still act on desire much of the time. If we become mindful of it, then even our action will teach us, instead of just reinforcing our habits. One Indian meditation teacher who had a powerful craving for sweets tried to let go of it in sitting without much success. So one day he went out and bought a huge plate of his favorite sugary sweets. He planned to eat the whole thing, trying to be mindful as he did so. Actually he could hardly begin. By the end of that plate he was sick of sweets and a lot freer of the desire. But we have to pay attention to learn. When desire arises, look at it and let it come and go of itself. If it is too strong and you are unable to be mindful of it, use a remedy to help bring the mind back to balance. But continue to pay attention. It is making these energies mindful that brings insight and wisdom in our practice.

How can we work with the opposite of desire, aversion? Again, we begin by making the effort to be mindful of it, experiencing it fully and noting it as "anger, anger." Anger presents us with the same opportunity to learn, to find greater freedom. So we should not fear it, but investigate it. How does anger feel? Where in the body do we feel it? What is its temperature, its effect on the breath, its degree of pain? How does it affect the mind? Is the mind smaller, more rigid, tighter? We can learn a lot from anger. Anger shows us precisely where we are stuck, where our limits are, where we cling to beliefs and fears. Aversion is like a warning signal lighting up and saying "attached, attached." The amount of attachment is revealed by the strength of our anger. Often we cannot change the conditions of our life, but we can always learn from them. Here, anger has come to teach us about its true nature, and our attention shows us the hurt, attachment, and identification that underlie it. Yet the attachment is optional. We can relate more wisely. When we stop and look at it, we will discover something fundamental about anger: conditioned by our viewpoint on that day, it is impermanent. It's a feeling with associated sensations and thoughts that come and go. We do not need to be bound to it or driven by it.

Of course, many of us have been conditioned to hate our anger. As we try to observe it, we will find a tendency to judge and suppress it—to get rid of it because it is "bad" and painful, or shameful and unspiritual. We must be very careful to bring an open mind and heart to our mindfulness. We need to let ourselves feel fully, even if it means touching the deepest wells of grief, sorrow, and rage within us. These are the forces that move our lives, and these are what we must feel and come to terms with. It's not a process of getting rid of something, but one of opening and understanding. So when anger or irritation or fear or boredom arises—any of these states rooted in aversion to experience—we must explore and observe it fully. We may need to actually let ourselves get caught up in it sometimes to understand it well. We will probably note anger or fear arising many times in practice before we have come to a balanced, mindful way. This is natural.

What we have to understand in working with anger and ill will is true of all the difficulties in our practice: that they are our strongest teachers. This became very clear in the spiritual community that G. I. Gurdjieff led in France. One old man who lived there was a personification of these qualities—irritable, messy, fighting with everyone, and unwilling to clean up or help at all. No one got along with him. Finally, after many frustrating months of trying to stay with the group, the old man left for Paris. Gurdjieff followed him and tried to convince him to return, but it had been too hard, and the man said no. At last Gurdjieff offered the man a very big monthly stipend if he returned. How could he refuse? When he returned everyone was aghast, and on hearing that he was being paid (while they were being charged a lot to be there), the community was up in arms. Gurdjieff called them together and after hearing their complaints laughed and explained: "This man is like yeast for bread." He said, "Without him here you would never really learn about anger, irritability, patience, and compassion. That is why you pay me, and why I hire him."

All these forces are part of our practice. Our main tool is to examine them with mindfulness. Still there are times when hatred and anger are too strong to watch. We can often balance them by developing thoughts of compassion and forgiveness. This is not just a papering over of anger; it is a deep movement of the heart, a willingness to go beyond the conditions of a particular point of view. When we feel anger toward someone, we can consider that he or she is a being just like us, who has faced much suffering in life. If we had experienced the same circumstances and history of suffering as the other person, might we not act in the same way? So we allow ourselves to feel compassion, to feel his or her suffering. We can also first reflect upon someone we love very much and let loving thoughts grow in our heart, and then extend that energy toward the person or situation that is the object of our hatred. In this way, we do not cut off from the power of love and compassion within us. It is a very real power and an accessible one when we can remember it, and we can use it to still the turbulence and confusion that often surround our anger.

Boredom, judgment, and fear are also forms of aversion that

we can learn to be mindful of. Usually we are afraid of boredom and will do anything to avoid it. So we go to the refrigerator, pick up the phone, watch TV, read a novel, busy ourselves constantly to escape our loneliness, our emptiness, our boredom. Without awareness it has a great power over us. Yet we need not let boredom run our lives this way. What is boredom when it is experienced in itself? Have we ever really stopped to look at it? Boredom comes from lack of attention. With it we also find restlessness, discouragement, and judgment. We get bored because we don't like what is happening and so don't pay attention. But if we stay with it, a whole new level of understanding and contentment can grow. In meditation we let boredom itself be an object of interest to explore. When it arises, feel the boredom. Note it, feel its texture, its energy, the pains and tension in it, the resistances to it. Look directly at the workings of this quality in the body and mind. We can finally stop running away or resisting it. Insight, consciousness, freedom, are to be found not in some other experience, in some other moment, but in any moment in which we really learn to pay attention. When the awareness is clear and focused, even the repeated movement of the in- and out-breath can be the most incredibly interesting and wonderful experience.

In the same way, we can become aware of judgment. If we observe, we can see that judgment is actually just a thought, a series of words in the mind. When we don't get caught up in the story line, we can learn a great deal about the nature of thought by watching the judging mind. We can learn a great deal about the nature of suffering in life as well. Start by simply noting "judging" when it arises—and noting it softly, like a whisper, not like a baseball bat, trying to get rid of it, because that's just more judging! At times in practice we find how incredibly active the judging mind is. We judge everything: too noisy, too fast, too hard, too long, too much, too little. This is bad, that's no good, and underneath, fundamentally, we ourselves are judged as not being good. It is helpful to bring a lightness and tenderness to observing this aspect of mind. For humor, we can also count the judgments, like counting sheep.

See if it is possible to discover three hundred subtle judgments in an hour of sitting. This can bring a tremendous leap in attention.

Fear will also come in practice. It comes strongly for everyone at certain times. Let yourself experience it mindfully, noting, "fear, fear, fear." How does it feel? Where do you feel it in the body? What is it like in the heart, the mind? Of course, there are times when we are really caught by it. We identify with it, we resist it and push it away. To work with it mindfully, we must soften the attention and let ourselves touch it with our heart. Try not to be afraid of it. Sit with it, be aware of it, and after much practice, at some point there will simply come the recognition, "Oh, fear. Here you are again. Now, that's interesting." We will have made friends with our fear.

As our capacity to be mindful grows more continuous, we can find ourselves filled with joy and rapture. These states are born out of wholehearted attention and deep interest in the present moment. The fullness of our being is what provides this joy, not the particular object of the moment. A sight, a sound, a taste—whatever it is, it is not the source. When this unique kind of joy is present, anger and fear have ceased to overpower us, and we can taste another level of freedom.

Sloth and torpor are the next difficult energy. Sleepiness has three causes. One is the tiredness that signals a genuine need for sleep. This often comes in the first few days of a retreat or at home after a long day, when we sit after a period of great business and stress. This kind of sleepiness passes after we take some rest. The second kind of sleepiness comes as resistance to some unpleasant or fearful state of body or mind. We don't want to feel something, and so we get sleepy. A third cause of sleepiness is a result of the imbalance of concentration and energy in practice.

Usually sleepiness comes upon us gradually. As we sit, we can feel the sleepiness begin like tendrils of fog curling around our body and then whispering in our ear. "Come on, let's just take a little snooze. It'll be really nice." The mind then becomes dissipated and depleted, and we lose heart for what we have undertaken. This can happen many times in our sittings.

Yet sleepiness is a workable state. To practice with sleepiness requires our full endeavor, because it is a powerful condition. Much of living is only half awake. Our life has been spent in sleep and sleepwalking; meditation means waking up. So we begin by noting it and bringing mindfulness to the sleepiness. Be aware of how the body feels when it's tired, the heaviness, the softening posture, the sense in the eyes. Of course, if we're sleepy and nodding off, it is somewhat difficult to watch. Observe as much as you are able. Pay attention to its beginning, middle, and end, and to the various components of the experience. See the impersonal conditions that cause it. Is it tiredness or resistance? Sometimes interested, penetrating awareness of sleepiness can itself arouse the energy to dispel the sleepiness and bring insight and understanding. Sometimes when we recognize that the sleepy or lazy mind is resistance in us, we can discover an important fear or difficulty just underneath it. Such states as loneliness, sorrow, emptiness, and loss of control are common ones that we avoid, and when we recognize them with mindfulness, our whole practice can open up to a new level. It is useful to know that some sleepiness can also be caused by the development of concentration and calm in the mind. If we get quite concentrated but have not balanced the mind by arousing an equal amount of energy, we will be stuck in a calm but dull state. This, too, requires careful attention.

There are other ways of working with this hindrance. Sit up straight and take a few deep breaths. Meditate with your eyes open wide. Stand in place for a few minutes or do walking meditation. If it's really bad, walk briskly or walk backward. Splash some water on your face. Sleepiness is something we can respond to creatively. When I was going through a long period of sleepiness in practice, my teacher, Achaan Chaa, had me sit on the edge of a very deep well. The fear of falling in kept me quite awake! Sleepiness is workable. When the mind is attacked by sluggishness and it becomes too constricted and heavy, our effort should be to balance the mind by making it more alive. We can accomplish this through continually trying to direct the mind to the object of this very moment, and then this very moment, and so on. The accuracy and immediacy of the watch-fulness—saying in effect, "Just this breath" or "Just this step," without trying to see beyond it, will steady the mind. If we can say, "Just this breath," in every single moment, from moment to moment, the mind will become expansive and refreshed, and sluggishness will disappear. When nothing at all seems to work, then it is time to rest.

The fourth common difficult energy is restlessness. When this comes on the inner radio, try not to judge it or condemn it. Like all other phenomena, it is conditioned and it comes and goes. Be mindful and note, "restless, restless." Let yourself experience restlessness without indulging or getting caught up in the content of its story. It can be terribly unpleasant; the body filled with nervous energy, the mind spinning with worry. Open to it and observe it without identifying with it or taking it as self. It is not "my restlessness," but rather an impermanent state born out of conditions and bound to change. If it gets very intense, think to yourself, "Okay, I'm ready. I'll be the first meditator in America to actually die of restlessness." Surrender and see what happens. Like everything else, restlessness is a composite, a series of thoughts, feelings, and sensations. But because we believe it to be something solid, it has a great deal of power over us. When we stop resisting and simply allow it to move through us with mindful attention, we can see how transitory and insubstantial the state actually is.

One antidote to restlessness is concentration. When restless-ness is too strong to simply observe, try relaxing and counting your breaths—one to ten, then start again at one—until the mind comes back to balance. If it helps, breathe slightly more deeply than usual as a way of collecting and softening the body and mind.

Part of understanding restlessness is understanding that meditation, like life, has its way of recycling. Some people don't like the aspect of life that has so many cycles. They want it to be very even and not have so many ups and downs. Unfortu-nately, on our planet, things don't work that way. There are constant changes. Our practice is to relate to what Zorba the

Greek called "the whole catastrophe," all the parts of it—the beautiful, the pleasant, the troublesome, and the unpleasant— with a certain amount of ease and humor.

This quality of acceptance is the ground out of which true insight and understanding develop. If we don't accept some aspect of ourselves—a feeling, a physical or mental sense of ourselves—then we cannot learn about it. We cannot discover its nature and become free in relationship to it. We become afraid, we resist, we judge, and we try to push away. We cannot look deeply and push away at the same time. When mindfulness is well developed and the ground of acceptance is laid, then the body and mind are filled with a sense of comfort. Even if something difficult or painful has arisen, this comfort is underlying it. The element of comfort is also an antidote to restlessness and anxiety.

The fifth hindrance is doubt. Look at it carefully and with detachment. Have we ever really observed the voice that says, "I can't do it. It's too hard. It's the wrong time to sit. Where is this getting me anyway? Maybe I should try some other practice?" What do we see? Doubt is a string of words in the mind, often associated with a subtle feeling of fear and resistance. When we become mindful of doubt as a thought process, when we note, "doubting, doubting," and when we do not become involved in its content, a marvelous transformation occurs: doubt itself becomes the source of awareness. We can learn a great deal about the impermanent, ungraspable nature of the mind through watching doubt. We also learn about what it means to be identified with and caught up in our moods and state of mind. When we are caught up in doubt, there is a great deal of suffering. And in the moment, when we feel it without grasping, our whole mind becomes freer and lighter.

One aspect of doubt that is especially difficult is the inability of the mind to focus on anything; the mind runs all over the place, considering possibilities, and remains indecisive. An antidote to this is to come fully back to the present moment, with a degree of continuity, a firmness and steadiness of mind. Gradually, this dispels confusion. Sometimes doubt is too strong, and we become muddled in it. Doubt can be balanced by developing faith. To strengthen faith we can ask questions or read great books. We can reflect on the inspiration of the hundreds of thousands of people in the spiritual life who have followed the path of inner awareness and practice before us. It has been valued by every great culture. To live with great wisdom and compassion is possible for anyone who genuinely undertakes a training of their heart and mind. What better thing to do with our life? A clear understanding of the teachings and wise reflecting upon them can inspire faith and help the mind return to a place of balance. It is natural for the heart to doubt. But let us understand it and let the doubt lead us to a deeper attention and a more complete seeking for the truth.

All of the kinds of doubt that come as a resistance—"It's not working today, I'm not ready, it's too hard"—could be called small doubts. After some practice we can learn to work skillfully with them. There also arises another level of doubt, which is very useful to us. It is called the Great Doubt, the deep desire to know our true nature or the meaning of love or freedom. The Great Doubt asks, "Who am I?" or "What is freedom?" or searches for the end of suffering. This doubt is a source of energy and inspiration in practice and is akin to the factor of enlightenment called investigation, about which we will speak in chapter 6. A spirit of true investigation and inquiry is essential to enliven and deepen our spiritual practice, to keep it from being imitative. Working with the spirit, we can even find that buried within each difficulty is hidden treasure. The difficulties of doubt can lead to the discovery of our Great Doubt. The hurt of anger can lead us to a deeper sense of strength and love, and underlying restlessness is a source of spaciousness and peace.

The path of awakening is our great and wondrous legacy as human beings. It will often be difficult and at times seem almost impossible. Thomas Merton writes, "True love and prayer are learned in the hour when love becomes impossible and the heart has turned to stone." When we remember this, the difficulties we encounter in practice become themselves part of the fullness of meditation, a place to learn and to open the heart. They are the juice, part of what makes us alive. Working with these hindrances will lead us to great insight and great understanding.

So the purpose of practice is not to create a special state of mind. That is always temporary. It is to work directly with the most primary elements of our experience, all the aspects of our body, our mind, to see the way we get trapped by our fears and desires and anger and to learn directly our capacity for freedom. If we work with them, the hindrances will enrich our lives. They have been called manure for enlightenment, and some teachers speak of them as "mind weeds," which we pull up and bury near the plant to give it nourishment. Our practice is to use all that arises within us for the growth of understanding, compassion, and freedom.

J. K.

### EXERCISE

## Making the Hindrances Part of the Path

Choose one of the most frequent and difficult mind states that arise in your practice, such as irritation, fear, boredom, lust, doubt, or restlessness. For one week in your daily sitting be particularly aware each time this state arises. Watch carefully for it. Notice how it begins and what precedes it. Notice if there is a particular thought or image that triggers this state. Notice how long it lasts and when it ends. Notice what state usually follows it. Observe whether it ever arises very slightly or softly. Can you see it as just a whisper in the mind? See how loud and strong it gets. Notice what patterns of energy or tension reflect this state in the body. Become aware of any physical or mental resistance to experiencing this state. Soften and receive even the resistance. Finally sit and be aware of the breath, watching and waiting for this state, allowing it to come, and observing it like an old friend.

# 5

# *Deepening Levels of Practice*

MEDITATION is a dynamic, living process out of which new perspectives, new ways of understanding and appreciating our lives, continually emerge. As we follow the path of meditation, we discover a process of deepening through observing, opening, and being.

### ARRIVING

Arriving, the first level, refers to what first happens after hearing the dharma and undertaking practice, to the process of working with the initial difficulties, and to the settling down of the mind and body. The beginning of practice can be very difficult. We have already talked about how the five hindrances—desire, aversion, restlessness, sleepiness, and doubt—seem to assail us, sometimes one at a time and sometimes all at once, as a multiple-hindrance attack. Part of the process of arriving is learning to work with these hindrances and use them to strengthen and deepen our practice. To arrive in the present takes skillful means in overcoming difficulties and an initial opening of the heart.

The first level of practice is illuminated by the qualities of courage and renunciation. To learn something really new is not a matter of planning or thinking and analyzing. What is required is a clearing or emptying of the mind and the heart so that we can listen in a deep and new way. The willingness to empty ourselves and then seek our true nature is an expression of great and courageous love. There are many struggles we will go through, and the willingness to persevere and explore so much new terrain, to uncover so much of what has been hidden, can only come from an unwavering love for the truth. This love gives us patience and gives us courage.

There is also a degree of renunciation that is required. Learning a new way, we cannot just act on our old habits and get lost as usual in our fears or desires. Instead, we must actually sit and face these forces directly. Such an opening up can be very uncomfortable, even overwhelming. We may feel unable or disinclined to risk losing what we know, however unsatisfying, for the unknown. But when we let go of the familiar and go forth with honesty and determination, everything we experience can serve to strengthen our understanding.

A major aspect of arriving is letting the body settle down. A variety of physical pains come as we begin sitting still for extended periods. Working with them takes a period of patient practice, stretching our legs and stretching our ability to be present. As we get used to our meditation posture, and as we learn to work more with physical pain by making it, too, an object of our gentle awareness, we begin to feel more comfortable and attentive. At this point we may experience the deeper "dharma pains" that come as we open to the release of tensions that have accumulated in our bodies, our shoulders, our jaws, our backs, or elsewhere over the course of our entire lives. With the growth of awareness, these knots held in the body begin to open more and more fully. Later on, at deeper stages, there may be still stronger physical sensations, startling releases of energy, hot fiery flashes, spontaneous movement of limbs, chills, prickles, powerful releases in our bellies, our throats, or around our hearts. A profound physical transformation often accompanies intensive meditation. For some, the opening of the body can be a long and fiery process. But for the first level what we most need to learn is to soften the body and allow the obvious knots and tension to release and open.

Just as the body gradually settles, so too does the breath. We don't try to control the breath; we simply pay attention to it as it changes naturally. We try to learn from it rather than direct it. Whether it is fast or slow, shallow or deep, we feel it, we watch it and allow the changes. This requires a surrender, accepting and getting used to the whole range of breaths from very powerful movements to its near-disappearance. Over time gradually the breath becomes softer, fuller, and more subtle. When this happens, we can use the gentleness and subtlety of the breath to draw down and carefully focus or refine our awareness.

As we let the body and breath settle down, the next aspect of arriving is settling the mind. What do we see when we look at the mind? Constant change. In the traditional scriptures the untrained and unconcentrated mind is referred to as a mad monkey. As we look for ourselves, we see that it is like a circus or a zoo in there. The parrot, the sloth, the mouse, the tiger, the bear, and the silent owl are all represented. It is like a flywheel of spinning thoughts, emotions, images, stories, likes, dislikes, and so forth. There is ceaseless movement, filled with plans, ideas, and memories. Seeing this previously unconscious stream of inner dialogue is for many people the first insight in practice. It is called seeing the waterfall. Already we begin to learn about the nature of mind. Its constant changes are like the weather; today it rains, tonight it may snow, earlier the sun was out. Sometimes it's muddy in the spring, and then the summer comes and the winds come. In the fall the leaves go; in winter the ice forms.

We're like that; we're part of nature. Our meditation isn't fulfilled by achieving some special state; it's beginning to find a genuine relationship to this organic change of body and heart and mind that we are. We can then discover our spiritual practice in every season.

So we practice and we see the waterfall and we see all parts of ourselves. For the mind to become settled in the present moment, in the midst of so much change, it is necessary to develop a degree of steadiness and stability; that is, concentration.

The type of concentration we are talking about involves a very careful attention to what is happening. Several years ago, a child was born to two friends of mine while they were far out in the country with no doctor, nurse, or midwife present. It was a long, hard delivery and a breech birth. The child came out feet first and blue from not breathing. The parents held their little boy and gave him artificial respiration, very softly and gently, blowing into his little mouth and lungs. After they did this for a while, they paused and watched with great attention, love, and caring to see whether or not he would begin to breathe and come into this world. They watched for the tiniest movement of his breath. After a long time finally he began to breathe. Imagine how closely we would watch the breath if our life depended on it. This quality of extraordinary attentiveness is an essential element of practice and a capacity we all share. Concentration means steadying the mind. It's like a candle flame in a windless place. It's learning to be wholehearted. Then we can sense in our most concentrated moments a unity of our body, spirit, and mind. To do things in this way is wonderful.

To be concentrated is to learn how to give ourselves fully. Of course, in the beginning, training the mind is like training a puppy. We put the puppy down and say, "Stay." What does it do? It gets up and runs around. "Stay." It turns around again. Twenty times, "Stay." After a while, slow though it is, it gets the point. Through practice, gently and gradually we can collect ourselves and learn how to be more fully with what we do. But remember, this bringing of the heart and mind to what we do builds slowly. At first we may be discouraged. After many sittings, we are mindful 10 percent of the time and 90 percent lost in thought. How we judge ourselves! Yet if we look, we may realize that when we began to meditate, we were here only 2 percent of the time, and now we are here five times as much! Fives times more present to touch the earth, to feel the breeze, to be awakened to our senses. This is no small improvement.

Finally, the development of concentration comes through nurturing an inner peacefulness. As our skill grows, we learn that the mind becomes concentrated, not through strain and struggle, but from letting go of anxiety about the past and future, and relaxing into the present. It is a natural process.

Through our paying attention, again and again, a quality of calm interest begins to grow and the mind settles lightly into the moment.

### OBSERVATION

So now we've arrived. We've begun to work with pain in the body, with the breath, with hindrances, and with concentration. We're here a bit more. Now what? The next step is to observe, to look carefully at whatever arises in each moment without grasping or aversion, to see it all with awareness and equanimity.

Observation means bringing the practice into the heart. It is a full receiving and experiencing of each new moment in a fresh way. Each moment is, in fact, unlike any other. There is nothing mechanical about this observing; it is always fresh and alive. In Zen it's called beginner's mind. The whole art of living a meditative life is to keep a beginner's mind, to keep a mind where, with each experience, at each time we sit down, we are willing to discover what is actually going to happen *this* hour, not what happened yesterday or what will happen tomorrow. It is a wonderful way to live.

It is like a botanist who is examining the plant life in some previously unexplored territory. The botanist's attitude would be one of intense interest and precise attention because each detail of what he or she sees would have something meaningful to say. How different an attitude this is from one that says, "Oh, there's an oak tree. I've seen a million of them." For the truth is that each oak tree—like each rose, each person, and each moment—is different from any other.

So as we learn actually to observe our experience in the present, we see how to bring to the breath and body a development of a finer and more constant attention. At first the breath is just an "in" or an "out." Then we see its beginning, middle, and end. Then we feel the coolness, vibration, pressure, tingling, or pulsing, and even notice the space between and around the breaths. We notice more its rhythms, its changes in intensity.

As we go on, we can start to see ten or one hundred aspects to the simple in- and out-breath.

To practice is to develop a continuity of attention that begins in a simple way, starting with the breath or walking, and is gradually expanded to other objects. We start by observing a rather solid world, the world of sight and sounds. At first our level of perception is inconsistent and dull, so that the body and mind seem intact and solid the way a movie does when we're lost in the plot.

Over repeated observation we begin to build a very powerful continuity of attention to see more precisely what makes up our sense perceptions, what makes up our world, and to be able to dissolve long-held conditioning and concepts. When we start to practice, the moments of awareness are quite far apart; then gradually they get a little closer together, and we are here more frequently.

As we continue to make gentle effort and carefully bring the mind back again and again, we begin to observe what at first seemed solid as a composite, as component parts. We begin to see that our whole being and all of our physical and mental universe is made up of moments, of six sense perceptions, sights and sounds, smells, tastes, physical sensations, and mental events. It takes practice to note the moments of physical senses such as seeing and hearing so as not to get lost in the story. Even more practice is needed to be able to observe our subtle sensations, moods, feelings, and thoughts. Our habit is either to cut them off and evaluate or to be lost in the plot. This happens particularly as we observe the movement of certain patterns, thoughts, feelings, emotions, and sensations repeating over and over like the top-ten hits of the week. Here it is difficult. There may be fantasies about relationships, about food, thoughts about one's health or some artistic endeavor. They all seem very important. Yet, as a matter of fact, most of the tunes are the same old ones for each of us. In this flow of phenomena there are some patterns that we like and hold on to, and some that we dislike and try to get rid of. "Oh, no. Not that tune again. Anything but that." In such cases we even try to use the practice to serve the judging mind. For instance, when something we dislike arises, the observing mind becomes like a baseball bat, beating away the unwanted object. This is not what is meant by observing.

With mindfulness, we are learning to observe in a new way, with balance and a powerful disidentification. We can begin to sense and observe the changing mind, body, and heart the way a meteorologist observes changes in the weather: "It's cloudy, the barometer is high, the temperature is eighty degrees, and the wind is from the southwest"—not "Oh, I hope it doesn't rain today. I wish it were sunny like yesterday. It's too warm, and the humidity is awful." We simply notice what is occurring.

We must learn that an essential characteristic of observing is acceptance. As we practice and watch, we begin to see that the mind can accommodate everything and that there is no need to struggle against ourselves. Thoughts come, feelings come, sensations in the body come—we simply watch, without judgment, without clinging or fear, but rather with a feeling of accommodating warmth and friendship with ourselves.

There are times when we don't know where we are, when we feel like ships that have left the shoreline, out in the middle of the ocean with no discernible reference point. At these times self-acceptance and compassion are the source of the spirit that allows us to continue with energy and interest. In Calcutta there is an old teacher, Dipa Ma, with whom I have had a chance to study. She is a great yogi and an embodiment of loving-kindness. She often gives blessings to people while they are practicing. She will come over and put her hand on your head and say, "Shhh," very softly and comfortingly. She has a tremendous power of heart, and there is a great field of kindness and love around her that's strong and quite tangible. Whatever you're going through, whatever difficulty you present her with, she greets you with, "Shhh, it's okay." You don't have to struggle to get rid of it, or hate yourself for experiencing it, she teaches. It, too, is all right.

What, after all, is an experience? It is a sight or sound or smell or taste of some flavor or a particular thought or physical sensation. We've somehow divided the world into the acceptable and the unacceptable, and feel frightened by some experiences and alienated and fragmented as a result. With observation and acceptance, we learn to be gentle toward ourselves and to feel connected and whole. We learn to listen to our entire being without judgment. We notice that meditation does not progress in a linear fashion, with one sitting better than the next. Instead we find ourselves sitting in the heart, sensing the waves of our body and mind, receiving and observing. Like anything else, this requires patience and practice. We are gradually developing a whole new order of balance within us—it is actually breathtaking.

There is a poster of Swami Satchidananda wearing a loincloth and standing in a yoga posture called the tree pose, with one leg up and his hands over his head. He is balanced there on one foot. This is nothing very unusual—except he is in this pose balanced on a surfboard riding down a very large wave. Underneath it says in big letters, "You can't stop the waves, but you can learn to surf." This is meditation. It's true, we cannot stop the waves of change; they are the very fabric of our lives. Yet we can learn to surf, to be aware, to balance. Then our lives are no longer based on fear, and the state of balance itself becomes a way of living with beauty and ease.

### OPENING

So at this stage we have arrived, trained our observation, and balanced the mind. We have learned to observe with ease and gentleness. Is this it, then? Have we come to the end of meditation? This balance and observation are not it. We cannot just rest here or try to establish ourselves in a calm meditative state. We can now use these powers to go deeper. The next level of the meditation is one of opening. We must go more fully into our bodies, more deeply understand the movement of our mind, the psychological patterns we have discovered, and open to the very process of life itself.

This opening involves a refining of attention and a deeper,

more careful noticing. As meditation progresses, the breath can become more and more of a teacher to us, demonstrating the laws of impermanence, of arising and passing. Careful observation shows us the physical elements in a thousand variations of texture, feeling, pressure, and warmth. We can even become so aware that we can answer the question Mahasi Sayadaw used to pose for students when he asked them whether they fell asleep at night on the in-breath or woke in the morning on an out-breath. As we observe the body more delicately, there is a deep unknotting and untangling. With refined attention we can open further and find a level of being where there is no solidity anywhere, only patterns of pressure, tingling, heat, or coolness. At profound levels of silence and awareness it is as if we can feel down to the cellular levels of movement. The boundaries of the body begin to dissolve, and so does our very deep identification and grasping. How can we hold on to quicksand that has no boundaries, that is dissolving under our fingers? At some levels of perception the body becomes filled with vibrations and fine waves of light and rapture. At other times our perception shows the body as fire, where each movement and sensation that arises out of stillness shows itself to be inherently painful and burning. The play of pleasure and pain, of continuous arising and dissolution, leads us again and again to understand very directly what the Buddha meant by the ungraspable, selfless nature of the body.

Just as our observing can lead us to a level of opening in the body, so too can we move to an opening of the heart and mind. The opening of the heart, like the breath, has many rhythms, of fear and closing, of grieving and sorrow, and of lightness and blossoming and joy. The heart is like a flower, which cannot be forced open. The moist rain of our kindness, the gentle sunshine of our attention, are the nourishing and healing forces for the heart. Even so, to open demands that we allow a full feeling of what is present and of what is held there, a full willingness to grieve and accept the pain of the heart in equal measure with the joy. This is what must be allowed to be human, to discover our heart of compassion. All these things are part of the heart.

Opening is difficult. There are pains that we have worked hard all our lives to repress and avoid, and now, as we open up, we experience them. It's like falling through the ice on a pond. We've been skating very, very fast, keeping ourselves moving so we won't fall through. Now we're going to let ourselves fall through and see what is there.

For the opening of the heart and the mind we need a delicate and fearless observation. This does not mean standing back. It is a full presence with our experience while we learn the truth it has to teach us. To observe and open to deeper levels in the mind, we must be able to work skillfully with the content that arises and also see the whole level of the process of mind.

As we observe our mental states, at first we simply allow them to come and go as they will. Sometimes we see particular thought types or knots or patterns that repeat themselves over and over. These may be planning or judging, or guilt and memory, or we may notice that particular melodramas about relationships, health, creativity, or work arise again and again. They begin to reveal to us familiar patterns in the working of our mind. Sometimes, more than thoughts, it is the moods and feelings that stand out in their repetition: fear, love, longing, worry, sadness, or some other such state. When we initially observe them come and go, this observation can remain superficial, especially of frequently repeated patterns. As we watch them come again and again, we begin to sense that these patterns are like layers of resistance, their constant movement concealing deeper aspects of ourselves. And so they pose to us some very exciting, difficult, and important questions: What keeps them going? What is specifically underneath our most frequently repeated mental patterns? Here we can take our awareness to a new level and work with the content of mind to learn the skills of a deeper attention. Let us use the example of repetitive thoughts. Repeated thoughts usually arise when we have not fully acknowledged the feeling that drives them. For example, we may notice that the mind is always planning. Now, if we pay very close attention, we can become aware of the subtle feeling that is present when we notice that our planning is accompanied by a state of fear, and when we fully acknowledge the fear, the need for all the repetitive planning usually stops. Instead, we are left with our fear, to feel it, to accept it, to come to see and understand it. Similarly, a repeated pattern about relationships or work will often stop when we become aware of the force of longing or anger or sadness or love or whatever fuels its arising. When the mind begins to move in one of these repetitive patterns, we can take that as a signal to look and feel deeply into it and get to the root of what is keeping us moving. It means bringing awareness to the deeper feelings and movements in our body, heart, and mind.

To see and then accept the feelings and states that produce our particular patterns and knots can allow us to stop and settle more deeply into the moment. It can bring understanding and a new peace of mind. But now our meditation requires us to look deeper still, to become aware of the very source of the movement of mind. What makes the mind move at all? What is it we are trying to avoid by all this hoping, planning, fantasizing, and remembering? What pain or loneliness or unworthiness do we try to escape? What do we want to gain by this movement? What is the nature of the wanting mind? More than just observe, we must now open and feel and uncover layer by layer, until we come to the very center of the patterns that keep the mind moving, and then let go.

So, for example, in observing a frequently repeated thought about a relationship, we might then notice that it arises because we feel longing, we want love. We feel the longing that comes with all the thoughts, and in that accepting, the thoughts quiet down. We observe it in our body and mind. We want love. But still there is more to observe. What makes this wanting of love? For some of us it is because we feel we are incomplete, or because we are afraid of being alone, or because there are parts of ourselves we can't accept and we want assurance that we are okay. These feelings keep us running and reaching and separate from the present moment. Underneath them is the sense that we are truly a limited and separate person. Still we long to break out of this prison of separateness and incompletion. If we let ourselves stop and silently face the fears, the emptiness, the loneliness, the space inside, a new level of awareness can grow. There is a deeper truth than this illusion of separateness. If we are willing to open completely, we can come to the source of the movement and free ourselves to be here with what is in a whole new way.

This kind of looking is not analytical or discursive. It is like being in the presence of a great mystery and becoming still and clear and completely wakeful, so as to see the very depth of it. The power of this level of practice, penetrating to the root of what is happening, is what brings us to freedom. It is a way through our emptiness and fears to discover a wholeness of ourselves and the world.

As we observe, open, let go, and become more powerfully present, the qualities of mindfulness and concentration naturally strengthen. Then, whether it is by observation of the general flow of our mental states or through a careful opening of our feeling states, we begin to see a shift from the content of our experience to the process. Just as the body begins to dissolve under the microscope of our attention, so too the mind reveals its evanescent nature. The more closely we examine our feelings, the more quickly they change from one to another to another: sadness to depression to fear to joy to peace to pride. If we make a mental note and feel them carefully, we find that they only last two or five or ten notings before the next feeling arises. The thoughts become even more like bubbles. At first in meditation our moments of awareness are far apart and we may only notice thoughts in the middle or even at their end, after many cars of the train have passed and we've taken a long ride. Over time our moments of awareness grow more frequent, and we begin to notice thoughts earlier on. Finally, in stages of meditation with very close attention, we become so aware that we can notice when thoughts first arise and sometimes even become aware of the subtle impulse to think that is felt before a thought comes out of its cave.

The simple exercise of counting thoughts can give us a sense of our capacity for observing thought, of making the thought process a part of our mindfulness. If we sit for just five minutes we can practice counting the thoughts as each one arises. Like a cat waiting for a mouse, we can count each word and picture thought as it arises. Many people will notice twenty or thirty or even sixty thoughts arise in just a few minutes' time. For a few minutes in this counting exercise, the power of awareness is usually strong enough that we don't get caught by the story or content of each thought. It arises, we notice it and count it, and as we do so it passes away and we wait to count the next thought. We can begin to study the whole process of the movement of mind.

At some point the general emphasis of our meditation begins to shift from content to process. Physically at first we will notice "knee pain" or "car sound." Later we start to experience these as different vibrations and textures in the areas of the knee or the ear, without names or solidity. In the heart and mind too, the feelings and thoughts themselves can become more like vibrations. We will notice movements of energy and sensations and thoughts without story and content attached. Just as the body boundaries dissolve, so the very nature of mind shows itself as constantly arising and dissolving. The more closely we look at mind, the less graspable it becomes, and more and more we see it as a rapidly changing process rather than anything static. It can happen that we observe so quickly that we cannot begin to note each experience, and the meditation becomes more like a fine shower of sensations and thought moments, like tiny bubbles. The whole solidity of ourselves, our body, our ideas and thoughts, begins to break down.

As we settled into practice we gradually became more and more proficient at observing our experience. At first it was as though there were a little person sitting on our shoulder. "Now he's thinking. Now he's sleepy. Now he's angry." Then, as we settled in further and mindfulness and concentration grew stronger, we learned to uncover and work with the psychological knots that bind us. But even there our stance is one of separation of observer and observed. The mental commentary may not be as loud as before, but there is still a subtle grasping after something, an experience of some sort that we can identify with and learn from or "own." But as we continue and the mind becomes more quiet and open, we see in the depths or our being how nothing at all lasts and nothing can be grasped.

### BEING

This leads us on to the fourth level of practice—being. We begin to see clearly the laws that govern this process of body and mind. We may notice moments of balance and then see the moments where our desires, even subtle ones, condition more sorrow, frustration, and struggle. As we look at moments of unsatisfactoriness and pain and at moments of pleasure and joy, we can see how we relate to each of them and what really brings us happiness. If we hold on to things and they're changing, does that bring us happiness? Or if we want things to be a particular way, if we want our mind always to be calm or silent or our body always to have certain kinds of feelings, can we do that? Has anybody been able to make a mental or physical state endure forever? We start to see and feel how it is our very wanting to be calm, our need to be free, our spiritual desires, our subtle fear of the actual present that keeps us in conflict, in chains. It is not a matter of finally getting some spiritual state or ideal, but rather of coming back to the center of our being, here and now.

We see how in one moment an attachment or our desire interferes with being able to be fully alive. We see the undirected emptiness of things, how thoughts come and go, moods come and go, body sensations come and go according to the laws of conditionality. We're not the owners of this process; we cannot control change. So we finally stop. We let go. Not because we're imitating someone or because we are supposed to, but naturally, because we can see for ourselves and we understand the nature of things. Suzuki-roshi says: "Nothing exists but momentarily in its present form and color. One thing flows into another and cannot be grasped. Before the rain stops we hear a bird. Even under the heavy snow we see snowdrops and some new growth."

The truth of our being is simply this process of flowing change. Everything is impermanent. Nothing is worth grasping because nothing lasts. It is all empty, without self, like clouds moving through the sky. Knowing that nothing is secure, that there is no solid place on which to stand, we can let go, let be, and come to rest. We discover the depths of what it means to let go. For as much as we grasp and hold the body and senses, the feeling, the memory, ideas, reactions, and observation, so much do we make a separate "self," and so much do we suffer through this attachment.

Once, in Sri Lanka, I visited a very old and much-venerated meditation master, Hina Tyana Dhammaloka. There was a wonderful feeling of joy and freedom about him, and people said they could not recall ever seeing him any other way. I bowed and paid my respects, and after we had spoken for a while, he asked, "So, you teach meditation, yes?"

"I try," I said.

"Tell me, what is the heart of Buddhist meditation?"

"There is no self," I answered, "just the play of phenomena. It is truly an empty process."

He looked at me and then broke into a great laugh. "No self, no problem," he said, and he laughed and laughed.

When the mind ceases to want and judge and identify with whatever arises, we see the empty flow of experience as it is. We come to a ground of silence and inherent completeness. When we stop struggling and let be, the natural wisdom, joy, and freedom of our being emerges and expresses itself effortlessly. Our actions can come out of a spontaneous compassion and our innate wisdom can direct life from our heart.

To come to this we must accept paradox. As T. S. Eliot beseeches, "Teach us to care and not to care." In meditation we learn to care with a full-hearted attention, a true caring for each moment. Yet we also learn to let go. We do not separate out only those experiences we enjoy, but cultivate a sense of harmony, opening constantly to the truth within us and connecting with all life. This is an energetic, committed way of practice. As the great Tibetan lama Karmapa said, "This is living the practice instead of just doing it."

J. K.

EXERCISE

## Moving from Content to Process

Sit comfortably with your eyes closed and resolve for five minutes to observe only the thought process. For these five minutes count each thought as it arises. Your thoughts may come as picture thoughts or as words, or both together. Some thoughts may also come associated with a feeling or kinesthetic sense.

Let your mind be blank like a clear screen or open space and wait carefully to count each thought, like a cat at a mouse hole. After noticing and counting a thought, just wait for the next one. Do not let yourself be fooled by them. Some of them are very soft whispers of words, like "It's quiet in here." Some appear from behind and say, "There haven't been many thoughts yet, have there?" Count each of them. They may hide a bit when you are first watching, but they will come. At the end of five minutes most people will have seen at least five or ten thoughts; and many will have counted fifty or sixty. You will see what types of thoughts predominate in your mind, words or pictures or whatever. And most important, you will get a sense of how you can actually observe the thought process with mindfulness, noticing the arising of thought without getting lost in each story. It is a powerful and freeing realization to see that you are not your thoughts, to observe the stream of inner thought and be aware of it without being identified and caught up in it.

# PART TWO

# Training the Heart and Mind

# 6

# *The Seven Factors*
# *of Enlightenment*

SOMEBODY once asked Lama Govinda how one could fit together various traditions that represent Buddha's teaching. He replied that one can think of Buddha's dharma as a wonderful seed planted in the earth, out of which has blossomed a tree with deep roots, great branches, leaves, flowers, and fruit. He said that sometimes a person might point to the roots and say that it is just here that we can find the real dharma, while someone else may say, "Oh, no, it's in the flowers," and still another will say that it is to be found in the fruit. But of course, these different parts cannot really be separated; the roots sustain the tree in their own way, the leaves nourish the tree in their way, and the fruit depends on the roots and leaves and branches as well.

There is a teaching of the Buddha called the seven factors of enlightenment. These seven factors of enlightenment are like the sap that runs through the Buddha's tree of liberation, nourishing all parts of it. They are the qualities of heart and mind that arise from spiritual practice and represent the core, the essence of where his practical and systematic teachings lead us. When understood, these point to inspiring and genuine experiences in our practice. They are not a remote or abstract description, but are relevant to how our meditation actually deepens and the development of a unified and full spiritual life.

The seven enlightenment factors are qualities of mind that, when cultivated in practice, profoundly affect our relationship to the world around us. They include three arousing qualities, three stabilizing qualities, and mindfulness, which serves as a balancing and linking factor. To understand them is to know the prescription for a powerful and healing medicine. We must then take the medicine, which in meditation is a matter of actually developing these mind states. As we practice, we can come to sense how these qualities operate in our minds and in our lives. The personal cultivation and awakening of these qualities brings freedom to the individual and provides actual living transmission of the dharma.

## MINDFULNESS

The first factor for our enlightenment, central to the whole practice of buddha-dharma, is the quality of mindfulness, a clear awareness of what is happening each moment. Mindfulness is where we start; it is the first ingredient in the Buddha's recipe for awakening. Mindfulness means seeing how things are, directly and immediately seeing for oneself that which is present and true. It has a quality of fullness and impeccability to it, a bringing of our whole heart and mind, our full attention, to each moment.

When we look at our lives, it's amazing to see how much of the time we live on automatic pilot, half asleep, unaware, oblivious to what we are doing and what goes on around us. We can walk down the street and all of a sudden find we've arrived at our destination, and yet remember nothing at all of what we saw or thought or heard while we were walking. If we reflect on how many things we have done halfheartedly, we can feel our hesitation, our distraction, our fears, and the deadening effect they have had on our life. When we are mindful, there is a quality of being total, of being wholeheartedly and fully present for any activity. In his teachings to Carlos Castaneda, the Yaqui Indian teacher Don Juan speaks of the value of keeping death as one's adviser. He points out that there are some people who are very careful about the nature of their acts; their happiness comes from acting with the knowledge that they don't have much time, and so they live with fullness, attention, and impeccability.

When we have given something our wholehearted attention, whether work or school or a relationship or dharma practice, there is a certain energy and joy that arise in the mind. It may not even matter so much what results we end up with, because in doing something completely—with awareness and in a wholehearted way—the very doing is in itself satisfying. To live with mindfulness is to live in a caring and heartfelt way.

Mindfulness has three functions. The first is that mindfulness sees clearly what is happening in the present moment. It is observing and experiencing without reacting. As we practice it, mindfulness allows us to notice what is just here, to receive each experience without judgment, without grasping or aversion. Then, when we are awake and aware, without having the mind move in relation to what it sees, a clear understanding of our world arises. Mindfulness permits us to perceive our senses directly without analysis, comparisons, or interpretation. With this attention we can discover the laws that govern our bodies, hearts, and minds. Through the freshness and immediacy of our attention, and with less identification, we can begin to sense a whole new inner spirit of freedom.

The second way mindfulness functions is that it develops all the other factors of enlightenment. This makes it an extremely powerful attribute of mind. As it grows, it brings with it steadiness, calm, and equanimity. It enhances our ability to investigate the whole nature of life. All of these grow out of our careful attention. Mindfulness can be called a universal quality. It helps in all circumstances: with meditation, with tennis and music, with science and lovemaking, in every human endeavor. When strengthened, it serves as a reference and protection for us and keeps us from being too caught up in the changing circumstances of life. Mindful attention is the ground out of which wisdom and love can grow.

The third function of mindfulness is to balance the mind. When we pay attention in the proper way, no matter what is going on, the mind comes to a sense of balance. In a moment of the worst fear or confusion or attachment or pain, when mindfulness arises, it sees our state clearly and brings us into balance in relation to it. Meditation students must have the direct experience of bringing mindfulness to a difficult situation to truly appreciate the power it has to bring balance to life. No matter how long or difficult an experience has been, a moment of mindfulness can bring us back to balance. Mindfulness balances the factors of enlightenment too. There may be some times when we need more serenity, other times when we need more enthusiasm and energy. At each moment that we are mindful, aware without reacting, the various factors of enlightenment come alive. For example, if we are very calm but a bit too sluggish, when we note "calm, calm," instantly the awareness of this calm state brings more energy. The awareness and investigation of what is present provide a balance for the calmness. Or, conversely, if we are restless or agitated and note "restless, restless," the very noting and accepting of it provides a calm and more open space of mind from which to experience the restlessness. In the end, mindfulness can help bring about an extraordinary balance, allowing us to be energized, focused, tranquil, and exploring, all at once.

There are four aspects or foundations of mindfulness that are central to the practice of awakening. That is to say, we can cultivate mindfulness on the four major fields of our experience.

The first foundation of mindfulness is mindfulness of the physical world, of the body and its senses. This means being aware of sights and sounds, of colors and tastes, of the breath, sensations, body posture, and movement.

The second foundation is mindfulness of feeling. Every time there is consciousness of a sense object, whether we are seeing, hearing, touching, smelling, tasting, or thinking, there is a feeling of pleasantness or unpleasantness or neutrality associated with it. Mindfulness of feeling is of great importance because it is in this aspect of experience that the mind gets stuck. When we come into contact with pleasant feelings, we are conditioned to become attached; when we come into contact with unpleasant feelings, we commonly react with aversion. Coming into contact with neutral feelings, we often blank out—we're not fully aware. Being caught by likes and dislikes, we try to perpetuate certain conditions and avoid other conditions, and so continually create the whole samsaric pattern of suffering and duality. Mindfulness can show us the nature of these feelings and our patterns of reaction so that we can live wisely.

The third foundation of mindfulness is awareness of the contents of the mind and heart. This means paying attention to all the states of the heart and mind. Whatever arises—doubt, fear, love, wisdom, clarity, sleepiness, restlessness, planning, remembering—the aim is to be mindful of these qualities, discovering their nature without judgment or interference, without trying to make them function according to our likes and dislikes.

The fourth foundation is mindfulness of the dharma. This means awareness of the laws that govern all the elements of the mind and body. Observation of these universal laws shows us that everything is impermanent, in constant flux. Everything is empty of self; there is no "I" behind the impermanent process of mind and body. We can see how attachment to the elements of mind and body causes suffering and dissatisfaction, because these elements arise and vanish according to the law of karma and not according to our wishes. All of this and more is revealed through our attention.

For anyone wishing to be enlightened, cultivating mindfulness is essential. Of course, in practice our level of awareness will go through many cycles. It may be more present during intensive retreats or at times of life crisis, when we are alone in nature or after we hear an inspiring talk. To practice is to nourish this quality. No matter what the level or situation, being mindful renews our balanced and nongrasping awareness. As practice develops, the frequency of this awareness will grow. During retreats and in intensive practice, after a period of settling down has passed, we actually find ourselves being present more frequently. While it may seem slow, any improvement in our ability to be aware is a major accomplishment. As we continue to reestablish and focus our attention, new levels of understanding will come into view. Eventually, mindfulness can get so precise that we can separate the process of perception, hearing the first vibration at the ear, followed by a moment of knowing its pleasant quality, followed by a moment of recognition—"bird song"—followed by an image of a bird and then a desire to hear more. We can learn to pay such fine attention that our whole solid world reveals itself to be a flow, an interactive process of body and mind, a dance of many moving pieces. What at first appears as just our "self" hearing a "sound" opens to show us moments of sense perception, moments of feeling, and moments of recognition and response. In this way, the very solidity of our world can be dissolved. Through very careful attention we can experience new levels of the instantaneous arising and passing of the whole body and mind. As we "dissolve," so do the boundaries between "us" and the "world outside," and we can come to experience the unity and non-separation of all things, and find a freedom not limited by any of them.

In daily practice, the power of mindfulness can grow too. Through attention to our bodies and minds and our reactions to outer circumstances, practice will deepen. This can be done through mindfulness while driving, in family life, at work or alone. As we look, we will see more and more clearly the patterns of habits and fears that have often run our lives. In coming more into the moment, we can actually experience the dynamic energy of our bodies and hearts. We can feel the difference between when we live with attachment and when we are at ease, when we are caught in compulsion and identification and when there is wisdom. Whatever level we attend to, mindfulness brings us the possibility of being free. It is possible to cultivate this wholeheartedness, this fullness of attention and being. As we do, the power of our awareness will bring to fruition all the riches of a well-lived spiritual life.

### EFFORT AND ENERGY

Mindfulness balances the mind. The next three enlightenment factors are arousing qualities. The first of these is the factor of energy or effort. Learning how to make the right effort is one of the most crucial questions for people. What does it mean to make proper effort?

First and foremost, it is simply the effort to be aware, to be mindful. Thus effort in insight meditation is not so much directed at changing the objects of our experience, but is the effort to see them directly with a clear mind and an open heart. Whenever we have a question about our effort, we can ask ourselves, Am I really paying attention?

Second, energy or effort grows as we find our capacity to be full in our practice. We tend to be stingy with our effort. We think, "Well, I only have so much energy, and if I really practice hard today, then tomorrow I'll run out of energy. So maybe I should just take it easy today." We are afraid, or perhaps we feel we are not ready, like Saint Augustine, who prayed, "Dear Lord, please give me chastity and continence, but not yet!" Do we want to be aware or not? Can we stand to open to it all, and will we have enough energy? There is a secret of practice and of life to learn here. The way energy works is just the opposite of what we fear. We are not like a battery that runs down. The more we open ourselves, the more our energy and effort in practice flow. We become a channel or conduit for energy. This energy is the power of expansion and opening, not an energy of struggle. It is a power of the heart. If we are willing to bring a wholehearted effort to every aspect of our practice, the very effort itself brings more energy as we touch this great capacity within us. As one Zen master teaches, "Cut all your bargaining!" Just do it.

This does not mean that we have to strain or fight in our meditation practice or in our lives. Effort has the characteristic of supporting, upholding, and sustaining us. It can be gentle, but it keeps us going forward uninterruptedly, without getting diverted or wasting our time.

Energy and effort breathe life into values that we respect or cherish. They bring power to our actions. A factor that greatly supports the opening of energy in practice is exercise and care of the physical body. At certain deep stages sitting meditation itself can bring energy and lightness to the body. But most practitioners find that this is not sufficient. Through mindful yoga, stretching, regular aerobic exercise, and movement we can help make the body a more supple vehicle for the powerful energy practice to open within us. As practice develops we must nourish mindfulness by learning to care for our bodies and live more fully in them.

There is another level of this quality, which we can master as our practice grows. Classically, the Buddha spoke of four great efforts. These go beyond the simple observation of the experience and express the potential we have for actually directing and purifying the mind. These are tricky practices because when misunderstood, they can inadvertently lead to an increase in judgment, aversion, and a gaining state of mind. Yet they are important for more experienced meditators to explore and understand.

The first great effort is to enhance and foster wholesome or skillful states that are already part of our makeup. So, for example, we may see that generous thoughts arise in our mind. We make the effort to protect them and develop them, like helping a sapling grow into a strong tree by taking care of it.

The second of the great efforts is the effort not to get entangled in unwholesome or unskillful states that have already arisen within us. So we may see, for example, that greed has come up in our minds, and understanding from our own experience the suffering of that mind state, we disentangle ourselves, we let it go. This doesn't involve a condemning attitude toward the mind state or toward ourselves—the energy is not a punitive or harsh one. Based on a clear understanding, we can simply move our minds in a direction of more happiness and peace.

The third great effort is to encourage skillful and beautiful states not yet arisen within us: to tap our enormous power and actively choose to develop qualities such as love and forgiveness and awareness.

The fourth great effort is the effort to avoid unskillful states not yet arisen. If we know that certain situations or circumstances produce unwholesome states within us, we can act with determination not to pursue them. We can manifest with our every action those things which we most care about.

Developing a sense of the inner power of effort and energy is a great blessing in practice. With proper effort, we can personally and directly touch our hearts, we can discover the highest truths, and we can bring them into action in our day-to-day lives.

## INVESTIGATION

The third factor of enlightenment is investigation of the dharma, investigation of nature. At times we may have a tendency to be complacent in practice, contenting ourselves with believing the words of a teacher or something we read in a book. Investigation of the dharma means not settling for secondhand knowledge or adopting someone else's opinion. It says, "I must see for myself what is true." What makes someone a true heir of the Buddha, what makes a buddha, is the courage and willingness to look directly and honestly into the body, the heart, and the mind without relying on or settling for what others say is true. Over years of meditation it is this quality that keeps practice alive.

The quality of investigation requires courage. It is an acknowledgment of what we really don't know and a willingness to examine the deepest questions in life. Don Juan explains that only by being a spiritual warrior can one withstand the path of knowledge. Practice requires courage, and while for ordinary people life is experienced as a series of blessings and curses, for one who wishes to become a man or woman of knowledge, life and practice is one continuous challenge. The spirit of investigation allows us to look into and be with whatever experience arises. As practice develops, we may go through periods of doubt, discouragement, and pain, even a dark night of the soul. We will certainly find ourselves exploring the powerful energies of greed and fear, of anger and sorrow. In undertaking our task to understand and free our minds and hearts, we must learn to observe and examine every realm and state that arises.

We may face a vision of our death in sitting, or powerful attachment and fear in our relationship. To investigate these conditions and discover the laws by which they operate is our task. When we actually investigate our experience, whether in sitting meditation or everyday life, we start to see that every experience is proclaiming the dharma, that life is always saying, "This is how things are!" Every experience is teaching the dharma: teaching about karma, teaching impermanence, teaching how suffering arises, and teaching about liberation. The poet Kabir says, "When the eyes and ears are open, even the leaves on the trees teach like pages from the scriptures."

This discernment into the true nature of this mind and body is not intellectual. As long as there is no insight into the truth of who we are, it is as if the mind is enclosed in darkness. If we were to walk into a dark room, we would be unable to clearly see the objects in that room and we could get filled with doubt and confusion—"Am I about to bump into something? Is it better to move or stand still?" In just the same way, we get terribly confused about how things are in our experience, and sometimes we're filled with paralyzing doubt. When investigation is developed, it is like a bright light that arises. We enter the dark room and our confusion is dissipated.

The power of investigation increases with the depth of our practice. We can investigate and actually explore all the elements that make up this body and mind. With powerful attention and investigation we can see the workings of the eight basic physical elements, the sixfold sense processes, the nature of skillful and unskillful factors of mind, and the ways to develop inner clarity and freedom. We can examine the moment-to-moment process of mental birth and death. We can discover our deepest fears and places of identification and clinging, and we can see their patterns of operation in our life. To do this we must be willing to open our hearts and minds, even to their secret corners. Sometimes in the place of greatest darkness, in opening to our deepest pains and fears, the most important truths are learned.

Over time in a variety of circumstances the spirit of inquiry can grow in us. Just as it can take us deeper, to see the very elements that make up this body and mind, it can also expand our vision of practice to inquire into our relationship with all the parts of the world around us. We can learn to direct it to every area of the four foundations of mindfulness. Maturity in practice will have us investigating our attachments and ideals, our understandings and our freedom in relationships, family, work—in all domains of our life. This investigation is supported by wise reflection, by associating with wise people, and by questions based on a sincere urge to discover truth. To look in this way does not mean asking circular questions or showing off, but is a way of keeping inquiry alive in us. Investigation and wisdom must he balanced with a proper level of faith or confidence. If investigation becomes excessive, it leads to over-intellectualization, or becoming lost in thoughts, analyses, and questions. If it is too weak, we become struck with blind faith. What is necessary is a faith or confidence in the possibility of awakening and the investigation to see how it actually can be done—a commitment to our own direct understanding.

### RAPTURE

The next factor of enlightenment is rapture, interest, and joy. It is learning to live and practice with a light heart. To find this lightness is essential to our opening in meditation. It can be fostered in all aspects of our lives when we learn not to take things too seriously. Of course, we will still go through every kind of experience, all sorts of phases and cycles of practice and of life experiences. But it doesn't take very much observation of the mind to see that it will make up any story or tell any excuse, and in a second transport us from heaven to hell. It is filled with the memories of old TV shows we have forgotten, of our second-grade teacher, of the noblest sentiments and pettiest gossip. The mind will do anything, and when we sit, it often does. It has no pride, and it is very slippery. Sometimes things will be dull and boring, sometimes very exciting, sometimes pleasant, sometimes unpleasant or terrifying. The quality of rapture is an ease and openness of mind that receives with interest every kind of circumstance. It asks, "What do I have to learn from this new experience?" or says, "Wow, this is pretty intense, isn't it?" To be in touch with this factor brings a capacity to look at our life with a playful yet caring interest and to say in difficulty, "Even this is something I can work with."

This quality of openness is based on being willing to expand and see things from a larger perspective. At times we become weighed down with our likes and dislikes and identification; our melodramas seem very solid and real and important. This quality of light-heartedness has been described as controlled folly by Don Juan. It is like looking at our small life on this earth from a great distance and from a great length of time. It is the recognition that all created things pass, and what matters then is not how much we collect or what we make or do, but how we live this short dance, and how well we learn to love. Let us learn to live wisely even though life passes like a flash of summer lightning and a dream.

When we get deeply concentrated in meditation, rapture becomes very strong and our whole energetic system is affected. This level of rapture and interest comes as the result of the altered and powerful states that steady concentration and a composed mind can produce. A whole range of pleasant physical states and an inner sense of extreme well-being arise. The physical effects of rapture can range from floods of joy like waves at a seashore, to transporting joy and feelings of floating, to suffusing joy, which pervades the whole body. All of this is different from the pleasurable feelings due to having a desire satisfied; it is born out of the unification of the mind, body, and heart as we enter our present moment's experience with strong concentration and interest. This is one of the wonderful aspects of practice, to discover and explore the range of rapture and the joys of lightness of heart.

## CONCENTRATION

The three arousing factors of enlightenment that we have considered—effort, investigation, and rapture—are balanced by three stabilizing qualities. The first of these stabilizing qualities is concentration, or samadhi. Concentration is the factor of enlightenment known as one-pointedness, arising when the mind is steadily focused on an object. It is a steadiness that gives the mind tremendous strength. Just as light, when concentrated in a laser, has the ability to cut through steel, the concentrated mind has the ability to penetrate deeply into the process of mind and body, and to explore widely other realms of consciousness.

One of the first insights that come to people who look within is a recognition that their mind is out of control; it is untrained and turbulent, filled with thoughts and plans and reactions and likes and dislikes. There is a constant barrage of sense impressions and a series of reactions to them. This constant stream of mental and physical events seems very solid. But as the mind becomes more concentrated, as it becomes focused and still, we begin to penetrate through the layers of thought and see how the thoughts and emotions simply arise and pass away moment by moment. We can examine the seemingly solid experience of body sensations and sound and sight, and see that, like the mind, they too are actually a process that is in constant change. The illusion of continuity that they give is called santati and is the result of the constant and rapid flow of activity. The concentrated mind is able to cut through this seemingly solid process and see its moment-by-moment impermanence.

There are two types of concentration generally used in Buddhist meditation. The first type uses concentration on a fixed single object to focus the mind and stop its discursive thinking, to bring about profoundly steady and peaceful states. There are many ways to do this, focusing on the breath, on a mantra, on a feeling such as loving-kindness, or on a light or visualization. This produces a profound steadiness of mind and a one-pointed stillness with the object of meditation. The second type of concentration is called moment-to-moment samadhi. It is also a development of a powerful and steady attention but is done by concentrating on whatever changing object arises in each moment. This concentration can shift between the breath, sound, body sensations, and mental states as they arise, but it brings an immediate, deep, and unwavering quality to each object it observes. It is this moment-to-moment concentration that is developed in insight meditation. For concentration to develop in this way, it is not the object itself that is important, but rather developing the quality of one-pointedness, stillness, and clear focus in each moment. When we use only one object—when we concentrate on the breath, a visualization, a mantra, or one of a hundred other objects—the single object serves the function of steadying the mind. But while concentration on a single object temporarily clears the mind of distraction and worry, it is in effect a temporary suppression of the hindrances. Moment-to-moment concentration focuses more on developing a steadiness of mind in all situations rather than the aspect of suppression and removal from distraction.

This type of concentration focuses attention on whatever is actually present. To learn to concentrate is central to mastering the art of meditation. Of course, the mind is quite difficult to steady, and the training of concentration requires determination and perseverance to bring ourselves back again and again to the object of the moment. After all, we have spent tens of thousands of hours (if not lifetimes) with our mind wandering. Each time we begin to concentrate, we will encounter the forces of this habit, the powerful desires, fears, and resistances that keep our mind in motion. These may include pain or tension in the body, states of anger, loneliness, grief, longing, and any unfinished business that our busy mind has protected us from feeling. To concentrate and calm the mind, we must learn the art of settling, releasing, or passing through these layers without adding to the resistance.

It is like learning a new language. We have to repeat it over and over again without judgment or rush. Only after a hundred times do we begin to learn. It is a steady and patient task most of us face to collect and train the mind. Yet it is not at all impossible. Many people have followed this path before us. What it takes is practice, consistency, and a discovery of the correct spirit, a sense of balance in the meditation. Then, when we begin to experience the fruit of even a little concentration, it becomes rewarding and exciting. There is a natural happiness and a feeling of well-being that arise when we have passed through the resistances and touch the first steadiness and clarity that concentration brings. It is even more exciting because we realize that this mind, which has been out of control for so long, can actually be worked with and can become aware, steady, and directed through our training.

As we become more experienced meditators, concentration becomes more of a skill we have developed than an obstacle to surmount. While we may not be always collected, we do learn ways to promote it. We learn the ways to settle ourselves, what postures to take, how long to sit, how to use the breath, and how to skillfully work with the hindrances as they arise. For some students most of their wisdom will arise while developing only mildly concentrated states. Insight will arise at the times when their attention is present and steady and they are able to carefully observe the normal movement of body and mind. For another group of students continued practice will bring them to much higher states of concentration. One level that is particularly worth noting is called access concentration. It is achieved when the mind has few discursive thoughts and almost no wandering from the present object. There is a deep steadiness and collection of attention on the present moment. At this point, most of the hindrances and restlessness have disappeared and the meditation flows very smoothly. The steadiness of concentration at this level can be used to gain access to the higher states of absorption. There is a spontaneous arising of light and rapture, and the factors of calm and profound steadiness become strong as one develops full concentration on a single meditative object. At other times, when the mind becomes concentrated we will sometimes experience a unification of the heart and mind. Here, the discursive mind quiets down and the sense of our center of attention moves from the head to the heart, as if all experience that arises touched us in the center of our being. Access concentration that focuses on our changing experience can be used in the way of vipassana to examine the mind and body. Through such concentrated examination we can see an almost microscopic level of arising and passing of all our senses, and the instantaneous changing of the whole body and mind. As we concentrate in this way, the whole illusion of solidity and separateness dissolves before our eyes. Whether from mild or powerful levels of concentration, insights can arise that bring understanding, presentness, and a deep capacity to let go and live more freely in our lives. Much more could be said about concentration, for it produces most of the altered states that arise in meditation—visions, lights, access to other states of consciousness and other realms of being, rapture, and much more.

At whatever level we work with it, in retreats or daily practice, concentration harmonizes and steadies our mind and heart. As we cultivate it, happiness and understanding grow along with freedom and a sense of disentanglement from the complex discursive mind. It is a wonderful part of our spiritual practice.

## TRANQUILLITY

The next stabilizing factor is tranquillity. In our busy world, we tend to overlook the capacity we have to allow the mind to settle down and rest, to become deeply silent and peaceful. This stillness is a great power in meditation, and through it we can learn to listen more fully to the world around us and to the wisdom of our own heart. To support tranquillity in practice we need to foster a stillness in the body, a calmness of breath, and an inner ease and restfulness. Exercising, breathing, sitting, calming, all of this can be practiced. Tranquillity is also fostered by our time alone and by time in nature. It is not by accident that the Buddha chose to live in the forests rather than in the cities of Benares or Rajagaha. Periodic retreats and other forms of outer stillness can powerfully nourish our inner tranquillity.

Mentally, the most direct way of coming to rest is to learn to let go of our likes and dislikes. This means to stop living so much in our desires and plans and regrets. Life can become so complicated and filled by preferences and plans that we miss the actual experience of things as they are. We can go for a hike on a beautiful trail in the mountains and spend three-quarters of our time thinking about what we're going to do when we get back. We are so attached to our judgments and plans and ideas, as though we really knew what is going to happen. We might be able to make a fair guess, but we really don't know. We don't know who's going to die today or who's going to be born; whether we'll get run over by a car or win the lottery. A great sense of tranquillity comes when we let go of the futile urge to control everything, and instead relate to each moment with openness and awareness. It is like the cool shade of a tree to a person previously affected by the sun's heat. It's not that it is somehow wrong to have plans and ideas—plans and ideas are fine—it is the attachment to these ideas or the excessive reliance on them that causes the trouble.

The Chilean poet Pablo Neruda expresses the spirit of this quality of tranquillity in his poem "Keeping Quiet":

> Now we will count to twelve
> and we will all keep still
> For once on the face of the
> earth,
> let's not speak in any language;
> let's stop for a second,
> and not move our arms so much.
>
> It would be an exotic moment
> without rush, without engines;
> we would all be together
> in a sudden strangeness.
>
> Fisherman in the cold sea
> would not harm whales
> and the man gathering salt
> would not look at his hurt hands.

Those who prepare green wars,
wars with gas, wars with fire,
victories with no survivors,
would put on clean clothes
and walk about with their brothers
in the shade, doing nothing.

What I want should not be confused
with total inactivity.
Life is what it is about; . . .

If we were not so single-minded
about keeping our lives moving,
and for once could do nothing,
perhaps a huge silence
might interrupt this sadness
of never understanding ourselves
and of threatening ourselves with
death.

Perhaps the earth can teach us
as when everything seems dead in winter
and later proves to be alive.

Now I'll count up to twelve
and you keep quiet and I will go.

Inner calmness is a way of being that can transform our lives. Taking one thing at a time as our focus, letting the imperfections of life be, fosters a sense of the present, a contentment with the moment. At first our meditation may develop in some ways but still be mixed with a quality of striving or judgment. As our skill in meditation grows, we can learn the art of letting go and finding a calm center in the midst of our changing sense. As we sit, extraordinary levels of silence and peace can open for us. We can feel as if the whole world had suddenly stopped moving. Our body can become light and transparent like a clear spring sky. The senses and the heart can open in a sweet and delicate way, and a powerful contentment can arise. We can learn how happiness comes from a heart at rest and not from changing outer circumstances. All of this can be discovered as a power and fruit of our practice.

### EQUANIMITY

The last of the stabilizing factors, the final factor of enlightenment, is equanimity. An image used to illustrate the quality of equanimity is that of a mountain. The mountain sits there as the sun shines on it, the rain falls, it gets covered with snow, struck by lightning. What does the mountain do? It remains unwavering. Equanimity is the power of mind to experience the changes in the realm of form, the realm of feeling, the realm of mind, yet remain centered and unmoved. Equanimity is developed as we learn to keep our heart open through the changing circumstances of our life and our practice. As we grow in wisdom our heart also matures from an outgoing exuberance of youth with its conditioned fears and desires to what is called a heart of greatness. Finding our heart of greatness comes through practice. Again and again we are challenged to return to this moment, however painful or pleasant or boring, and to let it into our heart—to greet it with balance. Often we are knocked off balance. Yet equanimity is but another moment away. Can we accept this moment with balance? In its strongest stages equanimity gives the feeling of unshakable stability, unable to be upset by any experience whatsoever. In another tradition it is called "shamanic equilibrium," which allows the shaman to travel to even the extreme realms of pain and death without fear of difficulty. We can find that a profound equanimity arises as we release our identification with this body-mind process. As our practice shows us how temporary and ungraspable is every aspect of life, we begin to feel a deep letting go of our attachment to various aspects of our self. Our ideas, our beliefs, our images, our feelings, our fears, and even our body are all temporary conditions. They are not ours! They are not graspable as I, me, or mine. To experience this truth in practice brings profound equanimity and liberation.

People often make the mistake of thinking that spiritual practice makes a person ineffectual or passive. In fact, qualities like equanimity have tremendous power. They are the inner strengths of the heart that our greatness draws upon, the forces that allow people like Gandhi or Mother Teresa to so powerfully affect even a very difficult circumstance.

There is a story in the Zen tradition that illustrates this very well. During a time of civil war in Korea, a certain general led his troops through province after province, overrunning whatever stood in his path. The people of one town, knowing that he was coming and having heard tales of his cruelty, all fled into the mountains. The general arrived in the empty town with his troops and sent them out to search the town. Some of the soldiers came back and reported that only one person remained, a Zen priest. The general strode over to the temple, walked in, pulled out his sword, and said, "Don't you know who I am? I am the one who can run through you without batting an eye."

The Zen master looked back and calmly responded, "And I, sir, am one who can be run through without batting an eye." The general, hearing this, bowed and left.

Equanimity, then, is a quality of mind and heart that, when developed, allows one to meet every kind of experience with both strength and a softness or fluidity that doesn't get caught by circumstances. To discover its power within is one of the great joys of practice.

The Buddha describes the seven factors of enlightenment as the fruit of practice and as the states of mind from which enlightenment arises. Over the years of our practice, in retreats and in daily life, we can begin to experience these qualities in our heart and mind: we can sense their strength within us. At the times when the fears and plans of the reactive and discursive mind become silent, we can begin to see how these qualities are our natural state, underlying the passions and confusions of the mind. To embody these factors of enlightenment is to awaken to our fullest inner potential. Yet we cannot attain them through grasping or forcing any more than we can make a flower grow taller by pulling on it. They are factors of the mind and heart that arise, like all things, according to certain conditions. Our way of practice is to water and weed, to sincerely nourish and support these qualities through wise attention in all the parts of our life. We need a long-enduring mind. For most of us, this is a process like the growth of a century plant—a long and slow opening to the magnificent bloom of our awakening.

It is beautiful to see how these qualities will manifest through each of us in a unique, individual way. We will all be different buddhas. Tall buddhas, short buddhas, John buddhas, Sally buddhas, Asian buddhas, New York buddhas. But anyone who awakens these qualities will discover the same freedom and the same joy. And any way of practice that develops these qualities leads us to this. There is no need to be confused by the outer forms of different spiritual traditions, by comparing Zen robes or Indian ceremonies to Hindu mantras or Sufi dancing. It is simple. Measured inwardly, any practice that leads to liberation will cultivate the qualities of mindfulness, effort, investigation, rapture, concentration, tranquillity, and equanimity.

Through the development and the balancing of these seven qualities we can break through the conditioned patterns of the mind and come to know the deepest truth for ourselves. That which was hidden becomes seen; that which was overturned becomes upright. We can live our lives in harmony, with a greatness of heart and a clear mind, and come to know peace.

J. K.

### EXERCISE

## Awareness of the Factors of Enlightenment

In traditional practice one takes a periodic review of the factors of enlightenment. In this exercise let yourself become aware of the presence of the enlightenment factors in your sittings. Pick a period of two or three weeks in your daily sitting, or else use one sitting each day during an intensive retreat, to review them. In the middle of each sitting, at a point when you feel relatively attentive, look to see which of the seven factors are present, which are strong and which are weak. Notice carefully what you see without any evaluation or judgment. In this sitting, is mindfulness strong or weak? Which of the three arousing factors are present? Are energy and effort there? Investigation? Rapture and interest? Notice to what degree or strength each of these qualities has arisen. Then examine the three stabilizing qualities. Is concentration present? If so, is it weak or strong? Tranquillity? Equanimity and balance? Which of the factors are present? Which are missing?

Sometimes in the very act of our being aware of qualities, they become stronger and more present. Notice if that happens as well. The factors of enlightenment are impersonal qualities arising out of certain conditions. Over the weeks that you observe them, become aware of the days when they are particularly strong and the days when they are noticeably absent. Become aware of what conditions block them. Try to get a sense of what ways you can embrace and nourish these qualities in your practice.

# 7

# The Life of the Buddha

A QUESTION for us to consider is whether we can relate to the life of the Buddha, both in our formal practice and in our everyday lives, in a way that is meaningful for us in these times. Can we relate to his life in some way that gives perspective and context to our own? One possibility is to see the Buddha as a particular historical figure, a person who lived in what is now northern India in the fifth and sixth centuries B.C.E., and who went through a powerful awakening transformation at the age of thirty-five. We can relate in a very human, historical way, understanding his struggles, his quest, his enlightenment, from the perspective of one human being to another.

Another level on which we can relate is to view the Buddha as a fundamental archetype of humanity; that is, as the full manifestation of buddha-nature, the mind that is free of defilement and distortion, and understanding his life story as a great journey representing some basic archetypal aspects of human existence. By viewing the life of the Buddha in both of these ways, as a historical person and as an archetype, it becomes possible to see the unfolding of universal principles within the particular content of his life experience. We can then view the Buddha's life not as an abstract, removed story of somebody who lived twenty-five hundred years ago, but as one that reveals the nature of the universal in us all. This becomes a way of understanding our own experience in a larger and more profound context, one that connects the Buddhas's journey with our own. We have undertaken to follow the same path, motivated by the same questions: What is the true nature of our lives? What is the root cause of our suffering?

In his book *Hero with a Thousand Faces* (New York: World Publishing Co., 1971), Joseph Campbell, the great scholar of humanity's myths and archetypes, explores the nature of the hero myth. He speaks of four stages in the great journey of the archetypal hero or heroine, and his discussion of the Buddha's journey in terms of these four stages is a wonderful interweaving of the personal elements of the Buddha's life and the universal principles they embody. Realizing how the events of the Buddha's life relate directly to our own experiences can give tremendous energy and inspiration to our individual journeys. Reflecting upon the life of the Buddha brings a sense of joy to the mind, because in recognizing the power and magnitude of the Buddha's spiritual quest, we reconnect with our own deepest impulses and motivations for practicing the dharma.

When we first contemplate the adventures of the world's great explorers, we are struck with a feeling of the mystery and drama of discovery. We might picture them venturing into uncharted waters or exploring strange, new lands, but we tend not to think about the countless daily hardships and inconveniences—the mosquitoes, the rain, the boredom, the bad food. Yet that is all part of the journey as well. In the same way, the countless irritations and difficulties that present themselves in the course of practice are part of the extraordinary exploration of the nature of our own lives. It is easy to get so caught up in the details of our experience that we may lose touch with the vast scope of the context in which we are working.

Campbell calls the first stage of the hero's journey the call to destiny. According to traditional accounts, the Buddha first heard this call many, many lifetimes before his birth as Siddhartha Gotama, when he was a forest-dwelling hermit named Sumedha in the time of the previous buddha, Dipankara. One day Sumedha heard that Dipankara Buddha would be passing nearby, and he joined the many people who were going to pay their respects. The people were preparing the road for Dipankara and the procession of monks and nuns, and Sumedha was given one small section of the road to prepare and make smooth. He had not quite finished and the road was still muddy when they were about to arrive, so at the last minute Sumedha laid his body down on the road for Dipankara to walk over.

It is said that when he saw Dipankara, Sumedha was so inspired by his presence and nobility that he resolved that he, too, would one day bring to perfection all the qualities of mind of a buddha. Dipankara saw this aspiration in the mind of the hermit and prophesied that many aeons of time in the future, Sumedha would be born a prince named Siddhartha Gotama and in that lifetime would attain to buddhahood. From the moment of hearing and responding to that call to destiny, Sumedha was a bodhisattva, a being destined to attain the awakening and perfection of a buddha. The *Jataka Tales* are a collection of stories telling of the bodhisattva's efforts through many lifetimes to bring to fulfillment the ten paramis, or perfections of a buddha: generosity, morality, renunciation, wisdom, effort, patience, truthfulness, resolve, equanimity, and loving-kindness. Likewise, the effort in our own lives to develop these paramis should not be undervalued. They are the powerful causes of all spiritual accomplishment.

In the lifetime during which the bodhisattva became the Buddha, he was born a prince in the small kingdom of the Shakyas near what is now the border of Nepal and India. At the time of his birth, wise men foretold that he would become either a world monarch or, renouncing the world, a buddha. The bodhisattva's father, the king, wishing for his son to become a worldly ruler like himself, contrived to surround Siddhartha with all the pleasures of the senses and to occupy him entirely with the delights of the world. There was a different palace provided for each of the seasons, with musicians, dancers, concubines, and the like, to entertain him. The king did everything within his power to banish unpleasantness from the experience of the young prince.

Siddhartha decided one day to leave the palace and go out into the city. Being concerned that Siddhartha would see something unpleasant and be prompted to question his life and renounce the world, the king ordered all unpleasant sights to be covered up, the city to be painted, flowers and incense to be placed all about, and all people who were suffering to be hidden away. But the bodhisattva's calling was not to be so easily denied.

It is said that four heavenly messengers, celestial beings, appeared to him as he rode throughout the city. The first of these messengers appeared to him as an old person, stricken with age, feeble in the senses. The second messenger appeared as a person suffering greatly with disease. The third appeared as a corpse. Each time, the prince was startled because he had never before in that life come into contact with sickness, old age, and death. Seeing these aspects of life for the first time touched him deeply. Each time, he questioned the charioteer about what he was seeing and whether everyone was subject to this fate. The charioteer replied that it is the inevitable fate of all who take birth to grow older, get sick, and die. The last of the heavenly messengers appeared to the prince as a wandering monk. Questioned again, the charioteer answered that this was someone who had renounced the world in order to seek enlightenment and liberation. These four heavenly messengers awakened within the bodhisattva the energy of countless lifetimes of practice; they awakened within him both the deep sense of inquiry—What is the nature of birth and death? What is the force that sustains it? How can the suffering of conditioned existence be brought to an end?—and the recognition of the possibility of freedom.

What was the impetus for our own beginning practice? Have we recognized the heavenly messengers in our own lives? Each of us, like the Buddha, has a story; we all share in having heard some call to awaken. Reflecting upon the first steps in our own journey, those powerful moments of intuition that set us upon the path of inquiry, connects us more deeply with our own source of inspiration and the original spirit of our quest.

The second stage of the hero's journey is called the great renunciation. Having awakened to the often hidden possibilities of life, we begin to give up our habitual ways of seeing and relating to the world and to live in a way more conducive to full realization. After the bodhisattva encountered the four messengers, he left the palace with all its pleasures and comforts in order to seek liberation. Siddhartha first went to different teachers of concentration meditation and mastered all the levels of absorption. Yet even after the highest level of attainment of this type, he realized that this did not constitute freedom. When he came out of those absorption states, his mind was still prone to defilements, and so he was not yet satisfied. He believed that even the highest of these states was not the unconditioned, that which was beyond birth and death.

He then spent six years practicing the various kinds of austerities and ascetic disciplines that were prevalent at that time—torturing and starving the body in an effort to subdue the ego and suppress the defilements of mind. It is said that for long periods he ate only one grain of rice a day, and that when he tried to touch his belly, his hand would grasp his backbone. So extreme was his asceticism that he would collapse from fatigue and hunger. After six years of such practice, he realized that this was not the path to freedom, to the end of suffering.

Siddhartha gave up this extreme ascetic discipline and, taking some food, nourished himself for the third great event in his journey, the great struggle. Having regained his strength, he seated himself beneath the bodhi tree with the resolve that he would not get up until he had attained supreme enlightenment. As he sat there with unwavering resolve and determination, all the forces of Mara, of illusion and ignorance, assailed his mind. Joseph Campbell describes this encounter in a mythopoetic way, which conveys very vividly the energy involved in that commitment to truth.

> [The Bodhisattva] placed himself, with a firm resolve, beneath the Bodhi Tree, on the Immovable Spot, and straightway was approached by Kama-Mara, the god of love and death.
>
> The dangerous god appeared mounted on an elephant and carrying weapons in his thousand hands. He was surrounded by his army, which extended twelve

leagues before him, twelve to the right, twelve to the left, and in the rear as far as to the confines of the world; it was nine leagues high. The protecting deities of the universe took flight, but the Future Buddha remained unmoved beneath the Tree. And the god then assailed him, seeking to break his concentration.

Whirlwind, rocks, thunder and flame, smoking weapons with keen edges, burning coals, hot ashes, boiling mud, blistering sands and fourfold darkness, the Antagonist hurled against the Savior, but the missiles were all transformed into celestial flowers and ointments by the power of Gautama's ten perfections. Mara then deployed his daughters, Desire, Pining, and Lust, surrounded by voluptuous attendants, but the mind of the Great Being was not distracted. The god finally challenged his right to be sitting on the Immovable Spot, flung his razor-sharp discus angrily, and bid the towering host of the army to let fly at him with mountain crags. But the Future Buddha only moved his hand to touch the ground with his fingertips, and thus bid the goddess Earth bear witness to his right to be sitting where he was. She did so with a hundred, a thousand, a hundred thousand roars, so that the elephant of the Antagonist fell upon its knees in obeisance to the Future Buddha. The army was immediately dispersed, and the gods of all the worlds scattered garlands. [p. 32]

This is a wonderful rendering of the bodhisattva's struggle with Mara; and in a very fundamental way, each one of us may be said to be sitting under the bodhi tree every time we strongly resolve to be aware, to be mindful. Mara may assail the mind with desire and anger, with restlessness and fears, with all the same forces personified in the imagery of myth. It is the same struggle, the same commitment, the same process of becoming free. The effort manifesting is heroic effort, because it resonates in an arena beyond just our immediate experience; we are expressing at that time the unwavering determination and courage of the hero and heroine.

The first stage of the archetypal journey is the call to destiny; the second is the great renunciation, the leaving behind of old patterns and habits, beginning to see our lives in a new way; the third stage is the great struggle with all the forces of delusion; and the fourth stage in this universal journey is the great awakening. After the hosts of Mara were dispersed, the bodhisattva spent the three watches of the night contemplating various aspects of the dharma. In the first watch he surveyed with his power of concentration the succession of births and deaths through countless lifetimes. Through seeing this process stretching back into beginningless time—being born into certain circumstances, going through the dramas of life, dying and being reborn—came a profound understanding of the impermanence and insubstantiality of existence. Life and death are arising and vanishing like bubbles on the surface of a stream. The long-range perspective of the cycles of lifetimes undercuts the seeming solidity and importance our attachments and preferences assume when we are identified with particular situations or experiences.

In the second watch of the night, he contemplated the law of karma. He saw how the karmic force of past actions propels and conditions beings through successive rebirths. Seeing beings driven by ignorance through the whirlwind of differing destinies awoke in him the energy of deep compassion. In the third watch of the night he contemplated the Four Noble Truths and the law of dependent origination. He saw how the mind becomes attached, and how through attachment there is suffering. He understood the possibility of deconditioning that attachment and coming to a place of freedom.

It is said that just at the moment of dawn, when the morning star appeared in the sky, his mind realized the deepest, most complete illumination. After attaining the great enlightenment, the Buddha uttered this verse in his heart:

> I wandered through the rounds of countless births,
> Seeking but not finding the builder of this house.
> Sorrowful indeed is birth again and again.
> Oh, housebuilder! You have now been seen.
> You shall build the house no longer.
> All your rafters have been broken,
> Your ridgepole shattered.
> My mind has attained to unconditioned freedom.
> Achieved is the end of craving.

The Buddha saw that in this world of samsara, of constant appearing and disappearing, being born and dying, there was great suffering. Craving, the builder of this house of suffering (the mind and body), was discovered; the defilements of mind, the rafters, were broken; the force of ignorance, the ridgepole, was shattered, and thus the Buddha realized nirvana, the unconditioned. It is said that the path to nirvana, the Eightfold Path, is a silent vehicle, like a chariot that drives smoothly and gracefully, without emitting squeaks and clatter. The people who ride on this chariot, however, those who have realized the truth, may be quite noisy. They are noisy in their songs of praise for this vehicle and for the completion of their journey.

In the *Theragatha* and *Therigatha*—collections of enlightenment verses of the early monks and nuns—we often find the refrain "Done is what had to be done." In attaining the great enlightenment, the bodhisattva experienced the completion and fulfillment of his long journey, a fulfillment of the potential shared by all human beings. He had become the Buddha, the Awakened One. He spent the next seven weeks in the area of the bodhi tree, contemplating different aspects of the truth. He had completed his own journey of liberation, and he now wondered whether it was possible to share the profound dharma he had realized with others, blinded as they were by their attachments.

According to legend, a celestial being, a brahma god, came down from the highest heaven realm and urged the Buddha to teach the dharma for the welfare of all beings, out of compassion for all beings. He asked the Buddha to survey the world with his eye of wisdom, stating that there were many beings with but little dust in their eyes who would be able to hear and understand the truth. The Buddha did as the brahma god asked and saw that what he said was in fact true, and out of deep compassion for the suffering of beings he began his forty-five years of teaching.

He first traveled to a place outside of Benares called Sarnath, where the five ascetics with whom he had previously practiced were living in a deer park. The Buddha gave his first sermon to these five ascetics, thereby setting in motion the Great Wheel of the Dharma. In this sermon he spoke of the Four Noble Truths and the Middle Way, that path between the extremes of sensory indulgence and self-mortification; and he thus laid the foundation for his teachings of the next forty-five years.

The Buddha continued his teaching travels, and when sixty of his disciples had themselves come to full enlightenment, he sent them out to begin spreading the dharma with this exhortation: "Go forth, O monks, for the good of the many, for the happiness of the many, out of compassion for the world, for the good, benefit, and happiness of people and devas. Let not two go by one way. Teach the dharma, excellent in the beginning, excellent in the middle, and excellent in the end. Proclaim the noble life, altogether perfect and pure; work for the good of others, those of you who have done your duty."

We can see from this statement of the Buddha that the whole thrust of practice and of understanding is to develop freedom in oneself, compassion for the suffering of the world, and an active sense of service for the welfare of others. Seeing the purification of our own hearts and minds in the context of working for the benefit of others inspires and gives energy to our practice. Practice is never just for oneself; the manifestation of truth is always one of greater connectedness and compassion.

The two chief disciples of the Buddha were Sariputra and Mogallana. Mogallana was very adept in meditation and he became an arhant, a fully enlightened being, in just one week. Among the Buddha's disciples, he was foremost in the development of psychic powers, and there are many stories of his exercising his powers to further the teachings. Sariputra was the disciple foremost in wisdom. Because his mind was more discursive, having to look at each experience from many different angles, it took him two weeks, a little longer than it took Mogallana, to get enlightened. Sariputra is said to have been second only to the Buddha in his understanding of the mind. According to tradition, it was through him that the abhidharma, the Buddhist psychology, took substance and form. It is said that the Buddha would visit the heaven realm where his mother had been reborn in order to teach her the abhidharma, returning periodically to give the gist of his teaching to Sariputra, who then elaborated and expounded it.

There are certain qualities that distinguish a buddha from other arhants. There is no difference between the freedom of mind of a buddha and that of an arhant; in the minds of both, greed, hatred, and ignorance have been completely uprooted. However, with his efforts through countless lifetimes, a buddha brings to perfection certain powers of mind and a range of understanding and compassion that is unique. The life of a buddha manifests the perfection of wisdom, compassion, and skillful means. In every situation a buddha knows exactly the right way to teach and the best way to open the minds of others. He is thus endowed with omniscient wisdom and practical compassion.

At the time when the hermit Sumedha encountered Dipankara Buddha, he already had the potential to be enlightened, but he chose to forsake this for the welfare of all beings suffering in their ignorance. Through his compassion for the countless beings needing to be led in safety across to the other shore, he was willing to sacrifice his own immediate freedom in order to spend the aeons necessary to develop all the perfections of a buddha.

The Buddha was endowed with three accomplishments. The first is called the accomplishment of cause, which refers to the extraordinary effort made by the bodhisattva through innumerable lifetimes to perfect the paramis; that is, he accomplished the cause for buddhahood. The second is the accomplishment of result, which refers to his enlightenment and attainment of omniscient knowledge. And the third is the accomplishment of service, seeing to the welfare of others. The Buddha was not complacent with his own awakening, but out of loving care for all beings he set forth to teach, and until he died he shared the dharma with all those who were ready to hear.

The heroic effort made by the bodhisattva to develop the perfections is only possible through the motivation of extraordinary compassion. Yet compassion alone is not enough; for it to bring effective results, compassion must be acted upon, and this demands a discriminating wisdom as to beneficial or harmful actions, knowing which paths will bring happiness and which will not. Great compassion requires great wisdom in order to bear fruit, and great wisdom requires deep compassion as the motivation and impetus for action to be undertaken for the sake of other beings. These two great wings of the dharma were perfectly fulfilled in the Buddha.

It is said that even if one were to combine the love and compassion of all parents on the planet for their children, it would not approach the great compassion of the Buddha. Parents may have a great capacity to love and forgive their children. In the Buddha, these qualities were boundless. Because of his practical compassion, he ceaselessly exhorted beings to give up the causes of their suffering and to avoid those actions that bring about harm and unhappiness. He encouraged and urged beings to follow that path that leads to happiness, well-being, and freedom.

One of the unique powers of a buddha is unobstructed vision. Every morning the Buddha would survey the world with his unhindered eye of wisdom, encompassing all beings in his net of compassion. With the ability to penetrate others' hidden tendencies, he would recognize all those who were ripe for awakening, and he would appear to them, offering the exact teaching that could open their hearts and minds.

There is a story of a monk who had been practicing meditation on the unpleasantness of the body, visualizing its parts—

internal organs, blood, hair, bone, flesh, sinew, and so forth—as a way of developing dispassion. Although he practiced diligently for several months, he made no progress, and his mind grew agitated and restless. The Buddha came to know of this, and he saw that for this monk that particular practice was not appropriate. Through his psychic power, the Buddha created a golden lotus, which he instructed the monk to contemplate. As the monk contemplated it, the golden lotus began to change and disintegrate, and through contemplating the process of change and decay in the beautiful flower, the monk was enlightened. In telling of this later, the Buddha said that this monk had been a goldsmith, working with and fashioning beautiful objects for five hundred consecutive lifetimes. The monk's mind was so attuned to beauty that although he could not relate to unpleasant objects in a balanced way, contemplation of the impermanence and insubstantiality of beautiful things was his own particular doorway to liberation.

One of my favorite stories is of a monk who was known as the dullard, because he couldn't learn or remember anything. His older brother, who was an arhant, tried to teach the dullard a dharma verse of four lines, but each time he learned a new line, it would push the previous line out of his mind. He worked for a time trying to remember these four lines, but he was unable to do so. His brother thought that there was no hope and suggested that the dullard leave the monkhood and return to a householder's life. Although he had a dull mind, he had a good and open heart, and this suggestion made him quite sad. He was walking down the road, feeling dejected, and the Buddha, having come to know what had happened, came and stroked his head consolingly. The Buddha then gave him an object of meditation: a white handkerchief. He told the dullard to take the handkerchief and rub it at a time when the sun was high. This was the meditation. Gradually, as the dullard did this, the handkerchief grew dirty, causing him to understand the impurities coming out of the body. Seeing how the handkerchief grew dirty by rubbing it led his mind to a state of dispassion, and out of that deep balance of mind he became enlightened.

The story goes on to say that with his enlightenment came all the psychic powers and knowledge of all the teachings.

The Buddha had seen that in a past lifetime the dullard had been a great king, who had one day gone out in the hot sun bedecked in his lavish finery, which slowly became soiled in the heat. At that time he began to see the unpleasant aspect of the body and to become detached from it. The Buddha touched on that seed which had been planted in him long before, and in a single stroke his mind emerged from its dullness.

There is a very touching story told of a woman named Kisa Gotami. Though she came from a poor family, Kisa Gotami married a wealthy man. In time she gave birth to a son, and they lived very happily until, after two years, her son died. She was overcome with grief. Refusing to admit that her son had died, she carried his small corpse around, asking people for medicine to make the baby well. She eventually went to the Buddha and asked if he could please do something to make her son better. The Buddha said that he could help her, and that in order to do so she must first go into the village and get some mustard seed from a house and bring it back. But he said that the mustard seed must be from a house in which no one had ever died. She went from one house to another asking for the mustard seed but each time was met with the same response. Although everyone gladly offered her the seed, there was not a single house in which there had been no death. By the time she got to the end of the village, her mind had opened to the fact that death is part of the universal experience, that nobody is free from it. Out of this openness to the fact of death, she was able to relinquish her illusions and finally bury her son. She returned to the Buddha, became a nun, and soon afterward attained to full enlightenment.

There are innumerable stories of people from all walks of life—beggars, merchants, artisans, courtesans, village people, nobles, kings and queens—each coming to the Buddha with varying degrees of faith and understanding, whom he helped come to freedom and peace through the power of his love, wisdom, and skillful means.

One discourse the Buddha gave that is particularly helpful in understanding the spirit of investigation and discovery in dharma practice is known as the *Kalama Sutta*. He was asked by a village people known as the Kalamas how they could know which among the many different religious teachings and teachers to believe. The Buddha said that they should not blindly believe anyone—not their parents or teachers, not the books or traditions, not even the Buddha himself. Rather, they should look carefully into their own experience to see which things lead to more greed, more hatred, more delusion, and should abandon them; and they should look to see what things lead to greater love, generosity, wisdom, openness, and peace, and should cultivate those things. The Buddha's teachings always encourage us to take responsibility for our own development and to directly investigate the nature of our experience. There was no desire in the Buddha's mind for fame, honor, or disciples. He was motivated by genuine compassion.

When he was eighty years old, the Buddha became quite sick and, knowing he was soon going to die, lay down on a spot beneath two trees. The legends tell us that these trees were flowering out of season, symbolizing the Buddha's final release into the unconditioned. Even on his deathbed he shared the dharma, showing the way to a renunciate of another sect. In his final words he exhorted those who had gathered around him—and all of us—saying, "All compounded things are impermanent. Work out your liberation with diligence." He then entered into a state of jhanic concentration and passed away.

As practice deepens and we come to a fuller appreciation and understanding of our own true nature, there develops a wonderful love and respect for the Buddha, both as a historical figure and as the archetype of the buddha-nature potential within us all. If we reflect on the three great accomplishments of the Buddha's life, we can become filled with a sense of deep appreciation for having the opportunity to walk the path discovered by such a being, a path of the greatest distinction and truest nobility. With mindfulness and insight we can reflect the Buddha's journey in our own.

J. G.

EXERCISE

# Recollection of the Buddha

Recollection of the Buddha can be an effective way of arousing and strengthening the spiritual faculties of faith and concentration. Contemplating the perfections of the Buddha (such as generosity, morality, concentration, loving-kindness, and wisdom) and investigating the ways in which he developed these qualities may serve as an inspiration to our own practice. In this regard, reading the story of his life, the tales of his previous births, and the direct teachings of his discourses will reveal his efforts and accomplishments. An important aspect for us in this recollection is to connect the Buddha's effort with our own.

Another way of recollection is to relate to images of the Buddha as if the Buddha himself were actually present. How does it affect our mind states if we are paying respects, bowing to, or sitting in front of the Buddha? Is there greater mindfulness in what we do? Does it help us to look more honestly at the nature of our minds? Perhaps there may also arise a deep feeling of love and devotion, which softens our mind and inspires our heart.

# 8

## *The Freedom of Restraint*

In order to understand our lives it is essential to understand the nature of the mind. Everything that we are, everything that we do, has its origin in the mind. Why do we live our lives in a particular way? Why do we like certain things and dislike others? Why are we in particular kinds of relationships? It all comes out of the power of mind. It comes out of our thoughts and visions and inspirations. What we are is the manifestation of mind. Rarely, though, do we take the time to create a space of silence to see how this mind of ours is working.

When we quiet the mind and look at our experience, we see that the mind is a process of constant change. One moment it is peaceful and calm, and the next it burns with anger or desire; now it is concentrated and clear, now entranced with fantasy. The nature of mind is a dynamic, changing energy conditioned and reconditioned in every moment of experience. It is conditioned by the input that we get through the senses—sight, sound, smell, taste, and body sensations—by our actions and reactions, by our thoughts and emotions, by what we do and how we manifest in the world.

As we begin to look carefully at the nature of this mind and at the forces that condition it, we begin to see certain patterns: what leads to more suffering, to more pain, to greater tightness and contraction, and what patterns of mind lead to openness and spaciousness, to a free and easy relationship with ourselves and other people. In order to see this clearly it is necessary to bring to the mind some level of stability and steadiness. As long as we're being barraged by our thoughts and emotions, liking this and disliking that, judging, comparing, evaluating, as long as we're caught in the whirlwind of action and reaction, it's very difficult to get a perspective that allows for clear reflection and deep wisdom. And so the first step in understanding is to work in some way to stabilize things, to allow the mind to settle down, to become centered.

The art and discipline of meditation is one way of bringing the mind into balance. We train the mind in awareness and concentration, steadying the attention so that it is not so restless and agitated. From this increased sense of calm and equanimity we can then look more deeply into our experience. We become aware in each moment of both what it is that's happening and our relationship to it. We ground ourselves in the reality of what is actually present, rather than being lost in our fantasies, thoughts, ideas, or interpretations. This steady and precise awareness brings profound stability because it excludes nothing. In each moment there can be balance because we practice opening to the full range of changing experience, without attachment or aversion. We see clearly what is happening in the moment, distinguishing the different elements of the mind and body, and also understanding the laws governing this unfolding process. *Dharma* (*dhamma* in Pali) is a Sanskrit word that means "law," and so dharma practice can be understood as a practice that refines our insight into the natural laws of our being.

One of the most fundamental laws that we begin to be aware of is the law of karma, namely, that our actions bring results, that they are not happening in a vacuum. When we investigate the nature of our experience, we can begin to understand how karma works directly in our lives, rather than seeing it as merely an abstract concept or an interesting theory. Through our attention and awareness we see how the quality of mind in each moment conditions both the present reality and the future.

When a strong mood or feeling is present in the mind, it is clear how much that can influence our experience at that time. If we are feeling very sad or angry or depressed, then we might be in the most beautiful place or with the people we care for the most, yet the whole situation will be colored by our mind state. Likewise, we may be facing extreme difficulties, yet if we are in love, or filled with a deep peace, then the situation is experienced very differently than if we are worried and agitated. It is fairly obvious that the quality of our mind conditions how we experience things. This could be called present or immediate karma, that is, the result or effect our mind states have on the quality of the present moment.

The law of karma can also be experienced another way. As we meditate it becomes strikingly clear that the mind retains impressions of all our past actions. When the mind becomes a little still, these impressions reveal themselves with a great force and immediacy. It's as if we were looking into a vivid reflecting mirror of our being. Our past actions then become a source of either great joy or deep remorse. We come face-to-face, in a very conscious way, with our own past actions. If we do this with gentleness and equanimity, then the experiencing of these karmic fruits of past actions can be very purifying.

We experience karma in how the mind conditions our present experience through our moods and emotions; we see the working of karma as we vividly reexperience our past actions, either in meditation or at other times when the mind is quiet and spacious. We can also understand karma directly as the development of certain habit formations, whether wholesome or unwholesome. Each of our actions of body, speech, or mind results in a strengthened tendency toward repeating that action. Finally, the law of karma can be understood as the specific and multiple results that an action will have in the future, just as a seed planted in the ground will, in time, bear many fruits.

When we deeply understand that actions bring results, it can motivate us to take active responsibility for our actions and our lives. We develop a wise reflection and consideration about where our actions are leading and whether that is where we want to go. But it is not enough to simply reflect on karma and the direction of our lives. We must have some force or quality in the mind that can directly apply the wisdom of our reflections. One of the great powers and strengths of mind that we can use for this purpose is the power of restraint.

It is important to understand what restraint means because it lies at the very heart of our practice. We should be careful not to confuse restraint with repression or avoidance. Restraint of mind does not mean pushing something away and denying its presence. It does not mean being judgmental or having an aversion toward certain aspects of our experience. When we suppress or avoid certain aspects of ourselves, the ignorance of not acknowledging what is present creates more tension and pain in the mind. With restraint, we are open to everything that arises, but we see with discriminating wisdom, without becoming lost or forgetful. With wisdom and awareness we can see that there are skillful activities that are conducive to greater happiness and understanding, and there are unskillful ones that lead to further suffering and conflict. Restraint is the capacity we have to discriminate one from the other, and the strength and composure of mind to pursue the skillful course.

Restraint also serves as a counterbalance to the addictive tendencies of mind. There is a story in the Buddhist texts of a monkey living happily and freely in a forest on the high mountains. One day he became curious about what it was like on the plains, so he went down to explore. Some hunters had laid out a tar trap, and the monkey, not knowing what it was, reached into the tar with his hand and got stuck. Unable to free himself, the monkey reached in with the other hand to pull out the first, and then both were caught. He tried pushing away with first one foot, which got stuck, and then the other. Finally, in order to free his hands and feet, he stuck his head in the tar and became thoroughly entrapped.

This is how we are with our addictions. Something gives us pleasure and we grasp it. Feeling the lack when it changes, we reach for it again or look for another source of that momentary satisfaction. We reach out for another source of pleasure. Then another and another, until we're totally entangled by the grasping and wanting state of mind. We become quite firmly entrapped by the force of our own desire. We become addicted not only to the gratification of our wants, but also to the mental habit of wanting itself. It is possible, though, to relate to desire in an altogether different way, a way of much greater freedom. It is possible to develop restraint, the gentle discipline of settling back and allowing the desires to arise and pass without feeling the need or compulsion to act on them.

In addition to restraining oneself from actions that are not very helpful or skillful, there is also the restraint from identifying with our inhibitions and fears. We have all been conditioned in various ways to fear different things and to be inhibited from contacting certain areas of ourselves or other people. Restraint in this sense means not buying into those patterns of mind that limit us and create more contraction and separation. It allows us to push at our limits, to take some risks.

An unrestrained mind is much like an unrestrained child: temper tantrums, fits of wanting, aversion, and the like. In both cases we need to develop a gentle kind of discipline, understanding that it is sometimes appropriate to say no. Just as a wise parent does not indulge a child's unhealthy tendencies, we need not indulge the mind's every desire and impulse: we can learn to say no to the mind, gently and with humor. True restraint is not cultivated through aversion and suppression. It comes from simply seeing what is harmonious and what isn't, and then acting accordingly, bringing our actions of speech and body into alignment with what we know to be true. And as we work with the quality of restraint, we find it to be a source of tremendous power and energy.

Restraint also functions as a way to conserve energy. As we practice meditation a strong energy begins to build—in our bodies, our emotions, and our minds. This sometimes becomes uncomfortable to feel. It is like a balloon being stretched as we blow more air into it. We are being stretched through our practice, and often we look for ways to release some of the energy to avoid feeling the discomfort, rather than relaxing and allowing ourselves to be with it. Particularly on intensive retreats it becomes very clear how creative the mind can be in devising ways to leak energy: extra cups of tea, planning the great American novel, notes to one's vipassana romance, and so on. This dispersing of the building energy is a big hindrance to the further deepening of practice.

Through the power of restraint we can learn that instead of letting every thought or feeling that goes through the mind be the cause of action, instead of letting all these impulses be energy leaks for us, it is possible to become aware of what is happening and have enough space and wisdom, enough reflective ability, to restrain the mind and conserve the growing energy momentum. It is from this conservation of energy that we generate enough power of mind to penetrate and open to the deepest levels.

The third aspect of restraint is one that leads to a profound change of understanding. Not only is it the letting go of unwholesome actions and the conservation and buildup of a strong energy momentum, but restraint of mind is also the matrix for seeing more clearly the impermanent, insubstantial nature of reality. When we are continually reaching out for sense objects, or expressing every impulse of energy, or identifying with each thought or feeling in the mind, we solidify our sense of the world and become deeply entangled in a strong sense of self.

Without a development or training of the mind, we find that much of our life is lost in thoughts and that we take these thoughts to be reality. How often do our thoughts condition reactions in the mind, as if the thought itself had substance? Yet the thought of a friend is not the friend; it is a thought. How many life scenarios have we created, directed, and starred in and, for those moments, taken to be the experience itself? We also may get carried away by the intense energy of our emotions, swept up in a typhoon of the mind and body. To be lost in emotions is to not be mindful of their energy; and when there is a strong identified involvement with them, there is no space in the mind for seeing clearly what is happening.

Through the power of restraint we can begin the process of disentangling our thoughts and projections from the reality of what is actually present. Vipassana means seeing things as they are; or, as one Thai meditation master said, it's learning to see what's what. Seeing what's what develops in a mind that is no longer compulsively driven by every desire or by the illusion of self. Restraint creates a spaciousness in the mind that can appreciate the emptiness and impermanence of phenomena. The Buddha expressed this ephemeral nature of experience in a short verse:

> See all of this world
> As a star at dawn, a bubble in a stream,
> A flash of lightning in a summer cloud,
> A flickering lamp, a phantom and a dream.

This wisdom opens up to us the possibility of simplicity in our lives, of what the Buddha called "the greatest gain"—contentment. We are so conditioned to want more, to think that we will be happier if we accumulate more money or possessions, more honor, fame, power, sex, and so forth, that we burden ourselves with acquisitions, both material and psychological. The underlying rationale of this wanting mind is that fulfillment will make us happy. If we stop to reflect upon our situation, we can see that the attitude of wanting more simply leads to greater craving and frustration.

The problem is not that we too rarely fulfill our desires, but that we so often do, yet are still left wanting. How many beautiful sounds, delicious tastes, wonderful sensations, exciting thoughts, rapturous feelings have we already experienced in our lives? Countless, too many even to remember. But all this has not yet satisfied the wanting mind. We have a desire, gratify it, and experience some pleasure, and when conditions change and the pleasure diminishes or goes away, we find a return of craving, wanting more, motivated by the same sense of lack. We try again and again to come to completion, but it doesn't work; we're never done.

What is it that we crave? Craving is hunger for pleasant feelings. Whether we crave pleasant sights, sounds, smells, tastes, bodily sensations, or mental states, what we are after is the feeling of pleasantness. The difficulty is that even when the pleasant feelings come, they don't last very long. We go around and around, looking for permanent satisfaction in phenomena that in their very nature are impermanent.

A story of Mullah Nasruddin illustrates this predicament. One night some of Nasruddin's friends came upon him crawling around on his hands and knees searching for something beneath a lamppost. When they asked him what he was looking for, he told them that he had lost the key to his house. They all got down to help him look, but without any success. Finally, one of them asked Nasruddin where exactly he had lost the key. Nasruddin replied, "In the house."

"Then why," his friends asked, "are you looking under the lamppost?"

Nasruddin replied, "Because there's more light here."

We are doing the same thing—seeking fulfillment in sense pleasure because that seems the obvious place to look. It is where everyone else is looking, believing it to be the place where happiness is to be found. But a more genuine happiness and peace lie in contentment and simplicity. We really don't need very much to be happy. Voluntary simplicity creates the possibility of tremendous lightness and spaciousness in our lives. As the forces of craving and acquisitiveness cool down and we are less driven by impulses of the wanting mind, we experience a greater and greater peace.

And rather than this being the cause of a withdrawal from the world, it creates a space in our lives in which we can move and act with greater strength and integrity. Generosity becomes a more spontaneous expression of our understanding, giving open-heartedly of our time, energy, material objects, kindness, care, and love. In addition to being a wonderful basis for our relationships with others, the practice of generosity also helps us to see more clearly into the subtle motives and attachments in our own behavior.

When I was practicing in India, the question of giving arose all the time because there are so many people who beg just to stay alive. And no matter how simply we may be living, or how little we may have, it is clearly far more than they. That reality could not be avoided. One day I was buying some oranges in the bazaar, and I was approached by a young boy begging. I handed him one of my oranges. He didn't thank me or smile or even nod—no acknowledgment at all. He just took the orange and walked away. This simple exchange helped illuminate an unconscious place of subtle expectation in the mind. Behind even the real desire to share there was also the expectation of some little response in return. With careful attention we can see and let go of even the most subtle expectations and learn to respond to situations with the simplicity of our caring heart.

At the end of his life, Aldous Huxley said that he had come to appreciate how most of spiritual practice is learning to be kinder to one another. Practicing kindness means that we connect with people rather than dismiss them; kindness breaks down the barriers between ourselves and others. When the attitude of kindness is strong, we cease to be preoccupied solely with our own self-concerns, and the circle of our caring expands to include all. Caring for the welfare of others directly expresses and cultivates freedom from the isolating prison of ego. But it is important not to create an ideal of how this should take place, because if we carry an attitude of loving care within us, then we need not wait for especially dramatic situations. Many times a day we may find the opportunity to manifest these qualities.

Valuing loving care, or metta, in our lives becomes a strong motive, then, for refining our understanding and practice of harmonious action, the nonharming of oneself or others. The five basic moral precepts of Buddhism—not killing, not stealing, not lying, refraining from sexual conduct that is harmful to oneself or others, and not clouding or confusing the mind with intoxicants—provide a simple and powerful guideline for harmonizing our actions with other people and with the environment. These precepts are the practice of a basic restraint; they express a conscious choice to refrain from those actions which create more fear and confusion. By demonstrating with our lives this commitment to nonharming and compassion, we are giving the rare gift of trust to everyone we meet, because we are clearly stating in our actions and way of being that no one need fear us.

Harmonious action generates tremendous strength of mind, because our energy is not bound up in aggressive action, deceptive behavior, or regret. By undertaking the training and refining of these precepts, we free ourselves from the danger of guilt and self-condemnation. Although in the busyness of our daily lives we may not always be aware of the extent of these feelings in the mind, as we become quieter through our practice, the impressions of our past actions become very intense and vivid. And it is easier for us to be forgiving and compassionate toward ourselves for the unwholesome things that we may have done in the past if we are now established in a strong and finely tuned sense of integrity and morality.

The motivation for living with morality is based on our valuing of metta, loving care, the quality of mind that wishes for the welfare and well-being of all; karuna, compassion for beings who are suffering or in distress; and mudita, the joy of delighting in the success of others. Being established in a morality nourished by these mind states serves as an authentic and outstanding adornment in our lives. As opposed to the artificial external adornments we may be drawn to, living with a kind consideration for all beings creates a true and enduring beauty.

It is essential that our understanding be translated into practice, not with an idealistic vision that we suddenly will become totally loving and compassionate, but with a willingness to be just who we are and to start from there. Then our practice is grounded in the reality of our experience, rather than based on some expectation of how we should be. But we must begin. We work with the precepts as guidelines for harmonizing our actions in the world; we live with contentment and simplicity that does not exploit other people or the planet; we work with restraint in the mind, seeing that it's possible to say no to certain conditioned impulses, or to expand when we feel bound by inhibitions and fear; we reflect upon karma and the direction of our lives, where it is leading and what is being developed; we cultivate generosity and love, compassion and service. All of this together becomes our path of practice. It leads to a place of deeper wisdom in the mind and greater love in the heart. From His Holiness the Gyalwa Karmapa: "If you have one hundred percent dedication and confidence in the teachings, then every living situation can be part of the practice. You can be living the practice instead of just doing it."

J. G.

EXERCISE

## Restraint

The practice of restraint is an essential element in the teaching of the Buddha. It provides great strength, energy, and composure of mind, and there are many ways we can begin to cultivate and develop it. In some sittings you might resolve not to move at all for a certain period of time, whether for twenty minutes, forty minutes, or an hour. This restraint in movement will arouse great effort and deepen concentration. When desires arise, practice letting go of them, saying no in a gentle and loving way. The desire may be for a simple thing like an extra cup of tea, or a desire to speak when it is not really necessary. Practicing restraint with small desires gives us the strength of mind to be restrained with more powerful desires when they are understood to be harmful. If we have a strong habit that is not serving us well, we can make a conscious practice of restraint in that area, perhaps, in the beginning, for a predetermined period of time. All of these exercises will develop this power in the mind, and we will begin to see for ourselves the very direct relationship between restraint and freedom.

# 9

# Suffering: The Gateway
# to Compassion

THE NATURE OF COMPASSION is a strong feeling in the heart to help others be free of their suffering. It is a wholesome movement of the mind and body that seeks to alleviate the pain and suffering of beings. Compassion is the spontaneous response of an open heart.

We don't have to look far to see how pervasive suffering is in the world. There is the suffering that people are experiencing right now due to poverty and injustice. The presence of starvation, disease, and oppression stringently defines many people's lives. As we pay attention to the world around us, we see how evident suffering is in so many arenas of life—in politics, economics, social structures, religious conflict, interpersonal relationships, in our own minds and bodies. It is vital that we remain connected and sensitive to this fact.

Even when we live on an island of relative peace and abundance, as many of us do, if we look closely at our own lives we can see the suffering that is always present, although sometimes disguised. There is the inevitable pain of the body: disease, decay, and death are an inherent part of the process of life. It is not a question of whether this happens to one person and not to another. If we have a body, it is going to get sick and older and die.

And when we pay careful attention to the mind, we also experience many different kinds of unease. Although we may find comfort and security in the habits and routines of our lives, beneath the comfortable surface there are often vague and disquieting feelings that there is something fundamentally incomplete or unclear or not quite right about our lives. There may be an uncertainty or a feeling or hollowness that drives us to fill our time with an activity. We might feel fragmented or dissatisfied or imprisoned. At times there are overwhelming feelings of anxiety, fear, depression, anger, jealousy, lust, and so forth. What is the source of these feelings? If we are to come to a true sense of wholeness, where compassion is the natural expression of our understanding, then we must be willing to honestly investigate these aspects of ourselves.

Seeing the suffering in the world around us and in our own bodies and minds, we begin to understand suffering not only as an individual problem, but as a universal experience. It is one of the aspects of being alive. The question that then comes to mind is: If compassion arises from the awareness of suffering, why isn't the world a more compassionate place? The problem is that often our hearts are not open to feel the pain. We move away from it, close off, and become defended. By closing ourselves off from suffering, however, we also close ourselves to our own wellspring of compassion. We don't need to be particularly saintly in order to be compassionate. Compassion is the natural response of an open heart, but that wellspring of compassion remains capped as long as we turn away from or deny or resist the truth of what is there. When we deny our experience of suffering, we move away from what is genuine to what is fabricated, deceptive, and confusing.

## PAIN

How does this movement away from suffering happen in our lives? What is it that we stay closed to? If we become aware of how we stay closed, we are already beginning the process of opening. One of the things we close ourselves to is sensations of physical pain. We don't like to feel them, and so the mind devises various strategies of avoidance. These strategies are often clearly revealed in meditation practice. One way we avoid the reality of painful feelings is by ignoring them and pretending they don't exist. This works for a while, but eventually the pain may become too great to ignore. The mind's next tactic might be to give the pain an occasional sidelong glance; that is, we're mindful of the breath, and just out of the corner of our mental eye we glance at the pain. This still is not opening to it with awareness and compassion, allowing ourselves to feel it fully. A yet more subtle form of resistance is the "project mentality," in which we are willing to be with the pain, but we are with it in order for it to go away. With this "in order to" attitude, or sense of anticipation, we are still not relating directly; we're pushing at the pain in the guise of awareness rather than truly accepting it.

When there is resistance in the mind, compassion cannot arise, because we have in some way closed ourselves off from what is present. In the case of physical pain, our conditioned responses and habits of mind can easily be seen. They range from these subtleties of manipulation to the extreme of panic and denial. If we cannot relate directly and compassionately with our own pain during meditation, how can we do so with other, more intense sufferings that we find in ourselves, in others, and in the world? An important aspect of our dharma practice consists in clearly comprehending suffering and our conditioned reactions to it, and practicing opening to what is unpleasant instead of turning away from it. In this sense the practice of awareness is the practice of compassion; we allow ourselves to feel what is there with openness, connecting directly to each moment's experience.

## UNPLEASANT EMOTIONS

Just as with physical pain, there is also a broad range of difficult or unpleasant emotional states and feelings that we don't accept and from which we remain cut off. This often causes fundamental splits in our minds and can create deep psychological conflicts in our lives. Feelings of vulnerability, loneliness, unworthiness, fear—these come to us at times as part of life experience. But how often can we actually be accepting of these feelings? Our habit is to react to unpleasant emotional states in the same way we react to unpleasant physical sensations. When a feeling of loneliness arises, we don't accept it. We feel aversion, we condemn it, and we try to push it away. How much of what we do in our lives is simply an effort to avoid loneliness or boredom? The unwillingness to be with and experience these feelings keeps us always reaching or grasping for something else. How much simpler it would be to just allow these feelings, letting them arise and pass away without struggle or resistance.

One of the most difficult emotional states we experience is the feeling of insecurity, of being vulnerable. What would it be like to be totally open? We think that if others saw us as we know ourselves to be, we wouldn't be loved or respected, that people would judge us harshly, that we'd lose all our friends. The fear of being vulnerable causes us to construct a self-image that we present to the world, one that we hope it will accept and love. We put that image out in front, while the dark, murky, unacceptable part of ourselves lurks behind.

When we investigate the fear of being judged, of not being accepted, we see that it does not have to do primarily with other people; instead, it has to do with our own unwillingness to experience certain of our feelings and emotions. It is we who are judging ourselves, not accepting ourselves, not loving ourselves.

If we can allow ourselves to feel vulnerable and insecure when that is what is arising, if we can be totally ourselves without any pretense, we will find a great inner strength. It is in just that moment when we acknowledge our shadow side, the side that we have kept hidden and under wraps, that our armor loosens. It becomes possible to breathe a little more freely. We begin to open the door of compassion, for ourselves and for the human condition.

Just as the mind has devised different ways of closing to physical pain, there are also different ways we are conditioned to avoid emotional suffering: denial, frantic activity, self-images. One of the most powerful conditioning factors in the mind that keeps us closed to what is true is the feeling of fear.

Although we have been deeply conditioned by fear, for the most part we have avoided directly exploring its nature, and because we are not aware of its workings, it is often an unconscious driving force in our lives. The Taoist sage Chuang Tzu said, "Little fears cause anxiety, and big fears cause panic." When fear arises, whether it's fear of pain, fear of certain emotions, or fear of death, our practice is then opening to the feeling of fear itself. What does it feel like? What are the sensations in the body? Where are they located? Are there images or pictures in the mind? We look closely to see what is the constellation of experience we call fear, to understand its true nature. We begin to see that fear is also a passing conditioned experience and that as we open to it with greater allowance and compassion, there is less identification with it as being "I" or "mine." It becomes much more workable.

From this foundation of awareness and acceptance, we can make choices about how to act with some degree of discriminating wisdom. Sometimes it is wise to retreat from a situation, and sometimes we move ahead despite the fear. We become more willing to take some risks because our energy is not so bound up in resisting feeling the fear itself. We learn that it is okay to feel fear. Our practice should challenge us to come to the edge of what we're willing to be with, what we're willing to do, what we're willing to open to. If we keep avoiding the feeling of fear, then we have to build barriers and defenses, closing ourselves off from every experience where fear might arise. Not only is this impossible to do, but it results in a narrow and restricted way of living. We close our hearts and close off the possibility of compassion.

As well as resisting painful sensations and emotions, we also resist difficult people and unpleasant situations. There are certain people we just don't like or situations that make us uneasy. Usually, when we find people to be unpleasant or abrasive, we react to their behavior and personality and get caught up in the dynamic of resistance, of shutting them out. But if we can drop beneath the behavioral level and allow ourselves to open to others—which sometimes can happen by simply looking at them caringly, without reaction—we can often see the suffering underneath. We can get a sense, perhaps, of that place of pain in them that is manifesting, often unconsciously, as unpleasant or obnoxious behavior. And when we open to and feel the suffering of another, compassion will have the chance to come forth.

### FEAR OF DEATH

Another aspect of our lives that we do not often bring to full awareness is the existential transiency of all experience. Every aspect, every element of our bodies and minds—sensations, thoughts, sense impressions, emotions, fantasies—every element of the world around us, is in constant change and flux, subject to birth, decay, and death. In our Western culture, we don't often look very closely at the face of death. We don't like to look at the process of decay and aging, and we rarely contemplate a dead body. One traditional Buddhist meditation is the contemplation of corpses in various states of decomposition. At first thought, this may seem morbid or extreme; yet it is one way of opening us to the reality of death, to the truth of what happens to the body, taking us beyond cosmetic pretentions. For many of us there may be a strong fear of dying. What is this fear of death about? When we don't clearly understand the nature of our mind and body, this fear and resistance to looking at decay and death may be very strong. We think that this mind-body is something solid and secure, that it is the person who we are—self, me, I. Naturally, when we have this viewpoint, the possibility of the death of "I," the death of self, can be frightening; it feels like a betrayal of our innermost beliefs about who we are and who is in control.

But as we open to the nature of the mind-body process, we see that it is literally—not metaphorically—being born and dying in every moment. We see that there is nothing solid, nothing static, nothing steady that goes from one year to the next, one month to the next, one moment to the next. The mind-body is a flux of constant creation and dissolution. Think for a moment of what your experience actually is from moment to moment: a sound, a sight, a thought, a sensation, an emotion, a smell, a taste. Moment to moment, these experiences arise and vanish, are being born and dying; the very nature of the process is constant, immediate, and continuous change. There is no possibility of holding on, although sometimes we try very hard to do so. When we experience this process of change in a very immediate and intimate way, then the fear of death begins to dissolve, because we see that there never has been anything solid or secure. We no longer consider death some kind of failure, apart from the natural order of things. We can be more at peace.

### OPENING THE HEART

These are some examples of the kinds of suffering we may resist or close off to in our lives. For genuine compassion to arise it is necessary to reverse the conditioned tendency of avoidance and to openheartedly experience the full range of our human condition. A beautiful expression of this possibility is found in the poetry of Ryokan, a wandering Zen monk who was born in the mid–eighteenth century. His poetry reflects a great willingness to be with what the Taoists call "the ten thousand joys and the ten thousand sorrows." And from this openheartedness to all experience flows a deep and boundless compassion. These are some of the poems of Ryokan:

> Once again the children and I are fighting a battle
>       using spring grasses.
> Now advancing, now retreating, each time with more
>       refinement.
> Twilight—everyone has returned home;
> The bright, round moon helps me to endure the
>       loneliness.
>
> The Autumn nights have lengthened
> And the cold has begun to penetrate my mattress.
> My sixtieth year is near,

Yet there is no one to take pity on this weak old body.
The rain has finally stopped; now just a thin stream
    trickles from the roof.
All night the incessant cry of insects:
Wide awake, unable to sleep,
Leaning on my pillow, I watch the pure bright rays of
    sunrise.

O, that my priest's robe were wide enough to gather
    up all the suffering people
In this floating world.

Why don't we, like Ryokan, open to all the joys and sorrows, to what is true in our lives? We stay closed to the full range of our experience because of a basic ignorance—an ignoring of the true nature of phenomena. We believe that happiness lies in the experience of pleasurable feelings, ignoring their fleeting, unfulfilling nature. This ignorance feeds the craving in the mind for more and more pleasant feeling. And although our desire for pleasant feeling is continually being gratified, we are never fully satisfied, precisely because of the fleetingness and insubstantiality of these feelings. The conditioning that is then happening in our minds is simply the nourishing and strengthening of desire, since, remaining unsatisfied, we are continuously wanting more. It is like trying to quench your thirst by drinking ocean water. The more you drink the thirstier you become.

An inevitable component of desire for pleasant feelings is the desire to avoid painful ones. Believing that our happiness lies in experiencing more and more pleasant feelings, we close ourselves to the full range of what arises in our lives. This ignorance and craving closes us off to an open awareness of suffering, and closes us off to compassion. Instead, the quality of compassion is subverted into sorrow. In sorrow there is an aversion to the suffering rather than an openness to it. Some people might believe that this aversion to suffering is the central motivation behind taking actions to alleviate it. But as we pay careful attention and begin to distinguish compassion from sorrow, we understand that in true compassion there is no attachment and no aversion; and that it is this state of openness to suffering which is in fact the greatest motive of skillful and effective response.

## COMPASSIONATE ACTION

Wisdom replaces ignorance in our minds when we realize that happiness does not lie in the accumulation of more and more pleasant feelings, that gratifying craving does not bring us a feeling of wholeness or completeness. It simply leads to more craving and more aversion. When we realize in our own experience that happiness comes not from reaching out but from letting go, not from seeking pleasurable experience but from opening in the moment to what is true, this transformation of understanding then frees the energy of compassion within us. Our minds are no longer bound up in pushing away pain or holding on to pleasure. Compassion becomes the natural response of an open heart.

We can see this very immediately and directly in our meditation. When we settle back and open to what's happening in each moment, without attachment or aversion, we are developing a compassionate attitude toward each experience. From this attitude that we develop in our practice, we can begin to manifest true compassionate action in the world.

There is no particular model for what form this action should take. The whole world becomes a field for compassion, beginning with ourselves and embracing all beings. Some people are moved to help alleviate the physical suffering of others, whether due to disease or poverty or injustice. Others may feel more responsive to the mental grief or anguish that people experience. And our response itself can be so varied, from a very direct intervention in a situation, to a creative work of art, to a vibration of love in the heart. Becoming a more loving person in our everyday relationships may be one of the most compassionate actions we can do—simply becoming a little kinder.

Compassion grows from proximity to suffering. It is a response to the obvious suffering that we can observe in the world around us, and it is a response to understanding the very deepest causes of our bondage. The Buddha's great compassion could bathe the festering sores of a dying monk, and to that very same monk teach the way to final freedom. Walking on the path of enlightenment becomes itself the greatest act of compassion, because it awakens in us an understanding of the deepest levels and root causes of suffering.

This understanding fosters and nourishes a compassion that is not limited to particular people or situations. We may have compassion for the victims of social or political injustice, but can we feel compassion for those who perpetrate that injustice? Our tendency might be to feel a righteous anger toward such people, forgetting that their actions are coming out of an ignorance which is not only causing pain to others, but sowing the karmic seeds of their own future suffering. Can our compassion recognize that ignorance and embrace them as well?

A poem by the Vietnamese Zen master and peace worker Thich Nhat Hanh expresses very beautifully the possibility of all-embracing compassion, without boundary and without discrimination. There is a seeing that all of it, all of life, is in us, and that we can relate to it all with an open heart.

*Please Call Me by My True Names*

Do not say that I'll depart tomorrow
because even today I still arrive.

Look deeply; I arrive in every second
to be a bud on a spring branch,
to be a tiny bird, with wings still fragile learning to sing in
    my new nest,
to be a caterpillar in the heart of a flower,
to be a jewel hiding itself in a stone.

I still arrive, in order to laugh and to cry,
in order to fear and to hope,
the rhythm of my heart is the birth and death
of all that are alive.

I am the mayfly metamorphosing on the surface of the
river,
and I am the bird which, when spring comes, arrives in
time to eat the mayfly.

I am a frog swimming happily in the clear water of a pond,
and I am the grass-snake, who, approaching in silence,
feeds itself on the frog.
I am the child in Uganda, all skin and bones,
my legs as thin as bamboo sticks,
and I am the arms merchant, selling deadly weapons to
Uganda.

I am the twelve-year-old girl, refugee on a small boat,
who throws herself into the ocean after being raped by a
sea pirate,
and I am the pirate, my heart not yet capable of seeing and
loving.

I am a member of the Politburo with plenty of power in
my hands,
And I am the man who has to pay his debt of blood to my
people dying slowly in a forced labor camp.

My joy is like spring, so warm it makes flowers bloom in
all walks of life.
My pain is like a river of tears, so full it fills all four oceans.
Please call me by my true names,
So I can hear all my cries and laughs at once,
So I can see that my joy and pain are one.

Please call me by my true names
So I can wake up and so the door of my heart can be left
    open,
The door of compassion.

J. G.

EXERCISE

## Cultivating Compassion

There are many levels on which we can strengthen and awaken compassion in our lives. We can practice it in silence as we sit. When thoughts or images of the suffering of other beings arise, either spontaneously or by intentionally calling them to mind, bring your attention to the area of the heart, letting yourself be touched by their pain and allowing a response of loving care and concern. Repeating the phrase "May you be free of suffering" also helps to develop the feeling of compassion within us. This phrase is directed toward the person who is suffering, and can be repeated for a few minutes or for an entire sitting period. Similarly, we can develop compassion toward ourselves when we feel our own suffering arise in meditation.

Outwardly, we can strengthen our response of compassion by working with another person. When you find yourself with someone in physical or emotional pain, take some time to be with that person, quietly if possible. Observe carefully all the different reactions that may arise in your mind and heart. Let all the movements of mind arise and pass away until there remains some inner space and silence. Look directly at the other person with a simple attitude of basic warmth. Can you see the other as a fellow human being in pain? Can you allow yourself to be touched by him or her? Is there a sense of connection or separation? Is the heart open or closed? Allow yourself to see and feel the other with the wish that he or she be free of suffering. If you can, stay with this process until you feel a sense of connection and compassion.

# PART THREE

# The Growth of Wisdom

# 10

# *Understanding Karma:*
# *Cause and Effect*

THE LAW OF KARMA is one of the most important laws governing our lives. When we understand it, and live our understanding, when we act on what we know, then we experience a sense of wholeness and peace. If we live in a way that is out of harmony, ignoring the nature of things, we then experience dissonance, pain, and confusion. The law of karma is one of the fundamental natural laws through which we create these vastly different realities. It is as though we are all artists, but instead of canvas and paint, or marble or music, as our medium, our very bodies, minds, and life experience are the materials of our creative expression. A great sense of fulfillment in dharma practice comes from knowing this and from actively creating and fashioning our lives.

*Karma* is a Sanskrit word (*kamma* in Pali) that means "action." The law of karma refers to the law of cause and effect: that every volitional act brings about a certain result. If we act motivated by greed, hatred, or delusion, we are planting the seed of suffering; when our acts are motivated by generosity, love, or wisdom, then we are creating the karmic conditions for abundance and happiness. An analogy from the physical world illustrates this: if we plant an apple seed, the tree that grows will bear apples, not mangoes. And once the apple seed is planted, no amount of manipulation or beseeching or complaining will induce the tree to yield a mango. The only meaningful action that will produce a mango is to plant a mango seed. Karma is just such a law of nature, the law of cause and effect on the psychophysical plane.

The Buddha used the term *karma* specifically referring to volition, the intention or motive behind an action. He said that karma is volition, because it is the motivation behind the action that determines the karmic fruit. Inherent in each intention in the mind is an energy powerful enough to bring about subsequent results. When we understand that karma is based on volition, we can see the enormous responsibility we have to become conscious of the intentions that precede our actions. If we are unaware of the motives in our minds, when unskillful volitions arise we may unmindfully act on them and thus create the conditions for future suffering.

The law of karma can be understood on two levels, which indicate the vast scope of its implications in our lives. On one level, karma refers to the experience of cause and effect over a period of time. We perform an action, and sometime later we begin to experience its results. We plant a mango seed, and many years later we taste the fruit. The other level of understanding karma has to do with the quality of mind in the very moment of action. When we experience a mind state of love, there comes naturally along with it a feeling of openness and joy that is its immediate fruit; similarly, when there are moments of greed or hatred, in addition to whatever future results will come, we also experience the painful energies that arise with those states. Our direct awareness of how the karmic law is working in each moment can be a strong motivation to develop skillful states of mind that create happiness for us in the moment, as well as produce the fruit of well-being in the future.

Another dimension of the law of karma helps in understanding how individual personalities develop. While it is true that there is no enduring entity, no unchanging self that can be called "I," it is also quite obvious that each of us is a uniquely changing and recognizable pattern of elements. This comes about because each of us has in our own way, both consciously and unconsciously, cultivated different mind states. If we cultivate loving-kindness, we experience its taste in the moment and at the same time are strengthening it as a force in the mind, making it easier for it to arise again. When we are angry, we experience the suffering of that anger as present karma and are also strengthening that particular pattern of mind. Just as we condition our bodies in different ways through exercise or lack of it, so we also condition our minds. Every mind state, thought, or emotion that we experience repeatedly becomes stronger and more habituated. Who we are as personalities is a collection of all the tendencies of mind that have been developed, the particular energy configurations we have cultivated.

We tend not to pay attention to this conditioning factor of our experience, thinking instead that once an experience has passed it is gone without residue or result. That would be like dropping a stone in water without creating any ripples. Each mind state that we experience further conditions and strengthens it. When we see how this is happening in our own minds, we begin to get an intuitive sense of something the Buddha spoke of often in his teachings, the conditionality of the six realms of existence. These six realms are the manifestations of strongly developed patterns of mind. They refer to the different realities we experience from moment to moment, and also to the actual planes of existence in which beings are reborn according to their karma.

The attitude in Western cultural conditioning toward rebirth and different realms of existence is often skeptical or disbelieving; there is a healthy strain of "Show me, I'm from Missouri" in our approach to these questions. It may be of value, though, to realize that along with all that we can verify directly in our practice, these concepts of karma and rebirth are very much part of what the Buddha taught, and that it is possible through meditative attainment to experience for oneself the truth of these teachings. For those of us with something less than perfect concentration or great psychic power, however, an attitude that helps to keep us open to possibilities beyond our present level of understanding is expressed in a phrase of the poet Coleridge: "the willing suspension of disbelief." With this attitude of mind we are trapped neither by blind belief nor by blind disbelief. In this way we acknowledge what we don't yet know for ourselves and stay receptive to new levels of understanding.

According to the Buddha's teachings there are six realms or planes of existence: the four lower realms of suffering, the human realm, and the higher planes of the various heaven worlds. The lower realms are conditioned by intense anger, hatred, greed, and delusion, and when we cultivate these states, developing them as a pattern of response to situations, they become a strong force in the mind. Not only do we then experience the present karma of the painful feelings in the moment, but we also create the conditions for possible rebirth in realms of terrible suffering.

The human realm is the first of the happy planes of existence. It is said to be the most conducive for developing wisdom and compassion because of its particular mixture of pain and pleasure. In the lower realms the intensity and degree of suffering is too great for most beings to develop wholesome qualities of mind, while in the higher planes of existence everything is so blissful that there is little inspiration to practice. It is precisely the combination of pain and pleasure in the human realm that provides the best circumstances for deep understanding and realization.

We take birth as human beings conditioned by a basic attitude of generosity and nonharming. These mind states create the powerful, wholesome karmic force that results in birth in this realm, and indeed, these qualities of mind reflect a true humaneness. When generosity and morality are practiced and developed even further, they condition rebirth in the deva realm, the heavenly planes of existence. In these deva worlds everything is pleasant, beings have refined bodies of light, and there are delightful sense objects on all sides.

The highest planes of conditioned existence are the brahma realms. They are characterized by great bliss, which is a happiness beyond sensual pleasure and is the result of the cultivation of a deep concentration of mind known as absorption.

These six realms are all karmically created. There is no one who judges, condemns, or elevates us to different realms, just as there is nobody who decides which mind states we are to experience in each moment. The great inspiration of the Buddha's teaching is that we must each take ultimate responsibility for the quality of our lives. Given certain volitional actions, certain results will follow. When we understand that our lives are the unfolding of karmic law, that we are the heirs to our own deeds, then there grows in us a deepening sense of responsibility for how we live, the choices we make, and the actions we undertake.

People sometimes wonder whether reflecting upon the law of karma will lead to feelings of guilt for past unwholesome actions. Guilt is a manifestation of condemnation or aversion toward oneself, which does not understand the changing transformative quality of mind. It solidifies a sense of self by being nonforgiving. Understanding the law of karma leads us to reflect wisely on the skillfulness or unskillfulness of our actions. In the infinite time of our births, through all the realms of existence, we have done so many different kinds of actions, wholesome and unwholesome. In view of karmic law, guilt is an inappropriate feeling, and a rather useless burden. It simply creates more unwholesome results. Coming to an understanding of karma is the basis for a very straightforward development of the wisdom to know whether our actions will lead to happiness and freedom, or to further suffering. When we understand this, it allows us to take responsibility for past actions with an attitude of compassion, appreciating that a particular act may have been unwholesome or harmful, and strongly determining not to repeat it. Guilt is a manifestation of condemnation, wisdom an expression of sensitivity and forgiveness.

The Buddha spoke often of the rarity and preciousness of human birth. There is a traditional metaphor illustrating how difficult it is to take birth as a human being after one has been reborn in one of the lower realms. Imagine a blind turtle living at the bottom of a huge ocean; floating on the surface of the ocean is a wooden yoke. Once every hundred years the turtle comes to the surface. It is said that the likelihood of the turtle's surfacing at just the place where it can stick its head through the yoke is greater than the opportunity for one reborn in a lower realm to take a human birth again. Of course, in the infinite reaches of time, just as the turtle will eventually stick its head through the yoke, a being born in a lower realm will also at some point take a higher birth; but it will probably take a long, long time.

Understanding that rebirth is karmically conditioned, we can understand why the Buddha so stressed the preciousness of our human state. For beings in the realms characterized by anger, fear, dullness, and desire, there is little opportunity to cultivate wholesome actions because of the intensity of the suffering. One unwholesome mind state conditions another in a downward cycle of greed, hatred, and delusion. Reflecting on the law of karma brings an appreciation of the preciousness of one's life and a sense of the urgent importance not to squander the rare opportunity we have to hear and practice the dharma. Countless times a day intentions arise in the mind creating the karmic force that brings results. With a careful attention and awareness of volitional activity, we can take active responsibility for the unfolding of our lives.

Once a man asked the Buddha what it is that makes for the different qualities, characteristics, and circumstances among people. Why is it that some people die young and others die old? Why are some rich and some poor? Why are some beautiful and others ugly? Some wise and some foolish? In response, the Buddha explained the actions that produce each of these various results.

Nonkilling results in long life. The result of taking the lives of other beings is that in the future one's own life will be shortened. Why is it that some people are healthy and others sickly? Nonharming is the karmic force for health, while hurtful actions create the condition for disease. Anger and hatred are the conditions for ugliness, and loving care, gentleness, and kind speech are the conditions for beauty. When someone is very angry, we can see what anger does to his or her expression. The energy that we see clearly manifesting in that moment has a continuing force and power. Previous actions motivated by generosity are the karmic conditions for wealth, and those motivated by greed create the conditions for poverty. Why are some people wise and others dull? The mind that inquires, investigates, and explores conditions wisdom. The minds of those not interested in understanding and insight become dull.

It is said that on the eve of his enlightenment, the Buddha, with the power of his mind, reviewed the births and deaths of countless beings wandering throughout the cycle of existence in accordance with their karma. His great compassion was awakened when he saw all those beings wanting happiness, striving for happiness, yet performing the very actions that would lead to suffering. When we do not understand the unfolding of karmic law, when we are deluded about the nature of things, then we continually create the conditions for greater suffering for ourselves and others, even when we are wishing and hoping for peace. There are those even today who have developed the power of mind to see karmic unfolding through past and future lifetimes. But it is not necessary to be able to see our past lives in order to understand the principles of karmic law. If we pay attention and carefully observe our own lives, it can become very clear how our actions condition certain results.

The Buddha spoke often about right and wrong view with regard to the effects of one's actions. Right view is the understanding that our actions do bring results, both in the present and in the future, while wrong view denies this cause-and-effect relationship. Our culture is generally geared to the pursuit of immediate gratification of desires, and this reinforces the view that what we do will not have effects, that there is no karmic result from our actions that will come back to us. But when we step back and take a broader perspective, we begin to understand that we are the heirs of our own motives and deeds and that our lives do not unfold randomly or haphazardly. It is important to see what our motives and volitions are and to understand the results they condition.

Mindfulness plays a critical role in understanding the unfolding of karma. Two aspects of mindfulness that are particularly relevant to this are clear comprehension and suitability of purpose. Clear comprehension means paying attention to what we are doing, being fully aware of what is actually happening. When we stand up, we know we're standing; when we walk, we know we're walking. Clear comprehension of what we are doing in the moment then allows us to consider the suitability of purpose. This means knowing whether the actions are skillful or unskillful, whether or not they will bring the results that we want.

When mindfulness is weak, we have little sense of clear comprehension or suitability of purpose. Not only may we be unaware of our intentions, we often are not even paying attention to the action itself, hence we may be propelled by habitual patterns into actions that bring painful results. The deep understanding that actions condition results creates a compelling interest in what we do. We begin to pay quite meticulous attention; we begin to awaken. Not only does each action, no matter how insignificant it may seem, condition a future result, it also reconditions the mind. If a moment of anger arises in the mind and we get lost in it, we are then actually cultivating anger. If we get lost in greed, we are cultivating greed. It is like a bucket being filled with water, drop by drop. We think each drop is so tiny, so insignificant, that it doesn't matter at all. Yet drop by drop the bucket gets filled. In just this way, the mind is conditioned by each experience in every moment, and moment after moment the mind gets filled. We should have a tremendous respect for the conditioning power of the mind, not only in terms of our present experience, but also in terms of our future direction.

For a moment now, imagine being on your deathbed and in your last moments looking back upon your life. How would you like to have lived? What would you have wanted to do? What qualities would you wish to have developed? Our lives are a dynamic process of energy transformation, constantly flowing and changing, and we each have the power to determine the direction of our lives and to live in accord with our deepest values. If we become more conscious and awake, developing the ability to observe clearly, we can begin to use our energy creatively and not be bound so blindly to past conditioning. We need not wait until we're dying to reflect on the course of our lives. Reflection on the law of karma, right now, can bring a very strong motivation and inspiration to practice and to live one's life in the best possible way.

The story of the great Tibetan yogi Milarepa is an illustration of how past unskillful actions can be transformed into a force for purification and enlightenment. Milarepa was born into a wealthy, landed family. When he was still a young boy, his father died and his aunt and uncle took control of the family's property, treating him and his mother as outcasts. Over the years a tremendous resentment and outrage grew in him, and when he was older he went off to study black magic. He proved to be an adept, and he returned home to put a powerful curse on his aunt and uncle, and on the land itself, causing great suffering. After achieving his revenge, he gradually began to reflect on the law of karma. He realized that because of his powerful, hate-motivated actions, he had accumulated much unwholesome karma, which would bear fruit over many future lives. Because of this he felt compelled to purify and free his mind in that very life. He came to recognize the preciousness of having the opportunity to practice the dharma, and it inspired him with an extraordinary sense of urgency. He sought out a teacher, and when he found one in the person of Marpa, he began years of remarkably strenuous and committed practice, which led him to a deeply liberating wisdom and compassion.

During a visit to the United States, His Holiness the Dalai Lama gave a talk about emptiness of self and the karmic law of cause and effect. In the course of the talk, he said that given a choice between understanding karma and understanding emptiness, one should try to understand karma. To many that was surprising, because the very heart of the wisdom of Buddhism is understanding the empty, selfless, insubstantial nature of phenomena. His point of emphasis, though, is extremely important for us to grasp, because without an understanding of karma, of the effect of our actions, the aspect of the emptiness of phenomena can be used as a rationale for not taking responsibility in our lives. To think that nothing matters, that we can do anything because it's all empty anyway, is a serious misunderstanding of the teaching and a poor justification for unskillful behavior. If we are sensitive to the law of karma and become responsible for our actions and their results, then it will help us come to a genuine understanding of emptiness.

Compassion, as well as insight, arises from understanding karma. When we understand that unfair, harmful, or hateful actions rebound in suffering to the person committing them as well as to the recipient, we can respond to both with compassion rather than with anger or resentment. This in no way means that our response is weak or indecisive. In fact, seeing people act out of ignorance in ways that cause themselves or others great pain can inspire a very strong and direct response to that ignorance, but it is a response of compassion.

The Buddha at one point remarked that only a buddha-mind could fully grasp the fullness and complexity of karmic law, the way in which it unfolds, not only within one lifetime, but over countless lives. There are, however, many stories illustrating how karmic destiny unfolded for various people according to their actions. Most are straightforward accounts of the very widespread understanding that we reap as we sow. There are some stories, though, that have particular twists in the plot. These stories are very simple, but they point out some of the complexities and subtleties of the law of karma. One story tells of a man in the Buddha's time who, seeing a monk passing by, thought to offer him food. The man offered the food to the monk but afterward regretted having done so, thinking that it was a waste. The monk was an arhant, a fully enlightened being, and it is said that offering food to an arhant has a very powerful wholesome karmic effect. The result of having offered food to the monk was that the man was reborn as a millionaire for seven consecutive lifetimes. But the karmic fruit of his having regretted his own generosity was that he had a miserly disposition throughout those seven lifetimes and was unable to enjoy his great wealth: the ironies of karmic justice. Each mind moment brings its own appropriate result, and an action can bring mixed results if the mind moments surrounding it are mixed. If a wholesome action is surrounded by a feeling of appreciation, the power of its wholesome karmic force is increased.

The karma generated at the moment of death plays a crucial role in determining the circumstances of rebirth. There are four different kinds of karma that can be operating at the time of death. The first is called weighty karma, and this refers to either wholesome or unwholesome actions done during one's lifetime that create so strong a karmic force that they take precedence over every other action in conditioning rebirth. Among those on the unwholesome side are killing one's father or mother. On the wholesome side, weighty karma is the development of jhana, or the realization of nirvana. Even the first glimpse of nirvana is powerful enough to close off any future possibility of rebirth in the lower realms.

If there is no weighty karma, then the mind states generated by the performance or remembrance of wholesome or unwholesome actions in the last moments before dying will condition rebirth. This is called proximate karma, that is, actions done near death. The dying moments play a critical role in the unfolding of karma and rebirth, and it is encouraging that today there is an increased awareness and sensitivity concerning the circumstances and surroundings of people's deaths. If there is neither weighty nor proximate karma operating, then rebirth is determined by the karma of one's habitual patterns, that which one has done over and over again, which comes naturally to the mind in the dying moment. This is usually the predominant karmic force. If none of these three types of karma is working, then any action one has done at any time in the past may come to mind at the moment of death. This last is called random karma.

The karma of a past action has a certain reach and will become operative or not in a given situation depending on the circumstances. This aspect of karmic law is illustrated by another story from the time of the Buddha. There was a man who had killed many people during his life. He was eventually caught and condemned to be executed. Just as he was about to be killed, he saw some monks walking by and remembered that he had once offered food to the Buddha's foremost disciple, Sariputra. Because his last thought was the remembrance of that act of generosity (proximate karma), he was reborn in one of the heaven realms. Someone reborn in those worlds experiences only the pleasant results of wholesome actions; the fruit of unwholesome karma cannot reach one while in that realm. Those beings also have the ability to see their past lives. This man, now a deva, a heavenly being, looked back over his past lives and saw the wholesome action that caused him to be reborn in that happy realm, and he also saw all those unskillful actions he had done, which would bear fruit when his time as a deva was finished. This realization motivated him to practice the dharma, and even though it is not easy to practice in the heaven realms because the temptations of sense pleasures are so great, in time he realized the first stage of enlightenment, the attainment of which closes off the possibility of rebirth in the lower realms. Thus, that fortuitous remembrance in his last moment before being executed allowed him to free himself from the net of suffering in which he would otherwise have been caught.

In explaining the workings of karma, the Buddha spoke of the potency of different actions. He spoke often of the great power of generosity, explaining that an act of generosity is purified and empowered in three ways. It is purified by the giver, by the receiver, and by that which is given. The purity of mind of the one giving and of the one receiving, and the purity of the gift itself (that is, the means by which the gift came into one's possession), strengthen the karmic force of each act of generosity.

And many times more powerful than giving a gift even to the Buddha and the whole order of enlightened disciples is one moment in which the mind is fully concentrated on extending thoughts of loving-kindness toward all beings. When we genuinely open our hearts, the deep feeling of our connectedness to all beings is a tremendously effective force, which can then motivate a wide variety of skillful actions.

The Buddha went on to say that even more powerful than that moment of loving-kindness is one moment of deeply seeing the impermanent nature of phenomena. This moment of insight is so profound because it deconditions attachment in the mind and opens up the possibility of true nonattachment. When we deeply see the impermanent, ephemeral nature of the mind and body, how they are in constant flux, we develop detachment and equanimity toward the dreamlike elements of our experience. Sometimes in meditation practice when we are dealing with the pain, restlessness, boredom, and other difficulties that come up, we may lose sight of the larger context of what the practice is about. It is helpful to remember that the karmic energy generated by the repeated observation and awareness of the changing nature of things is a tremendously powerful karmic force that leads to many kinds of happiness and to freedom.

Understanding the law of karma is known as the light of the world because through this understanding we can take responsibility for our destinies and be more truly guided to greater fulfillment in our lives.

J. G.

EXERCISE

## Equanimity Meditation

Although it grows naturally through vipassana practice, the quality of equanimity can also be cultivated in meditation in the same systematic way that is used for loving-kindness and compassion. Equanimity is usually paired with and used to balance the spirit of compassion. Even though we may cultivate a boundless compassion for others, and strive to alleviate suffering in the world, still there will be many situations we are unable to affect. As Reinhold Niebuhr's well-known prayer says, may I have the strength to change the things I can, the patience to accept the things I cannot, and the wisdom to know the difference. Having the wisdom to know that all beings are heir to their own karma, that they act and receive the fruits of their actions, brings an understanding mind together with a compassionate heart.

To cultivate equanimity as a quality, sit in a comfortable posture with the eyes closed. Bring the attention to the breath until the body and mind are somewhat calm. Then begin by reflecting on the benefit of a balanced and equanimous mind. Let yourself feel an inner sense of balance and ease. You may repeat such phrases as "May I be balanced and at peace. May I be undisturbed by the comings and goings of all the events of the world. May I be peaceful." Acknowledge to yourself that all created things arise and pass away; joys and sorrows, pleasant events, unpleasant events, people, buildings, animals, nations, even whole civilizations. "May I learn to see the arising and passing of all nature with equanimity and balance. May I be open and balanced and peaceful." Acknowledge that all beings are heirs to their own karma, that their lives arise and pass too, according to conditions and deeds created by them. "May I bring both compassion and equanimity to the events of this world. May I find balance and equanimity and peace."

# 11

# *Understanding Karma: Liberation*

THERE IS another level of understanding karma, one that is not primarily concerned with creating particular conditions of happiness, such as being reborn in a higher realm or in some wonderful circumstance on earth. This other level is concerned not with the particulars of rebirth, but with the process of complete liberation from the entire round of birth and death.

The jewel of the Buddha's teaching, the essence of its wisdom, is insight into anatta: selflessness or emptiness. According to the teaching of anatta, there is no entity, no self, no "I" to which our momentary experience refers; what we are is an evolving process in which all elements, both physical and mental, are constantly changing. That which we call a being, a self, is the grouping together of what are called the five aggregates, or skandas in Pali.

The first skandha is the aggregate of form, the material elements that we experience as physical sensations: hardness, softness, heat, vibration, heaviness, lightness, and so forth. The second is the aggregate of feeling, which is the quality of pleasantness, unpleasantness, or neutrality that is inherent in each moment's experience. The third aggregate, perception, is that quality of mind which can distinguish and recognize different objects. For example, through perception, we can recognize a sound as a car or as a dog's bark. Memory is one of the functions of this skandha. The fourth is the aggregate of mental formations, including volition, and all the other mental factors besides feeling and perception, those two already having been singled out because of the particularly essential role they play in our conditioning. For example, mindfulness, concentration, greed, aversion, love, compassion, wisdom, and delusion are all different mental factors in this fourth aggregate of mental formations. The fifth skandha is consciousness, the knowing of an object that has come into contact with one of the senses. What we are is the interaction of these five aggregates. Such terms as *me*, *you*, *woman*, or *man* are just the conventional and convenient expressions used to describe particular patterns of changing aggregates.

For example, in a moment of hearing a sound, the knowing of it is consciousness. The ear, which is the base for hearing, is the aggregate of form. The unpleasant or pleasant quality of the sound is the aggregate of feeling. The recognition of the sound as the horn of a car is perception; and the aversion or attachment that may arise in the mind is the aggregate of mental formations.

An important Buddhist text entitled *The Questions of King Milinda* tells of a dialogue between King Milinda, a Greek king ruling one of the Asian provinces of Alexander the Great's conquest, and a renowned monk named Nagasena. At one point, the king asks Nagasena about the teaching of anatta, saying that in conventional reality there certainly seems to be a self. Nagasena then points to the king's chariot and asks, "O Sire, what is the chariot? Where is the chariot to be found? Is the axle the chariot? Is it the wheels? The spokes?"

As Nagasena mentions each part, the king replies, "No, that is not the chariot."

"What then is the chariot?" Answering his own question, Nagasena responds that "chariot" is a concept describing the coming together of these parts in a certain relationship. Apart from this relationship of constituent elements, no chariot exists. In the same way, that which we call self is a concept applied to the interplay of the five aggregates of form, feeling, perception, mental formations, and consciousness, which are in reality arising, passing away, and re-arising in each moment. Their very nature is continuous change, dissolution, and reemergence.

We look in the mirror today, and the aggregates appear more or less the same as they did yesterday. They certainly go by the same name. We get the impression that there is something unchanging and enduring; and even when we do perceive changes, we think of them as happening to someone. But when we look more closely, and it is for this that meditation practice is so useful, we see that consciousness or knowing itself is a process of change and that everything we call "self" or "I" is only the continually changing process of these five aggregates, with nothing substantial or enduring behind them.

The unfolding process of the aggregates does not happen randomly; it is not chaotic. It happens in an ordered way, with continuity, according to certain laws. The laws governing the unfolding relationships of the elements of mind and matter are analyzed in the body of texts called the abhidharma, the Buddhist system of psychology. According to the abhidharma there is a basic unit of experience called a thought process. Thought in this case does not refer to discursive thought or words in the mind, but rather to a series of seventeen distinct mind moments. When we hear a sound, for example, the basic unit of the experience of hearing is a thought process composed of these seventeen mind moments, all having the same object, in this case, the sound. This is how our experience of seeing, hearing, smelling, tasting, touching, and thinking unfolds: seventeen mind moments of one thought process followed by seventeen mind moments of another.

Some of the mind moments of each thought process are called resultant moments; that is, they are the karmic results of past actions. We experience these results as the feeling aggregate of pleasantness, unpleasantness, or neutrality. For example, if we are hearing an unpleasant sound, the unpleasantness of that resultant moment is the karmic fruit of some previous action. Others of the seventeen mind moments are called active moments, and these moments produce new karmic seeds depending on how we are reacting to the object of experience. When we hear an unpleasant sound, the unpleasantness is outside of our control since it is simply the fruit of past actions.

But the remaining mind moments within this thought process, the active moments, will condition future results depending on our response to the unpleasant feeling. If there are moments of aversion and condemnation for the unpleasantness, the karma they generate will bring further unpleasantness in the future. If we respond with awareness, openness, and insight in the active moments, then we are generating new, wholesome karma, which will produce happiness in the future.

Present feelings of pleasantness, unpleasantness, and neutrality are the result of past karma. Reactions to present feelings create new karmic results, conditioning the future, which will then be experienced as new feelings. It is a cycle: as the karmic result of past actions, feelings arise in the present; because of these feelings there are reactions; and because of these reactions in the present, which are creating new karma, there will be new feelings in the future; because of these feelings in the future, new reactions, and around and around. This cycle of karmic conditioning is the wheel of samsara seen on the level of mind moments.

The teaching of vipassana meditation stresses both the awareness of what is happening in each moment and how we are relating to it, because it is in our relationship to experience that new karma is being created. Are we relating to each moment's experience in a way that simply keeps the whole cycle of conditioning going? Or can we use each moment's experience as a way of deconditioning the reactive mind and finding freedom?

The key to liberating ourselves from this cycle of conditioning is mindfulness. Mindfulness means awareness, openness, and acceptance of whatever arises, without attachment to the pleasant, aversion to the unpleasant, or forgetfulness of neutral feelings. If we can experience present feelings, which are the result of past actions, with a mind that is not grasping, not condemning and not deluded, then we are creating the conditions for enlightenment and freedom.

Even one who is fully enlightened experiences the result of past wholesome and unwholesome actions. There is a story from the Buddha's time about a man named Angulimala, who had murdered nine hundred and ninety-nine people. He was called Angulimala, which means "garland of fingers," because he collected the fingers of all those he had killed in a garland around his neck. One of the actions productive of weighty karma, discussed previously, is killing one's mother or father. Angulimala was about to make his mother his thousandth victim. The Buddha, through the power of his mind, saw Angulimala running after his mother, and he appeared before him to prevent it. As the Buddha walked slowly and mindfully, Angulimala ran after him as fast as he could. No matter how fast he ran, he was unable to catch up to the Buddha. Finally Angulimala shouted, "Stop! Stop! Why can't I catch you?"

The Buddha replied, "Angulimala, I have stopped. It is you who have not stopped."

And Angulimala stopped, really stopped, impressed by the fearlessness and compassion of the Buddha. Soon afterward he was ordained as a monk and eventually attained full enlightenment. He still had a great deal of unwholesome karma as a result of his past murderous deeds, and every time he went into the towns and villages, he would be beaten and stoned. He experienced in this way the karmic fruit of his past actions, but his mind had been freed and there was no angry reaction, no new karma being created. He understood that his painful experience was the playing out of the law of karma.

Everything, from the lowest of the hell realms to the highest brahma realm, is a manifestation of mind. Through understanding the laws governing the unfolding of our lives comes the enormous power to choose our destiny. We need no longer feel helpless in this awesome process. We can walk on a path that leads to wisdom and happiness; and through understanding karma on the mind-moment level, the samsaric chain of conditioning can be broken. Through the power of mindfulness, of not clinging, condemning, or identifying with what arises, we break that chain of conditioning and open to the possibility of genuine freedom.

J. G.

EXERCISE

# Observing Intention

To understand karma, it is essential to see how the motivation or intention preceding an action determines the future karmic result of that action. Thus, if an act is motivated by true kindness, it will necessarily bring a positive result, and if an act is motivated by aggression or greed, it will eventually bring an unpleasant result. Because karmic results do not always bear fruit immediately, it is sometimes difficult to observe this process.

Speech is one area in which karma can be seen in an easy and direct way. For this exercise, resolve to take two or three days to carefully notice the intentions that motivate your speech. Direct your attention to the state of mind that precedes talking, the motivation for your comments, responses, and observations. Try to be particularly aware of whether your speech is even subtly motivated by boredom, concern, irritation, loneliness, compassion, fear, love, competitiveness, greed, or whatever state you observe. Be aware, too, of the general mood or state of your heart and mind, and how that may be influencing your speech. Try to observe without any judgment or program of what you should see. Simply notice the various motivations in the mind and the speech that flows from them.

Then, after discovering which motivation is present as you speak, notice the effect of the speech. If there is competitiveness or grasping or pride or irritation behind the speech, what response does it elicit from the world around you? If there is compassion or love, what is the response? If your speech is mindless, as if you were on automatic pilot, what is the response? If there is clarity and concern, how is this received and responded to?

With the law of karma we have a choice in each new moment of what response our heart and mind will bring to the situation around us. In discovering the power of our inner states to determine outer conditions, we are able to follow a path that can lead to genuine happiness and freedom.

# 12

# *The Five Spiritual Faculties*

In his teaching, the Buddha spoke of five spiritual faculties, qualities that bring power and balance to our minds and form an essential part of the path to freedom. Meditation is a process through which we develop these qualities so that they become strong and enduring forces, touching every aspect of our lives.

## FAITH

The first of these spiritual faculties is usually translated into English as "faith," but no one English word captures the full scope of the Pali term *saddha*. This quality of mind includes trust, clarity, confidence, and devotion. Saddha has several different levels. The first level arises when we encounter something that inspires us. It may be a religious symbol, a work of art, a talk, a scene in nature, or a meeting with an unusually inspiring person. This feeling of inspiration can fill the mind with brightness, love, and devotion. It is possible, though, for this inspiration to arise without wisdom and so be the cause of blind faith.

A deeper level of confidence is the kind that is born out of wise consideration, when we use our intelligence and discrimination to investigate our experience. This is known as "verified faith" because our original inspiration has begun to be verified or reinforced by the faculty of discriminating wisdom. An example of this might be our faith in particular aspects of the teachings—in the truth of impermanence and selflessness, or in the possibility of liberation as exemplified by the Buddha or other enlightened beings—not simply because of what we have been taught but because of our own investigation, reflection, and insights.

There is also a faith that we can have in the direction of our life's journey, a direction not in time or space, but in the dimension of our understanding. In Asia there are often situations when one is in the midst of tens of thousands of people. In the middle of a swirling mass of humanity, of countless people all busily engaged in the day's activities, often one feels very directly the circular, whirlwind nature of samsara. We are born, live out our lives desiring, hoping, interacting, and reacting according to our conditioning, getting sick, getting old, and ultimately dying. Questions arise in the mind: Where is it all going? Is it leading onward in any way? Of course, there is no need to be in Asia to be struck by these basic questions. They are the starting point of our inquiry. It is in the journey of understanding ourselves that this swirling whirlwind of life takes on a deeper meaning. With faith in the process of deepening insight, every aspect of our lives becomes our practice; there is no fragmentation or separation of practice and life. We do not have to live our lives motivated by fear or desire; we can appreciate each moment as a vehicle for developing wisdom.

And when we open to an experience of truth beyond the realm of ideas and feelings, our verified faith becomes even stronger. If we develop meditation practice to the point of deep and genuine realization, then our faith is no longer dependent on any external object or situation for reinforcement. We experience the power of unshakable faith, verified not only by our hearts and intellects, but by the deepest levels of intuitive wisdom. This deep level of faith and trust is symbolized by a magical gem, which when dropped in water has the unique power to cause all impurities to settle to the bottom, leaving the water clear and sparkling. Faith has this power in the mind. It settles doubt and agitation, creating a mental environment of inspiration, confidence, and purity.

We develop deepening faith by learning to stay open and connected in each moment. Why is it, though, that we often find this difficult to do? What has happened to our magical gem? What keeps us from trusting and opening to our own experience? One way in which we prevent ourselves from opening to the simplicity and directness of each moment is by seizing upon some past experience and projecting it into the future. If it was a pleasant experience, we try to repeat it; if it was unpleasant, we try to prevent it from arising again. In either case, our practice becomes a process of struggling and striving with past and future, rather than being fully attentive to what is happening right now. We may cling to pleasant experiences of rapture or insight. One sitting period feels wonderful, with the mind concentrated and clear. We begin the next period with the expectation of taking up where we left off, but this time it's all pain and confusion: "If only I could get back to where I was before." We might spend a great deal of time in our practice resisting our present experience in order to regain something that has passed. This struggle diminishes the healing, deepening power of faith.

Every experience, no matter how wonderful or terrible it may be, will change and pass away. What we are is a process that is continually unfolding into the unknown of each new moment. In striving to regain what has passed, we keep ourselves prisoners of what we already know. Think of yourself as having set out on a long journey through terrain never before explored. You come to a mountain and climb to its very peak. The view is fantastic, and the chill in the air is exhilarating. Extraordinary though it is, eventually you push on and continue the journey. The trail takes you up other peaks, down into desert valleys, through swamplands and forests. Each place you come to is unique, and it is all to be explored. But this is only possible if you travel light, without attachment to what has gone before, without comparing, and without giving up. Faith means trusting the unfolding process of our lives. It is a willingness to let go of fears and attachments, and open ourselves to the unknown in each new moment.

### EFFORT

Once we have developed enough faith to at least begin the journey, it is then necessary to apply effort and energy to our investigation. The quality of heroic effort is the second of the five spiritual faculties. It is the root of our practice and the source of all accomplishment in our lives. But if this quality of effort is not correctly understood, it can also lead to ambition, tension, and the creation of more goals and models at which to grasp. We need to understand effort and energy in a way that generates them from within us, rather than imposing them from the outside by some ideal that demands that we be a certain way. If we try to fit ourselves into a model of how we should be, our practice will be one of constant struggle and resistance. Yet it is possible, and indeed necessary, to nurture a sense of urgency and commitment within ourselves, which then generates a tremendous effort and energy for discovery.

One way that we impose limits on our energy is by settling into comfortable patterns—patterns of eating, of sleeping, of relationships, of work. We assume certain boundaries and limits for ourselves and find comfort staying within their familiar confines. But when we are willing to extend beyond these limits, we find great reservoirs of energy available in our lives. A wonderful rediscovery of something that we all know but often forget is that effort creates energy. Think of times when you may be feeling very tired but then make the effort to do some vigorous exercise. The very effort involved in doing that creates a feeling of energetic well-being. We can each experiment to find ways of cultivating and strengthening effort and energy, not being afraid to push at limits or to take some risks.

Effort may be divided into three aspects. There is launching, or preliminary effort, which is the courage and willingness to begin on a genuine path of discovery; there is liberating or transcending effort, which is the diligence not to falter or be dissuaded in times of difficulty; and there is developed or progressive effort, which is that quality of energy that does not decrease or stagnate, but which continually grows in power, leading us on to liberation.

Effort in practice can be aroused by a meditative reflection that is common to all schools of Buddhism, that is, a reflection on the certainty of death and the uncertainty of the constantly changing circumstances of life. We don't know how things will unfold. Consider the precariousness of our lives right now, with so many disruptive forces in the world and so much potential for destruction. The fleeting, uncertain nature of our lives makes the dharma, the truth, a most precious and rare gift that should not be neglected; we don't know when the opportunity to practice will arise again.

## MINDFULNESS

Effort is directed toward the development of mindfulness—the third of the spiritual faculties. What captures the sense and meaning of this mind state is the understanding of mindfulness as "fullness of mind." In this fullness of attention there are no barriers, no exclusions; it includes and encompasses every aspect of experience. Nothing lies outside the field of awareness. Whatever we are doing and wherever we are, it is possible to arouse this quality of awareness.

In the *Satipatthana Sutta*, which is the discourse the Buddha gave on the four foundations of mindfulness, four fields or areas of mindfulness are described. The first is mindfulness of the body, which includes awareness of posture, whether standing, walking, sitting, or lying down, as well as movements of the body such as turning, stretching, and bending. As mindfulness of the body deepens, we begin to go beyond the concepts of body or foot or leg, to the experience of the body as different sensations: hardness, softness, temperature, vibration, tingling, tension, throbbing, and so on, where there is no longer any sense of solidity or static form. We dwell repeatedly in the awareness of the body, developing the power of clear and unhindered observation.

This first foundation of mindfulness is particularly appropriate for the development of a deep and grounded attention in our daily activities. The body is always there as a clear object of awareness. As we walk down the street, can we be carefully feeling the sensations of movement, or are we lost in thoughts about past and future? Opening doors, brushing our teeth, drinking a cup of tea—all these simple acts provide ongoing opportunities to be significantly strengthening our practice.

The second field of mindfulness is awareness of feelings. These are not feelings in the sense of emotions, but refer in this meditative context to the quality of pleasantness, unpleasantness, or neutrality arising in every moment of experience. The awareness of these feelings is so important because they condition our reactions of grasping, aversion, and ignorance. It is because something is pleasant that we grasp it, and because something is unpleasant that we condemn or dislike it. And when an experience is neither pleasant nor unpleasant, we often become forgetful or our mind wanders. If this second foundation of mindfulness is cultivated, then we can feel the pleasantness or unpleasantness of different experiences without having a conditioned reaction. We have a greater ability to feel what is going on with balance and equanimity.

Awareness of feeling in this way also provides a key for unhooking the mind once it has already been caught in a reactive state. Suppose the mind is lost in a lustful state, with strong and delightful images enticing the attention. In addition to noting the bodily sensations and images that are present, if we can clearly and precisely notice the pleasantness of these sensations or pictures, then we can see very directly that it is the feeling of pleasantness which is capturing the mind and conditioning the grasping. By meticulously noticing and noting this aspect of pleasantness, the mind unhooks from the object, lets go of the grasping, and is aware of the pleasant feeling simply as another object of observation rather than as something to hold on to. When we understand how desire is conditioned by feeling, we see that underneath the wanting mind is a place of choice. In situations where we find ourselves caught in a reaction of strong clinging or aversion, this second foundation of mindfulness can be a powerful tool of investigation and freedom.

The third field of mindfulness is awareness of the mind and mind states; that is, becoming aware of the mind as it is colored by different emotions: love, joy, anger, hatred, interest, boredom, and so on. The meditative balance is to be able to feel them with openness and softness, without getting lost or wallowing in them. Emotions, like all other parts of our experience, are not "I," not self, but part of the passing show of phenomena.

When there is a strong emotion present, it is often helpful to ground the awareness of it in the first two fields of mindfulness; that is, to become carefully aware of the specific bodily sensations associated with the emotion and whether the feeling is pleasant or unpleasant. This grounding helps us stay mindful and open to the emotion without getting lost in our personal story. From the meditative perspective, we are more interested in discovering the nature of anger, for example, or joy, than in an analysis of the particular content. In this way we come to a deep and profound understanding of the nature of the mind, which goes beyond our personal history.

The fourth foundation of mindfulness is mindfulness of the dharma, the awareness of the functions of different mental states. We become mindful, for example, of how desire functions as a hindrance, or how faith functions as a spiritual ally. As this application of mindfulness grows, we also become aware of certain basic laws and relationships: the Four Noble Truths, the Eightfold Path, the relationship of the sense bases to the sense objects. Many aspects of our growing understanding are revealed by this foundation of awareness. The effort to be mindful from moment to moment brings our wisdom to life and infuses our faith with understanding.

The characteristic of mindfulness is one of nonsuperficiality; it is penetrative and profound. If we throw a cork into a stream, it will just bob up and down on the surface, while a stone thrown into the water will immediately sink. If we are mindful of an object, our awareness will sink deeply into it. As long as mindfulness is present, the object of observation is kept in view; we are not forgetful or half-hearted in our attentiveness. The mind comes face-to-face with the object, with directness, focus, depth, and sensitivity. Mindfulness also manifests as a protection, because when we are mindful we are protected from the force of the conditioned habits of grasping, condemning, and forgetfulness which create pain and confusion in our lives.

## CONCENTRATION

Concentration is the fourth of the spiritual faculties. It is the quality that brings strength and intensity to one's practice. The cultivation of concentration can be approached in numerous ways. In the context of insight meditation, concentration is a steadiness of attention to the flow of constantly changing objects. Even when we are keeping our attention on the breath, we can feel the continually changing sensations of the air touching the nostrils or the different sensations in the movement of the abdomen. The key to developing concentration is a persevering continuity of mindfulness. We can see an illustration of this in the primitive means of creating fire by rubbing two sticks together. Were we to rub the sticks together for a few minutes and then get tired and give up, rub again for a little while, get diverted by a distraction and stop, rub for a few moments more and get lost in reflection, then the momentum of heat generated would continually be lost, and we would never even get a spark. Likewise, if we are mindful for only a few minutes at a time, with many breaks in continuity, we cannot develop the power to go deeper. When we practice developing an unbroken stream of mindfulness, the hindrances to concentration are set at bay, and the mind becomes calm and clear. As mindfulness becomes enduring, the mind remains steady, without becoming scattered or distracted, and concentration becomes strong and well established. If we are willing to make the effort to bring continuity to practice, we will naturally enjoy the power, depth, and wholeness that come from deep concentration. When the mind is not scattered, there is a feeling of completeness and nonfragmentation, which brings about a happiness that is completely different from the pleasure we conventionally experience.

In the course of practice there are often times when we feel lazy and uninspired. This may conflict with our model of what it means to have steadiness of mind, and so we think, "Well, since it's just not happening, I might as well not even try." Rather than give up when you feel disheartened or depressed, allow the attention to open to that feeling in the mind and body. Let the experience of discouragement become the object of awareness and inquiry. The very effort to be mindful at these times energizes the mind and makes possible a steady focus of attention. If we don't limit ourselves by thinking that in order to practice we must be in a certain frame of mind, then steadiness of mind can be developed whatever the circumstances. Concentration, like the other spiritual faculties, is not something we must struggle to attain at some remote point in the future. It is present naturally in each moment that we are fully attentive, and it is something we can cultivate right here and now.

## WISDOM

The fifth of the five spiritual faculties is wisdom. The term *vipassana* means insight, seeing things as they are. Wisdom, or insight, means seeing clearly the nature of experience. When concentration and mindfulness are well developed, insight will unfold by itself. It is an intuitive understanding, which no amount of reasoning or intellectualizing can bring about in a genuine way. In Buddhism this insight is spoken of in three aspects.

One aspect of wisdom is seeing clearly the impermanent nature of all phenomena. Impermanence can be seen with varying degrees of refinement depending on the degree to which the mind is concentrated. But on whatever level we look, we see that things are in constant change: the earth, the seasons, the weather, societies and civilizations, our relationships, our bodies, our thoughts and emotions—everything. As the mind becomes more focused, awareness of impermanence becomes more subtle. When concentration and mindfulness become strong enough, as is often the case during periods of intensive meditation, the perception of impermanence becomes so precise that the body/mind process is experienced as a continual pulsation of energies, each element of experience instantaneously arising and dissolving. There is nothing at all solid that we can hold on to.

Another aspect of wisdom is understanding suffering. When we quiet the mind and look carefully at our experience, we see that this world of consciousness and object is a world of constant change and insecurity. Once an object has arisen, no matter how hard we try to keep it stable, it will pass away. Whatever appears is so transitory that it doesn't even last a moment. Consciousness and object reveal themselves to be continually dissolving. We see that whatever appears is not dependable, that there is no refuge, no safe haven in conditioned phenomena. The poet Rilke calls the kind of happiness that is based on these fleeting experiences "that quick gain of an approaching loss."

The Buddha said that coming to realization is like swimming upstream, going against the current of many popular worldly beliefs. If we are to come to an integrated understanding of who we are, it is essential that we investigate the nature of suffering—how it arises and how we stay bound to it. We begin to see how attachment to that which is continually changing is a source of great pain in our lives. But how to let go of our attachments, how to let go of our suffering? It is as though we are holding a hot burning coal in our hand. Do we stop to consider how to let go? We drop it quite naturally as we become aware that it is burning.

By closing ourselves off and suppressing what is unpleasant, we continue to hold the burning coal. The extent to which our culture avoids and denies the truth of suffering is striking. It is as though we think that only a few people get old, become sick, and die. We live as if this will only happen to others, not to ourselves; or we romanticize these experiences, not feeling the actuality of disease in the body or the loneliness and alienation so often felt in old age. This attitude keeps us closed off from a true relationship to life.

So much of our time is spent trying to experience and capture moments of satisfaction. But there is an ephemeral, dreamlike quality to our experience that we all sense yet rarely explore in depth. We get up in the morning, get dressed, go to work, do our jobs, talk with people, come home, eat dinner, read the newspaper, go to the movies, go to sleep, wake up the next morning, and start all over. We go through the endless cycle of our daily routine, busying ourselves with fantasies of happiness and security, and often out of touch with, or unwilling to accept, the ever changing and unpredictable nature of things.

Acknowledging the truth of unsatisfactoriness is the key to the deepening of wisdom and compassion. Awareness of suffering lights a fire within us, a fire of motivation to awaken, a fire that can consume all obstacles. The more we open to suffering, the greater is our freedom from it, allowing a natural sense of joy and a genuine fulfillment to arise in our lives.

As insight into impermanence and suffering deepens, the third aspect of wisdom emerges: awareness of the selfless nature of phenomena. Seeing deeply into the nature of the mind-body process reveals the fundamental and transforming truth that there is no self, no "I," no one to whom experience occurs. What we are is this changing process moment to moment. There is no one behind it to whom it is happening.

Although all that we experience is in a process of continual change, our concepts about experience are static. The reality of the mind-body is that of a process in constant flux; the names we use to describe it stay the same. We are misled by the static use of concepts and are conditioned by them to view the world as a collection of solid things, all in relation to a solid ego, "me."

As an experiment, hold your hands together and experience the sensation of them touching each other. What do you feel? (Please take the time to do this.) There may be warmth or moisture or pressure, but is there any sensation that could be called "hand"? When we stay just with our direct experience, we see that "hand" is a concept, an idea we apply to a certain collection of sensations. That which we take to be "self" is also just a concept. "I" is an idea, a name we apply to a constantly flowing pattern of ephemeral mental and physical phenomena.

Imagine yourself outside at night looking up at the stars and seeing the Big Dipper, that big constellation pointing to the North Star. Is there really a big dipper in the sky? There is a group of stars in a particular pattern, which we separate out from all the other stars in the sky, and to which we attach the concept "Big Dipper." But apart from the name, there is no big dipper, just all the pinpoints of light in the vastness of space. In exactly the same way, "self" is a constellation of sights, sounds, smells, tastes, bodily sensations, and mental events, all continually changing. These phenomena form a pattern that we call "I." But just like the Big Dipper, "I" is a concept, a conventional term of communication.

Some evening, go outside, look up at the sky, and see if it is possible *not* to see the Big Dipper. It is very difficult to do because we have been so conditioned by that concept. If it is so hard not to see the Big Dipper, you can appreciate how difficult it is to let go of the concept of self. The sense of "I" is so deeply conditioned in our minds, our identification with it so basic and subtle, that its influence pervades our lives. Because of our identification with the concept of self, we become preoccupied with pleasures to gratify it or defenses to protect it. We come to view the entire world of our experience—thoughts, emotions, the body, or work—in relationship to the "I." But as we settle into the experience of each moment, this false sense of solidity, of selfhood, begins to dissolve and with it its attendant burdens, the continual struggle to protect, defend, and maintain the fiction of self.

As wisdom develops we become filled with faith, because we have seen for ourselves the true nature of our bodies, our minds, and our lives. The path of insight, of understanding the nature of our being, is a journey that encompasses every aspect of our experience. And the journey is always right here, right now. There is no need to struggle or be in conflict with what is happening. By bringing a precise attentiveness and quality of openness to the whole range of our experience, moment to moment, the nature of reality will reveal itself. Dharma understanding will unfold according to its own laws, just as in springtime the flowers open in their own time.

The five spiritual faculties—faith, energy, mindfulness, concentration, and wisdom—are our greatest friends and allies on this journey of understanding. These qualities are most powerful when they are in balance. Faith needs to be balanced with wisdom, so that faith is not blind and wisdom is not shallow or hypocritical. When wisdom outstrips faith, we can develop a pattern where we know something, and even know it deeply from our experience, yet do not live it. Faith brings the quality of commitment to our understanding. Energy needs to be balanced with concentration; effort will bring lucidity, clarity, and energy to the mind, which concentration balances with calmness and depth. An unbalanced effort makes us restless and scattered, and too much concentration that is not energized comes close to torpor and sleep. Mindfulness is the factor that balances all these and is therefore always beneficial.

There are some other ways of developing these five spiritual faculties and bringing them into balance. The first is to reflect, and remember in the moment, that whatever arises will pass away. When we can accept that this constant flux is the way things are, we can be more fully with our experience of the moment without reacting.

The second aid in strengthening these faculties is to meticulously and carefully carry out the meditation with respect for its value in our lives. The dharma is a great and noble treasure; the practice of it on all levels is the cause of our great happiness. If we deeply honor the practice, the respect we feel for it brings a caring, loving, and impeccable quality to how we live.

We do not have to live in a world of illusion if we are committed to realizing the truth. We can approach our lives with a sense of spiritual urgency, with a great desire to understand this body and mind before we die, developing the strength of mind to go straight ahead without abandoning our sense of purpose. And in both intensive meditation practice and our daily lives, the refining and deepening of the five spiritual faculties can make real our aspiration to make best use of our lives.

J. G.

# 13

# The Three Basic Characteristics

As we have seen, Buddhist teachings often speak of cultivating certain beautiful qualities of mind—awareness, equanimity, kindness, faith, and so forth—that the mediator perfects as he or she progresses along the path of practice. We can describe the very fabric of the path as the development and maturity of these qualities. The path does not exist apart from this development; it is the essential nature of our endeavor. While this systematic view can be helpful to understanding the process in which we are engaged, it can also confuse us by fueling our fantasies about what is supposed to happen. Judging and measuring our actual experience against an idea—oftentimes erroneous at that—about what should and should not occur in spiritual practice can lead to confusion and pain, rather than a sense of peace and authentic conviction. Instead of providing the vast source of inspiration and energy that such a framework is intended to offer, our goal-oriented and comparative thinking can make it lead to striving, doubt, and bitterness.

What can we most truly rely on for guidance in our practice? Only our direct experience. Most fundamentally, our life is composed of six experiences: sights, sounds, tastes, smells, physical sensations, and mental events. From this perspective, our life is very simple. Our whole complex world is only this: changing sights, sounds, tastes, smells, touch, and thoughts and feelings. In practice we make the effort to be aware of our direct, immediate experience of life, of these six senses, including the mind as a sixth sense. As we do this, we come to understand more and more clearly what in Buddhism are called the three basic characteristics of all created phenomena: suffering, impermanence, and selflessness. Our practice is a constantly deepening personal and intimate sense of these three characteristics, and they provide for us a framework that is powerful and enduring. The realization of these characteristics can cut through all grasping and goals and can guide us to wisdom in all spiritual experiences, inside and outside of retreat.

### SUFFERING

In looking further at these three characteristics, let us begin by considering suffering because that is where the Buddha began his teaching. Suffering also includes that which is unsatisfactory and unreliable. Speaking of the importance of understanding suffering, he said: "There is one thing, O monks, the not seeing of which keeps us unfree, keeps us bound on this cyclic wheel of becoming. That one thing is the truth of suffering."

To stop and again seriously consider the enormity of the suffering experienced by many millions born on this earth—the poverty, hunger, violence, and cruelty—is a sobering and powerful reflection. It is important to acknowledge and come to terms with this worldwide suffering in our spiritual life, through understanding and through compassionate action. Yet to understand suffering deeply, we cannot just look outside of ourselves. In our practice and our own hearts, we can find an understanding of suffering that is even more immediate and discover how it affects and touches us in each moment. Let's consider our own direct experience of this. Our first observation must include the many times we experience life as being uncertain, unstable, and oppressive, when we feel anxious or depressed, or even at the best of times the uneasy feeling that certain happiness is somehow eluding us, that something is just not quite right. Of course, there is more to it than this. Even the joyful process of birth has its attendant pain for the mother and baby, and as we grow up, each period of childhood, adolescence, trying to become an adult, aging, sickness, each step in making our way through this complicated world, has its great share of suffering. Still, to understand suffering is more immediate than this. If we watch carefully during the course of an ordinary day, we will see that there is dissatisfaction, discontent, or fear, loneliness, judgment, or irritation, physical pains, disappointments, or insecurity in the moments of much of our experience. This fundamental suffering can affect many of our actions and move us through our day.

Let's say we wake up one morning and we have the whole day off with no obligations. We lie in bed for a while, but soon we experience the discomfort of having to urinate. We get up and quickly take care of that, but then leave the bathroom to avoid the unpleasant smell, then get back under the covers to avoid the cold. We think, "Now I'll be comfortable and happy." But after a while, we begin to feel hungry, so we must get up to relieve the unpleasant sensation of hunger. When we have finished eating, we have to wash the dishes and straighten the kitchen to avoid the unpleasantness of the food going bad and attracting flies. Next we decide to sit in our most comfortable chair, and we think, "Now I'll be happy." But even here we have to move continually or the body starts to ache, to hurt. And even though we may feel relatively comfortable, pretty soon just sitting in a chair becomes boring. We have to look for entertainment to avoid that. So we get up and go for a walk, and before you know it, we're tired, so we have to sit back down to avoid the painful feeling. Then we're hungry again. Then we're bored. Then we're tired. It's true, isn't it? Look at ourselves right now: we scratch to relieve an itch, move to relieve an ache, squirm because of restlessness. It is not at all that we shouldn't do these things, but only that we should look clearly and penetratingly at them so that we can understand this aspect of our lives. It is this sense of suffering that drives much of our actions.

It is everpresent. It is a central experience of our lives, like water to a fish. As we come to see the pervasive nature of dissatisfaction in our lives, we also see our consuming preoccupation with avoiding it. We create elaborate dramas around our routines, desires, and relationships, just so we can lose ourselves in them and not face the underlying hunger—hunger for contact, for love, for food, for happiness, for comfort—from which they all arise.

If we look closely at this hunger, allowing ourselves to experience it fully, we can see that we are constantly driven by it. We can also see the fundamental, existential pain in which it is rooted. It is this raw and open painful place in ourselves that we spend our lives trying to cover up and avoid. We keep running away from the immensity of it.

Any moment in which we stop doing our dance of running away from it, we can come in contact with this basic, primal pain. And if we are ever willing to investigate it with our full attention, if we allow our practice to open to it, and feel it completely, in that moment something extraordinary happens— that hunger that drives us and keeps us constantly moving falls away. This falling away happens not because the hunger is bad, nor because we shouldn't have it, nor because we try to get rid of it. It falls away because in the pure openness of that moment, we no longer need it.

That hunger and movement is how we distract ourselves from facing our most fundamental pain. But when we allow ourselves to look into it, we can finally come to rest. Not that it is easy to face; it isn't. In fact, it is very painful. But when we allow ourselves to experience it fully and directly, we find that there opens all around this raw and hurting place a feeling of surprising spaciousness. When we don't add identification and reaction to it, the pain is just there, as it is, bearable. This is our task. The Sufi teacher Pir Vilayat Khan put it this way:

> Overcome any bitterness that may have come because you were not up to the magnitude of pain that was entrusted to you. Like the mother of the world who carries the pain of the world in her heart, each one of us is part of her heart, and therefore endowed with a certain measure of cosmic pain. You are sharing in the totality of that pain. You are called upon to meet it in joy instead of self-pity.

We have a hard time believing that we are actually able to face our own pain. We have convinced ourselves that it is something to fear and avoid at all costs. We have been conditioned to believe that, and so our society has been built around this fear. We put people in old-age homes and mental hospitals, in part to avoid their pain. We have freeways so that we can drive around the ghettoes, and even our dead we make up and dress up as if they were going to a party! If we stop running, it will overwhelm and destroy us. But there is no need to fear our pain. In fact, the fear is just as another story with which we distract ourselves! There are countless meditation techniques that have developed in Buddhism's history, yet the point of them all is to direct us back to the fact of our suffering, because that is what keeps us running. Facing it directly, we can come to freedom.

We try hard to overcome the fact of how quickly pleasure passes. Even though pleasant sense experiences pass, we hope to string enough of them together to make them seem to stay. Yet all this gets very tiring. This is a fragile and illusory security in a world where so much changes so quickly.

It is important to understand that our vision of these basic characteristics gets clearer as we continue to practice. If we look to meditation to lead us only to quiet and bliss, we will become disappointed. Naturally, more peaceful and balanced states develop when mindfulness grows in us. For many people there arise periods where the mind and heart open into great and tender silence. There arise periods of stillness and times when the heart and mind are filled with light and a profound sense of peace and well-being. Yet this clarity and contentment develop *together* with a deeper and deeper ability to see and allow suffering. As we pay attention we grow to experience more fully the suffering of the body. Superficially, we find periods of aches, pains, progressive aging, and illness. More profound attention reveals patterns of much more deeply held tensions: powerful fires, releases of heat, cold, throbbing, pressure, vibration, and the forces within us that grasp and hold this body. Even more careful and concentrated attention can bring us to feel a cellular level of fire and suffering.

As we examine the mind in the present, its thoughts and feelings, additional suffering reveals itself. At first, this may be through touching our painful moods and feelings: grief, sadness, past wounds, fear, anger, jealousy, and more. Then awareness grows to see how it is not just these feelings but any movement of mind whatsoever that creates suffering. Any wanting, the very tension of liking and disliking itself, is suffering. As we continue to practice, our suffering shows itself in another profound form as our awareness touches the senses more keenly. In very silent moments we can experience how the objects that contact the senses themselves are sources of suffering. We notice how as each object touches the sense doors, pressure on the body, sounds on the ear, even light on the eye, there is pain in contact. At the very deepest level we see that our identification with and grasping at any of the five processes of life (body, feelings, perception, reaction, consciousness) is the source of suffering. Seeing the extent of this suffering can be enormously freeing—but seeing it alone is not enough. We have to soften our bodies and hearts to receive it, to open to its truth in a wise and tenderhearted way. This is a big part of our practice. Only through acknowledging and opening to suffering can we stop and come to rest, can we find stillness and a deeper ground of goodness and well-being. It is this suffering that prompts us to let go, to live more lightly. By touching this suffering we can awaken the fullest compassion within us.

An old monk in Thailand drew a picture of a happy, smiling buddha on the wall of his cave and under it a most peculiar saying: "O joy to discover there is no happiness in this world." What could this mean? It is an acknowledgment that there is no *lasting* happiness, because of the eternal truth that nothing lasts. Only when we stop running and accept life with all its dance of change, its ten thousand joys and ten thousand sorrows, with its inherent suffering, only then can we find peace and wisdom.

## IMPERMANENCE

The second of the three basic characteristics, which become clear to us as we progress in meditation, is impermanence. Just as we have avoided looking at suffering, so do we try to avoid impermanence. In the Indian epic called the *Mahabharata*, it is asked what is the most wondrous thing in the world. The reply is that the most wondrous thing in the entire world is that people can see other people all around them growing old and dying and somehow think that it will not happen to them!

Impermanence—look at it right in this moment. A sound comes and then it's gone. A thought arises and so quickly passes away. Sight, taste, smell, touch, feeling—they are all the same: impermanent, fleeting, ephemeral. Where is yesterday, where is last year, where is our childhood? It all vanishes so quickly. If we want to understand death, we have only to look at the present, because in each moment we are being born and dying. The sound we just heard is already gone—it died, and we died with it. To live fully is to let go and die with each passing moment, and to be reborn in each new one.

Out of the misconception that it is possible, we try to make things solid and secure. We create the illusion of stability in our minds: "I'm this sort of person. These are my opinions. My body is like this. I'm going to go to live this way and do that thing." It is like winding our watch on the way to the gallows; we live as if we could continue this way forever. But those are the stories we make up to give ourselves something to hold on to. The raw experience of our lives, the basic stuff, is constant change: changing sights, changing sounds, changing smells, changing tastes, changing sensations, and changing thoughts. When we look, is there anything else?

We find it difficult to accept the truth of impermanence. If we would stop and look carefully, we would see that it is the very nature of our lives. We cannot stop the body from constant change, and we cannot stop the mind from constant change. When we want things to be other than the way they are, we are bound to be frustrated. Have you ever met old people who are bewildered and resentful that age came so quickly? Because of this frustration, people often feel betrayed by the unfolding of their lives.

There is an alternative. Instead of trying to deny the flow of change and living in conflict, we can understand it deeply and live in harmony with the seasons of life. Instead of creating solid "things," solid relations, a solid, unchanging world to try to hold on to, we can let go and open to the actual truth of each changing moment. This is learning to live by what Alan Watts called "the wisdom of insecurity." There is no pretending, no complacency, and no bleak grasping and groping for some secure thing that will not go away.

As practice develops, the vision of impermanence deepens. As we learn to acknowledge our aging and our death, we live more fully now. We can see through observation how our opinions, thoughts, feelings, and sensations all change so quickly. Jack Engler, a Harvard psychologist who has studied meditation, described the growth of wisdom as a process of grieving. Outwardly, our spiritual life brings us to acknowledge the temporality of life, to accept aging, death, and the temporary nature of even the most beloved people and experiences around us. As practice grows in us, our visions, our reflections, our hearts, are required to come to terms with this. Often, actual visions of our death and the deaths of those around us will arise. To come to terms with outer change at this level involves a tremendous process of letting go. Yet it is a task of all humans and an immediate necessity for anyone who would live with a wise heart in this world.

As meditation progresses, another, more inward process of letting go and grieving becomes revealed. To come genuinely into the moment means that our sitting must actually teach us to die. We must die to our attachments, our hopes and plans, to all our fears and expectations. To be here fully we have to let go of it all. Of course later we can pick much of it up again, but we still touch our life more lightly and wisely. But let's not speak of that too soon. Most of practice is a relentless process of letting go. We have to see our self-images, our psychological process, the way we have structured our life, our whole sense of self, and see how it is all constructed of temporary images, thoughts, and fears. To face our death, to go beyond this small sense of self, we must grieve and leave it behind.

As mindfulness and concentration get more highly developed in our meditation, we can use this strong awareness to examine our world more closely. Under a constant and powerful attention that keeps focusing on the present moment, our life dissolves into fleeting moments of sense perceptions, changing every instant. This level of insight can be called "dissolving the rapidity." It brings into vision each momentary arising and passing of experience at the sense doors, so that what has ordinarily appeared as a solid movie of ourselves and the world around us literally breaks apart under the gaze of this refined attention. With strong concentration, we can actually perceive the individual moments of sense impact and of our recognition and reactions to them, like seeing frames arise one by one very rapidly on a movie screen. This is a dramatic and liberating level of practice. Wherever in the body or mind we turn our attention dissolves into microscopic moments, granules of life arising and dissolving—even the observing dissolves moment after moment, passing too quickly to count or grasp. Now we can actually experience what is meant by the stream of events and feel directly how life is impermanent on every level.

### SELFLESSNESS

As we practice, the third characteristic that grows in our understanding is no-self. All phenomena are empty of self. There is no entity separate from the flow of experience, no "self" to whom it is happening.

While the depth of this truth of selflessness is profound, we begin to experience it early on in our practice. Sometimes we have the experience in meditation of the mind settling down and becoming still and quiet, and then immediately there arises a sense of fear and anxiety, and suddenly it's busy again with ideas and plans and opinions. It is a common experience, one that happens to almost everyone. But why should a quiet mind frighten us so?

Our primary delusion, one whose influence pervades all aspects of our lives, is the belief that there is an "I," a self, an ego, that is solid and separate from everything else. But actually this sense of "I" is made up only of the process of identifying: "This is me. This is what I do. I like this. I'm going there. I want to be this way," and so on. It is created entirely by thought and has no substance. It's just thought-bubbles.

The only way to effectively maintain the illusion of the self's solidity is to keep churning out thoughts, plans, programs, and the rest. If we keep them coming, we can quickly paste it all together and it seems to make something solid. But when the mind begins to quiet down, the whole structure begins to slip, and from the ego's point of view that is scary. It's very simple. When thought begins to disappear, who else disappears? We do. Our sense of self is created by our thought process and by the habit of grasping in the mind.

If we are not caught up in all our thoughts about our experience, there is simply experience in each moment: just seeing, hearing, smelling, tasting and touching. It is all emptiness, all without self. Of course, it is not that we have to get rid of thoughts to experience emptiness, because thoughts are empty in themselves, thoughts are merely a process, words and pictures, conditioned by certain causes and composed of constituent elements. We don't have to make things empty of self; emptiness is their true nature. We have only to experience each moment directly; each moment is a manifestation of the empty, unpossessable nature of reality.

We can see this for ourselves. When we sit, it is often as if someone left the radio on and we can't turn it off. We don't even choose the programs. Thought, sounds, sensations—they all just arise and pass by themselves. Do we ask our thoughts to come? Do we truly control them? They just come into being and then die away. They are not us, nor are they ours to control. The same is true with body sensations. They arise and change spontaneously of their own accord. Can we tell the mind not to think, or the body not to grow old? Would it listen? All that we think of as "me" or "mine" is a flow of changing experience, happening according to certain laws, with no enduring entity behind the scenes controlling the show. In truth what we are is this changing process; there is nothing substantial or solid.

As our awareness grows in practice, this truth becomes clearer and clearer. We see how the thought process just thinks, the feeling process just feels, the sense process just senses, all according to conditioned laws. And even we, the observer, are seen by awareness in a new light. There are objects of experience that arise for a moment together with a process of knowing or consciousness, each object and knowing arising and dissolving moment after moment. To see consciousness in this way is like learning about photons and then experiencing the particle nature of light. This can actually be experienced in subtle levels of practice.

The realization at the center of this practice is the experience that none of the five processes which make up our life—the body, the feelings, the perceptions, the reactions, the consciousness itself—none of them is enduring or possessable. We are part of a waterfall. Through thought and ego-sense, through habit and conditioning, we have grasped them for many years as our self, yet none of the processes can be held, and the very identification with them is false, the cause of our suffering. It is all a phenomenal show of light and color, gone as soon as it arises. Everything comes out of the amazing void, each day and each moment, coming out of nothing and returning to nothing.

Achaan Chaa often called our life "just this much." We continually look and hope for a new, special thing that is going to last or make us happy, fulfill our needs, answer all our questions. In actuality, what are we going to get? We will get more seeing, hearing, smelling, tasting, touching, and thinking. That's it; that's what life is. We might like it to be otherwise, but it is just that much.

When Zen master Seung Sahn visited Bodh Gaya, he wrote a

poem about the Buddha's enlightenment under the bodhi tree, which says:

> Once the great man sat under the bodhi tree,
> He saw the morning star and was enlightened,
> He sat there and absolutely believed his eyes,
> his ears, his nose, his tongue, his body, his mind.

Sometimes the deepening experience of the three characteristics becomes confusing. We may have practiced for a number of years and become a bit more calm and balanced as result of it. But in the back of our minds, we think of how our practice should develop further. After all this time, shouldn't we be experiencing more of the factors of enlightenment? We expect more bliss or stillness or profound clarity, more ease and joy. Yet what do we actually see? More impermanence, more emptiness, more unsatisfactoriness and suffering. We see it, we feel it more clearly, and we think something is wrong with our practice.

Practice is the deepening realization of these basic truths. Each of them is a gate to liberation, a gate to freedom, if we can understand and fully accept it. At the very deepest level of meditation, a moment of full acceptance of one of these gates and of full letting go brings us to what is beyond it, the unconditioned, to nirvana.

Furthermore, as we sit and the initial insights deepen, for a majority of yogis the characteristic that becomes the most powerful over the years is that of suffering. The suffering of grasping, the suffering of identification, the suffering inherent in life. To touch the full flame of this suffering with our awareness is what finally brings us to let go. Touching the full flame of it with our heart brings the deepest compassion. So when we feel that our practice is not going well, we must look to see if we are facing more of the impermanent, insecure, and painful aspects of life. If we are seeing them more clearly and learning to accept them, we are on the right track and our practice is going well indeed.

When we cultivate a powerful and direct awareness, the truth is so clear that we ordinarily can't believe it. We want our lives to be more. We want our experiences to be permanent, fulfilling, to finally suit our fantasies. For most of us, this is our deepest, most heartfelt desire. Are we still trying to find this completion through external experiences, through the ever-changing world of our senses and relationships? Our heart cannot be fulfilled through the senses or through relationship to something external. It is not possible, for these experiences are impermanent and without self. Look at it closely, feel it directly, be aware of it. This is what all forms of our practice lead us to.

Even in spiritual practice, we hope that someone will give us something more. We want that special, esoteric whispered-in-the-ear teaching that brings instant repose and joy. But that hope just binds us further. The way we will find freedom, harmony, and happiness is by discovering in ourselves what is fundamentally true: impermanence, suffering, selflessness. Only when we see and accept these basic characteristics of our life are we ready to find what we seek for our heart, only then can we come to rest, can we find our imperturbable and joyful buddha-nature. This experience is the secret of the teaching. As T. S. Eliot puts it, "We shall not cease from exploration, and the end of all our exploring will be to arrive where we started and know the place for the first time."

To sustain our exploration of these three characteristics, we need great faith in our ability to face the world directly. Outwardly, we take refuge in the Buddha and our own buddha-nature as a symbol of this faith. To take refuge in our buddha-nature is to sense within our hearts the full potential of wisdom, compassion, and true freedom. We take refuge in the dharma, meaning the teachings and the truth or universal law. To take refuge in what is actually *true* in each moment is to live according to this law. We align ourselves with a practice of awareness that brings us to look directly and deeply at what makes up our world and our lives. We take refuge in the sangha, in the community of those practicing, and in our inherent connectedness with all life. To liberate ourself is to contribute to the liberation of all we know. Faith in the sangha cultivates a sense of unity and enables us to practice with a sense of protection and direction. Hundreds of thousands of yogis have gone before us, in every age and every great culture. We join this great journey in each moment that we look at how things truly are.

We must have faith in ourselves and the insight of our own experience. Are we willing to trust ourselves and what we find? Are we willing to be independent, to drop our hopes and expectations and see what is true? We cannot rely on the secondhand words of others. This is an important issue in developing our practice. It is not easy to be self-reliant, to trust oneself. "Someone else must know better. How can I trust my own confused or greedy or angry mind?" We are afraid to really look. We fear our shadow side. Sometimes we feel that if we don't keep all the bad stuff down and under control, we will be overwhelmed by it. We imagine that purity will be found somewhere else.

But let's look succinctly at the problem. If we don't face the difficulties in our life directly, won't we have to keep running away? How else can we actually learn to find a heart of compassion but to face our deepest greed and fear, attachment and sorrow and pain? Where do all those qualities we judge so harshly come from? They come from a sense of incompletion, a hunger and desire that we spoke of earlier. This feeling of being incomplete is based on the fundamental misperception that there is a separately existing self. We hunger to gratify the self, to give it pleasure. We react with fear and hostility when it is threatened or doesn't get what it wants. Over and over this conditioned reaction continues. Yet these are not our true self. They arise based on our illusion of separateness, and so we seek security based on this illusion.

When we open to trust things as they are—impermanent, unsatisfactory, without self—a whole new relation is possible. We need courage and faith to look into this deeply. Can we see and open to the three characteristics in our life, in every part of our practice? By seeing them, we awaken. There is no self to hold on to. We are not separate, and nothing about us can be grasped. When we stop running away from what presents itself in each moment, our loving care for ourselves and one another can flow unimpeded. Through our attention the hunger and illusion that obscure the truth fall away, and our real nature expresses itself wonderfully and naturally. If we open ourselves to deeply accept the impermanent, unsatisfactory, and insubstantial nature of all things, we come to a kind of completion. There is none of the hiding and not quite knowing what we are hiding from. There is no weariness of maintaining a pretense. There is no forlornness of endless neediness. In the place of all this comes the acceptance and wisdom that we have admired in so many other wise ones. And quite naturally there arises a heart of love and compassion. All this is the direct expression of a life lived in harmony with these simple truths.

J. K.

EXERCISE

## Observing Discomfort in Our Conditioned Response

Spend half a day observing the arising of discomfort and pain in your normal life and in observing your responses and reactions to it. It is important to do this exercise without any judgment and without any attempt to change yourself. The task is to simply observe and understand what you see.

Starting first thing in the morning, determine to pay attention every time you change posture. Be aware each time you stand up, sit down, move your arms and legs, or go from one place to another. Notice particularly if you are moving in response to a discomfort or pain, to alleviate hunger, to scratch an itch, to avoid boredom or loneliness, to ease your tiredness, to stretch a cramped muscle. Try not to change posture or move without first observing the cause. Try to be aware of more than just the desires such as "I want to get something to eat," and notice also the hunger pangs to which the desire is a response. Be aware of how many desires and movements arise in response to the power and frequency of discomfort and pain in daily life. Study this aspect of the characteristic of suffering. Let the awareness be gentle and heartfelt, understanding the suffering that reveals itself and acknowledging it with softness and true openness.

# 14
## *Perspectives on Reality*

THE WORD *dharma* can be understood in a number of ways. It is the truth, the true nature of things, reality, the moral and spiritual law. It also denotes each of the individual mental and physical elements that together comprise the phenomenal world. *Dharma* also means "teaching," and in the context of Buddhism it means specifically the teachings of the Buddha. Dharma practice, then, is the process of coming to understand the moment-to-moment unfolding of reality on all the different levels of our experience, and bringing ourselves into harmony with the truth of our lives and the laws of nature.

We are each a mandala of ever-changing experience that can be viewed from a variety of perspectives; we are a process of continuous transformation in which nothing is fixed. In recognizing ourselves to be a part of this interconnected, changing reality, we seek to find a sense of equilibrium and an understanding of its nature. We need subtlety to understand and work with different levels, to learn to be open and fluid in going through our experience from whatever perspective is appropriate.

One of the fundamental aspects of dharma practice is understanding the creation of dualistic perception. How is it that the mind creates an orientation of fragmentation and separation? How is it that through making distinctions and separations we limit ourselves and create a prison of duality? In his book *The Spectrum of Consciousness*, Ken Wilber synthesizes a broad range of spiritual and psychological wisdom to describe with great clarity the progression of dualities the mind creates. He outlines in the following four stages the movement from nondual awareness to a narrow identification with one aspect of the mind.

The primary dualism we perceive is that of self and other, subject and object, inside and outside. This first level of dualistic thinking is the separation of ourselves from the environment, separating out the mind/body organism from the totality of experience. It is well described in Benoit's phrase "a rent in the seamless fabric of the universe." From this division of oneness into subject and object arises the second level of dualism: the duality of mind in the body. This is the development of a separate ego sense within the total organism. It is the feeling of someone having a body.

The next level is the fragmentation of the mind itself into "persona" and "shadow." The persona is all the mental phenomena that together create our image of ourselves, who we think we are. It is all the conditioned patterns of mind with which we identify. Those elements of mind which we discard and repress, the dark and unpleasant ones, are what comprise the shadow. Even though we try to repress them, these negative qualities follow us about, like a shadow, and we can't get away from them. Because we don't recognize and pay attention to it, we are unconscious of the shadow and the ways in which it motivates and manipulates us.

Through the power of ignorance in the mind, we restrict and narrow our sense of who we are as we go from a nondual awareness of the wholeness of the universe through the progressive levels of separation. First we separate the mind/body from the environment and limit ourselves through identifying with the organism. There is then a further narrowing in which we identify with the ego-mind, that one to whom all experience is happening. Finally, the mind itself becomes fragmented into those aspects we identify with because they are acceptable in light of our self-image, and those which we repress because they are not. At each level our lives become more fragmented and limited.

The path of dharma is to heal these divisions, to understand the true nature of our lives. This does not mean that we dissolve into an undifferentiated mass of cosmic oneness, but rather that we fully understand the different levels so we can act appropriately and freely. Just as we might know that at the subatomic level of existence most things that appear to be solid are predominately empty space, still we're willing to accept that on another level of experience the chair we sit on will support us. The awareness of the subatomic level, however, allows us access to more fundamental and powerful energies. In just the same way, we can relate from a conventional understanding of self and other, but imbued with a quality of freedom that comes only when we realize the relative nature of that division and are no longer caught up in an identification with it.

We begin the process of reintegration on the level of persona and shadow by opening to the full range of mental phenomena—emotions, thoughts, impulses, feelings—without judgment or evaluation. We investigate the arising and projecting of self-images, that process of identification with certain aspects of the mind, with particular patterns of conditioning. We also develop a dispassionate attitude toward the shadow, allowing all parts of it to come into consciousness. Identification with certain aspects of the mind and rejection of others inevitably creates a sense of conflict and tension. As we develop acceptance and detachment toward all that arises, we begin to live with less fear and aversion.

As the process of unification continues, integration of the next level of duality, the split of mind and body, can begin. Here, great care in understanding is necessary because the mind and body are, in fact, two distinct processes, and insight into this distinction is fundamental in our deepening practice. The duality to overcome is not the difference between the mind and body, but rather the fragmentation that occurs when we identify with the ego-mind as being "I," that sense of someone "having" a body. Implicit in this view is that there is someone, a self, to whom the body belongs. This gives rise to, and reinforces, mental projections based on the felt need to protect and defend this sense of self. Feelings of separation are rooted in this identification with the ego-mind, as are the mind's tendencies toward attachment, aversion, fear, judgment, and comparison. These tendencies, in turn, sustain the complex fiction of a separate and enduring "I": if there are feelings of attachment, aversion, and so on, then there must be a self that is "having" them. Until we can see and penetrate this Möbius-strip conditioning, we stay bound in an endless cycle: identification with the ego-mind within the body creates a sense of self and separation; the sense of self then conditions feelings and reactions that further strengthen the identification with the ego-mind.

Another result of identifying ourselves as someone who has a body is the tendency to mistake the projections of this ego-mind for reality. Because we don't fully experience ourselves as a total being, we become immersed in seductive mind-worlds of fantasy. Walking meditation can be particularly revealing in this respect. The simple experience of touching the earth is so clear and grounding that it becomes obvious, in contrast, how we create, through our thoughts and images, conceptual worlds that have nothing to do with our actual experience in the moment. Between one step and the next the mind can create Los Angeles, an entire relationship, an argument, or any one of a limitless number of scenes and scenarios, each eliciting its own emotional responses, judgments, and reactions. Countless times each day we become lost in fantasies, forgetting that they are only thoughts. It is as though we were watching a movie and become so absorbed in what we're seeing that we jump up to the screen and begin to interact with the characters.

In the *Zen Doctrine of No Mind*, D. T. Suzuki writes: "All is mind made. It is like a person painting a tiger. He paints it, looks at it, and is frightened. There is, however, nothing in the painted figure which is fearsome. All is the brushwork of your own imagination." Thought forms arise, last for a while, fade away, and dissolve. As we observe the mind, we begin to see how much of our reality is the brushwork of our own thinking. As we look at the particular patterns and conditioning that arise in the mind, insight into how each of us creates our world from this sense of self begins to grow. We investigate the orientation that refers everything back to "me," and we see the qualities of mind that arise from that way of viewing things. Fear, aversion, attachment, judgment—all arise from the perspective of self. Through the simple and direct observation of how this happens, without judging and comparing, we begin to let go of our identification with the patterns that reinforce the "I" within the organism.

Dharma practice is coming to an awareness of the completeness of experience in each moment. When we are no longer identifying with just a part of the total organism—that is, with particular thoughts, emotions, or even with a silent knowing—then there is a unified wholeness to our experience, and we can begin to heal the last dichotomy of subject and object, inside and outside, self and other. With refined perception we see that what is true in each passing moment is just the experience of that moment, the "suchness" of it. The sense of self, of an "I" separated from experience, is extra.

In one sutra the Buddha says, "In seeing there is just what is seen. In hearing there is just what is heard. In sensing (smelling, tasting, touching) there is just what is sensed. In thinking, there is just what is thought." This is the direct and simple experience of things as they are, free of the artificial boundaries of separate selfhood. When we hear the sound of a bell, is the hearing inside us or outside us? When we perceive something with a silent mind, where are the boundaries? There is a short poem by Sasaki-roshi illustrating this:

> As a butterfly lost in the flower,
> As a bird settled on the tree,
> As a child fondling mother's breast,
> For sixty-seven years of this world,
> I have played with God.

As a butterfly, as a bird, as a child: subject and object are one.

The abhidharma gives a clear explanation of this in terms of the interdependent arising of elements in a particular moment.

For a moment of seeing-consciousness to arise, what are the necessary components? What factors must be present for seeing to occur? There must be the working organ of sight, the eye. There must be color appearing before the eye, there must be light, and there must be attention. If any of these elements is missing, seeing will not take place. When the conditions come together, there is a moment of seeing-consciousness. There is no "one" who sees, no silent observer waiting for objects to come. There is just the coming together of certain conditions which result in a moment of consciousness arising.

As long as we separate out and identify with any one part of the totality, we imprison ourselves in the limits we create in that very process. The path of dharma, of freedom, is to understand and integrate each level of dualism and limitation. The key to doing this is mindfulness and wisdom.

There is an intermediate space leading from the level of separate identity to the level of nonduality. Practice at this intermediate stage has to do with allowing the expansive quality of love to grow in the mind. Love, in this sense, is not particularly a matter of doing something, or of finding an object for one's affection, or of sentimentality. It is not an attempt to gratify the ego, but is rather an attitude of openness and receptivity, of deep and profound appreciation. It is love in the sense of total and complete acceptance, which is the underlying principle of unification.

Shortly before he died, when Shunryu Suzuki-roshi, the founder of the San Francisco Zen Center, was quite sick with cancer, he was asked if he was suffering badly. He replied that it was okay if there was suffering—that's suffering Buddha. Mother Teresa of Calcutta similarly expressed this remarkable sense of appreciation in saying that even in very painful situations, what one is seeing is Christ in his distressing disguise. These statements illustrate something far more profound than mere tolerance. This kind of love and appreciation is the intimacy that leads beyond fear, attachment, and judgment. It is the space in which divisions are healed, in which two become one.

The Hindu guru Neem Karoli Baba often said to his disciples, "Don't throw anyone out of your heart." Not throwing anyone out of our hearts means not separating ourselves. This quality of openheartedness includes within itself all aspects of the psyche, every experience of the mind and body, and the total environment.

The receptive quality of love allows every experience to enter us, to touch us. It allows us to be touched by the wind and the sun, by other people and by each part of ourselves, by the trees and the birds and all of nature. Dharma practice is the practice of intimacy with all of life. From this receptivity can come an outflow of energy that is appropriate and responsive to each experience, rather than reactive.

It is the open and receptive space of acceptance that leads from the ego-centered, relative perspective to an understanding of the nondual. The power of this acceptance is the power of complete honesty and deep detachment—not denying or pretending things are other than the way they truly are; not relating to experience through the filter of our desires, wanting or needing things to be a certain way. Desirelessness is the path to wisdom, because with desirelessness we can perceive reality without any distorting lenses. The power of love, in this sense, is the power of dispassion.

Going from the ego center to the zero center means seeing things as they are without an artificial separation. When we see ourselves as substantially existing within the boundaries of our body, separate from everything outside it, we are imprisoned by the limits of that vision. Realizing the zero center of our being, not holding on to any particular aspect of experience as being self, we are connected to the totality of the experience of each moment. There are no static limits, no rigid postures toward what is arising and passing.

When we know from our own experience that we are not thoughts, emotions, or sensations, not the body, not sights or sounds, not love, not wisdom, not consciousness, not anything at all, then we can understand everything exactly as it is. Because we haven't identified ourselves with any one thing, we come to understand the dreamlike fabric of this world of phenomena, of knowing and object. We see how essenceless, ephemeral, and insubstantial all conditioned existence is. Because we do not isolate out a part of the dream and say, "this is the real me," because we are not deluded, we can move freely and unafraid through our lives. Because we are zero, there is peace with all that is.

There is a poem by the Taoist sage Chuang Tzu:

*Starlight and Non-Being*

Starlight asks Non-Being
Master, are you or are you not?
Since he received no answer whatever
Starlight set himself to watch for Non-Being.
He waited to see if Non-Being
Would put in an appearance.
He kept his gaze fixed on the deep void
Hoping to catch a glimpse of Non-Being.
All day long he looked and he saw nothing.
He listened, but heard nothing.
He reached out to grasp and grasped nothing.
Then Starlight exclaimed at last,
This is it, this is the furthest yet
Who can reach it?
I can comprehend the absence of being
But who can comprehend the absence of nothing?
If now, on top of all this,
Non-being is,
Who can comprehend it?

Sometimes the various expressions of the dharma are confusing because of apparent contradictions. Such contradictions occur because what seems true from one perspective may not seem true from another. This paradoxical situation was expressed very succinctly by Zen master Seung Sahn: "There is no right and no wrong. But right is right and wrong is wrong."

In order to be completely free, we cannot cling to anything. And even as we come to understand the deepest levels of reality, we also must learn to function freely within the relative ones. The Buddha spoke of right thought, thoughts that lead to peace, to happiness, to wisdom, and to liberation. He spoke also of wrong thought, those which lead to contradiction, ignorance, and suffering. This is the level of wise discrimination—right is right and wrong is wrong. But from another point of view, all thought is empty. When thoughts arise in the mind and we don't identify with them or get lost in them, the very idea of right and wrong dissolves as we see thought as simply thought. Thought arises, it's there, it passes away: empty phenomena rolling on. In that openness to all experience, there is no right and no wrong. But in manifesting and directing our energy, we must take a careful look both at what we do and at the results of our actions, because right is right and wrong is wrong.

One of the basic pairs of opposites influencing our lives is yes and no. What is the attitude of yes? Yes is positive. When we say yes to things we are open to them, and in that openness is a sense of fearlessness. In dharma practice, in coming to understand our lives, the attitude of saying yes to thoughts, emotions, other people, the world, brings a wonderful sense of richness and fullness. We are engaged and committed. But yes can also lead to craving and attachment. Yes can lead to clinging, to identification, to a strengthening of the sense of separate selfhood.

What is the attitude of no in practice? What is the wisdom of no? The wisdom of no is that attitude which says, "Not this, not this. This is not self." Thoughts are not self, emotions are not self, the body is not self, the world is not self. No means letting go of all conditioning, all phenomena, letting go of the thought of selfhood. No also means restraint. There is great wisdom and power in the no of restraint, in saying no to unskillful impulses and desires. Following habitual desires and impulses that lead to suffering is not freedom. It is simply being carried away on a wave of conditioning. Practicing the no of skillful restraint is the expression of a free mind. But there is also a danger in no, because restraint, when wrongly understood, becomes suppression. And when no is not understood, when restraint becomes repression, it fuels the condemning mind. Just as yes can lead to attachment, no can lead to aversion.

There is freedom in yes; there is fearlessness in yes. There is freedom in no; there is fearlessness in no. Yes and no are not mutually exclusive, and when our practice embraces both, we get a sense of the wholeness of the dharma, the wholeness of the power of the mind.

The *Prajnaparamita Heart Sutra*, one of the texts of Mahayana Buddhism, leads with another pair of opposites central to practice: form and emptiness. All existence manifests as form. Existence is not possible without form. Existence is form, whether it is a body, an emotion, thoughts, rocks, plants, the earth, a relationship, societies—it is all in form. And all form is empty, in constant change; there is nothing solid, substantial, or enduring about it. It is essenceless, conditions coming together to create a momentary reality and then dissolving, changing into something else.

If we become attached to form, to its apparent solidity, we react by clinging to those forms we like and pushing away those we dislike. If we can see the emptiness of forms, how they arise, change, and dissolve, we can learn from them and move gracefully with them. But we should also not get stuck in the perspective of emptiness. We can become attached to the idea that everything is empty and so abdicate responsibility for how we manifest in the world by not seeing the interplay of form and emptiness. The Buddha used many images to suggest the relationship of form and emptiness. He described life as being like a dream, an echo, a rainbow, a drop of dew on a blade of grass: phenomena arising from causes and vanishing as the conditions change; existing, yet without endurance or inherent substance; arising and passing, so fragile and insubstantial.

Practice begins, continues, and ends in each moment. As we begin to observe what is happening in the moment, we find that our perspective may be limited through having become identified with one side or another of various pairs of opposites. We identify with yes or with no, with form or with emptiness. That identification is the perspective that creates the idea of solidity and of the ego center.

In the *Verses on Faith in the Mind*, by the Third Great Ancestor of Zen in China (translated by Richard Clarke, Universal Publications, 1974) it says:

> If you wish to see the truth then hold no opinions for or against anything. To set up what you like against what you dislike is the disease of the mind. When the deep meaning of things is not understood the mind's essential peace is disturbed to no avail.
>
> The Way is perfect like vast space, where nothing is lacking and nothing is in excess. Indeed, it is due to our choosing to accept or reject that we do not see the true nature of things.
>
> Live neither in the entanglements of outer things, nor in inner feelings of emptiness. Be serene in the oneness of things and such erroneous views will disappear by themselves. When you try to stop activity to achieve passivity your very effort fills you with activity. As long as you remain in one extreme or the other you will never know Oneness.

The richness of dharma practice is in the exploration of the different perspectives on reality and their relationship to one another: we explore the level of separation and the sense of personal identity, and how that creates the world. We develop the open space of love and deep appreciation of all things. And we experience the level of nonduality. Commitment to dharma practice is the commitment to honestly exploring and working with all aspects of our experience, developing gracefulness and compassion in the movement through the various perspectives.

By investigating and integrating the different levels at which we create duality—the shadow and persona, the identification with the ego-mind and the body, the dichotomy of self and other—we come to the experience of freedom.

J. G.

# 15

## The Path of Service

ONE OF THE MOST important questions we come to in spiritual practice is how to reconcile service and responsible action in the world with a meditative life based on nonattachment, letting go, and coming to understand the empty nature of all conditioned things. Are the values we hold that lead us to giving and serving and caring for one another different from the values that lead us deep within ourselves on the journey of liberation and awakening?

In considering this question we must first learn to distinguish among four qualities central to practice—the divine abodes of love, compassion, sympathetic joy, and equanimity—and what might be called their "near-enemies." Near-enemies are states that seem to be very close to these qualities and may even be mistaken for them, but the two are not fundamentally similar. Let us consider them one by one.

The near-enemy of love is attachment. Attachment masquerades as love. It says, "I will love you if you will love me back." It is a kind of "businessman's" love. So we think, "I will love this person as long as he doesn't change. I will love that thing if it will be the way I want it." But this isn't love at all—it is attachment. There is a big difference between love, which allows and honors and appreciates, and attachment, which grasps and demands and aims to possess. When attachment becomes confused with love, it actually separates us from another person. We feel we need this other person in order to be happy. This quality of attachment also leads us to offer love only toward certain people, excluding others.

True love is a universal, nondiscriminating sense of care and connectedness. In it we can include even those whom we may not at all like or approve of. We may not condone their behavior, but we can cultivate understanding and forgiveness toward them. True love becomes a powerful tool for transforming any situation. Love is not a passive acquiescence. Love is inclusive and powerful, and when we touch it in our practice this becomes a direct experience for us. As the New Testament teaches, and Meher Baba put so well, "true love is unconquerable and irresistible." There is no hardship and no difficulty that enough love cannot conquer, no distance that enough love cannot span, no barrier that enough love cannot overcome. Whatever the question, love is the answer. This is a universal law and a lesson in spiritual practice that our hearts must learn. The Buddha said it clearly: "Hatred never ceases through hatred. Hatred only ceases through love."

The near-enemy of compassion is pity. Instead of feeling the openness of compassion, pity says, "Oh, that poor person over there is suffering!" Pity sets up a separation between ourself and others; it has a sense of distance and remoteness from the suffering of others as if we ourselves were different. Compassion, on the other hand, experiences the suffering of another as a reflection of one's own pain, "I truly understand that; I suffer too. It is part of our life." It is a sense of our shared suffering.

Compassion is the tender readiness of the heart to respond to one's own or another's pain, without resentment or aversion. It is the wish to dissipate the suffering. Compassion embraces those experiencing sorrow and brings them into our heart.

The next divine abode is sympathetic joy, which is the ability to feel joy in the happiness of others. Its near-enemy is a sense of comparison—concluding that our experience makes us superior, inferior, or equal to someone else. This is the force of assessing ourselves in relation to someone else's experience. We separate ourselves and in our separateness measure, evaluate, and affirm ourselves in relation to someone else's life. Comparison itself, regardless of the conclusion we draw, is a source of pain and delusion in the mind. When we touch the spirit of sympathetic joy in our heart, it connects us with the happiness of all life. Sympathetic joy embraces all those enjoying happiness themselves and brings us together with them. Their well-being is our own.

The near-enemy of equanimity is indifference or callousness. This can arise in regard to ourselves, our families, our work, or world problems. The voice of indifference says, "Who cares? To be spiritual is to be unattached. What does it matter anyway? It is all transitory!" This is the voice that fears commitment and finds it difficult to stick with a spiritual practice or a relationship or a job. Genuine spiritual life requires great commitment and a willingness to engage in a full and intimate way with our life. In a mistaken way we can use the attitude of indifference to bring a temporary sense of peace. But because it is an attitude of not caring and a withdrawal from experience, it actually separates us from the energies of life.

True equanimity is not a withdrawal, it is a balanced opening to all aspects of life. It is an engagement in the whole of life with composure and with balance of mind, seeing wisely the nature of all things. Although everything is empty, we must nevertheless honor the reality of form. As Zen Master Dogen says, "Flowers fall with our attachment, and weeds spring up with our aversion." When we have touched equanimity in our heart, we can know deeply that the world of conditioned phenomena is insubstantial, and still be fully present and in harmony with it. Equanimity embraces all of life equally: loved and unloved ones; agreeable and disagreeable things; and pleasure and pain; touching them all with balance.

The near-enemies are ways of separating ourselves from life out of fear. True spirituality is not a removal or escape from life. It is an opening, a seeing of the world with a deeper vision that is less self-centered, a vision that sees through dualistic views to the underlying interconnectedness of all life. Liberation is the discovery of freedom in the very midst of our bodies and minds. A Zen master recently gave a simple talk on this teaching of nonseparation at an international peace conference. He explained it by making his two hands into two different

people. One he called Gertrude and the other Harry. He en-
acted a conversation between Gertrude and Harry about what
they liked and what they didn't like. Everyone started to laugh.
He went on and on about it. He said, "That's what we do.
Somehow we actually believe we are Harry or Gertrude, separate from one another." This sense of separation creates all the
sorrow and suffering in the world. In pursuing our spiritual
practice we must learn how to put them all together, to bring
the whole world into our heart. When we undertake this practice in a genuine way, we become what is called a bodhisattva,
a being (*sattva*) committed to liberation (*bodhi*). Suzuki-roshi
says, "Even if the sun should rise in the west, the bodhisattva
has only one way." In the worst circumstances, even if our
world turns upside down, the bodhisattva has only one way—to
continue to express compassion and wisdom there too.

Once while in India I spoke with a meditation master named
Vimala Thakar about the question of meditation and activity in
the world. Vimala had worked for many years with the follow-
ers of Gandhi in Indian rural development and land redistribu-
tion projects. She was then asked by Krishnamurti, of whom
she had been a long-time student, to teach meditation. After
devoting years to teaching meditation, she has in recent years
returned to development work and helping the hungry and
homeless, teaching much less than before. I asked her why she
decided to go back to the type of work she had been involved
with years before. Did she find meditation too limited and feel
a need for more direct action? In responding to the question,
Vimala resisted any attempt to separate the two parts of her
life. She replied, "Sir, I am a lover of life, and as a lover of life,
I cannot keep out of any activity of life. If there are people who
are hungry for food, my response is to help feed them. If there
are people who are hungry for truth, my response is to help
them discover it. I make no distinction."

The Sufis have a saying, "Praise Allah, and tie your camel to
the post." This brings together both parts of practice: pray, yes,
but also make sure you do what is necessary in the world. Have
a life of meditation and genuine spiritual experience and, at

the same time, discover how to manifest that here and now. Realization brings a balance between understanding emptiness and having a sense of compassion and impeccability guide our lives. Seeing emptiness means seeing that all of life is like a bubble in a rushing stream, a play of light and shadow, a dream. It means seeing that this tiny blue-green planet hangs in the immensity of space amid billions of stars and galaxies, that all of human history is like one second compared with the aeons of the earth's history, and that it will all be over very soon. This context helps us to let go amid the seeming seriousness of our problems, to discover what Don Juan calls our controlled folly and to enter life with a sense of lightness and ease.

On the other hand, the quality of impeccability entails realizing how precious life is, even though it is transient, and how each of our actions and words do count, affecting all beings around us in a profound way. There is nothing inconsequential in this universe, and we need to personally respect this fact and act in accordance with it. Even if a person meditates in a cave somewhere far away, it has a power and a value far beyond what we ordinarily assume, because what each part of this whole does affects the rest. We are not ultimately separate.

How can we actually bring together these two sides of practice—the development of compassionate and caring attention with the fleeting and empty nature of life? Taken separately, each point of view is compelling. One could make a very convincing case for just concentrating on meditation and nothing else, and then make another convincing argument for devoting oneself entirely to service in the world. Let's look at it from the first vantage point. Does the world need more medicine and energy and buildings and food? No. There is enough food and medicine, there are enough resources for all. There is starvation and poverty and widespread disease because of human ignorance, prejudice, and fear. Out of greed and hatred we hoard materials; we create wars over imaginary geographic boundaries and act as if one group of people were truly different from another group somewhere else on the planet. Although political and economic change is important, it alone can never be sufficient because the ongoing source of war and poverty is the power of these forces in the human heart. What the world needs is not more oil, but more love and generosity, more kindness and understanding. The most fundamental thing we can do to help this war-torn and suffering world is to genuinely free ourselves from the greed and fear and divisive views in our own minds and then help others to do the same. If we cannot do that, how can we expect it from others? Spiritual practice and transforming the heart are the most important task in our life. From this point of view spiritual life is not a privilege; it is our basic responsibility.

The other side of this question is also compelling. We have only to consider the recent horror of Cambodia, the violence in Central America, the starvation in Central Africa—situations in which the enormity of suffering is almost beyond comprehension. In India alone 360 million people live in poverty, where one day's work can mean that night's meal. I once met a man in Calcutta who was sixty-four years old and still pulled a rickshaw for a living. He had been doing it for forty years and had ten people dependent upon him for income. He had gotten sick the year before for ten days, and after a week the family ran out of money and had nothing to eat. How can we possibly let this happen? Each day we build more nuclear missiles. As you read this, forty children per minute will die from starvation while $15 million per minute is spent on weapons. Today there are hundreds of millions of people who are starving and don't have enough to eat, who are malnourished. That's happening this very day, to people like us—people with eyes, ears, hands, bodies, stomachs, hearts. There are hundreds of millions of people who are so impoverished that they have little or no shelter and clothing to protect themselves from the sun, wind, and rain. There are hundreds of millions of people who are sick with diseases that we know how to cure, that just take a simple kind of medicine. But they can't afford the medicine or don't have access to it. Here today, on this small planet, these things are taking place. Clearly we must respond. We cannot hold back or look away.

At times we may have painful dilemmas about what path to take, where to put our energy. There are so many possibilities—even choosing which type of meditation to practice can be confusing. How are we to decide? It all requires an act of listening to the heart. There are two steps to this process. The first requires that we be willing to touch and feel directly the problems and possibilities in ourselves and the world around us.

This is the beginning of the teaching of the Buddha, and the beginning of our own understanding of the problem of world peace. Then the second step involves this same deep listening and touching of the heart, and from it the allowing of an immediate and spontaneous response.

To look directly at the situation is not a question of ceremonies or religion. The mandate is to look in some very deep way at the sorrow that exists now in our world, to look at our personal and individual and collective relationship to it, to bear witness to it, to acknowledge it, instead of running away. But nuclear war, ecological devastation, broken families, and even the unavoidable growing pains of our children and our own hearts are often overwhelming. The suffering is so great that mostly we don't want to look. We close our minds. We close our eyes and hearts.

Opening to all aspects of our experience is what is asked of us if we want our hearts to grow, if we want a difference. This means looking at the world with honesty, unflinchingly and directly, and then looking at ourselves and seeing that this sorrow is not just out there, but also within ourselves. It is our own fear and prejudice and hatred and desire and wanting and neurosis and anxiety. Our own sorrow. We have to look at it and not run away from it. In opening to suffering, we discover that we can connect with and listen to our own hearts.

This is the source of compassion and the basis for choosing a path with heart. Choosing our path is the second step, though it may need to be taken many times. Each time it is the same process: allowing sorrow to touch our hearts and listening to our hearts, listening to our individual response of wisdom and compassion. One of the difficulties with our busy modern culture is that we don't take time to listen to our hearts. Our immediate problems, our plans and thoughts, fill our minds and, lost in thinking, we lose our connection to our hearts and our true nature.

When we take the time to listen, from deep inside, we hear a voice that guides our journey. Some of us may respond by choosing the path of simplicity, developing an ascetic or isolated or monastic practice to purify our hearts. The hermit yogis who even today still live in caves in the North Indian Himalayas have chosen this path. And the exquisite silence and inner purity they cultivate is their powerful connection and contribution to the whole world around them. Others may choose a path of surrender and devotion, inspired by love of the Buddha or Jesus or Krishna, and live a life of kindness and nonattachment through this devotion. Some may choose a path of service, of heartfelt and active social and community involvement, giving to others as their path to awakening. Others may choose a path that involves study, reflection, and a spiritual use of the intellect. There are as many paths as there are hearts to awaken. The spiritual journey does not present us with a pat formula for each of us to follow. It is not a matter of imitation. We cannot be Mother Teresa or Gandhi or the Buddha. We have to be ourselves. We have to discover and connect with our own unique expression of the truth. To do that, we must learn to listen to and trust ourselves to find our path with heart.

A great potential exists in the heart of each person for the realization of truth, for the experience of wholeness, for going beyond the shell of the ego. We can discover a wholeness of being that will express itself both through meditation and through sharing ourselves with others. When we listen to our hearts, the course to take can become clear and immediate. Whether it is an inner or outer path, it has enormous power to affect the world.

For most of us, our practice will express both of these dimensions at different times. Initially many of us have focused our practice on inner meditation, retreats, and silent sitting.

Through this comes centeredness, wisdom, and an increasing ability to open the heart. We can learn from our sitting the power of awareness and touch a level of purity and freedom unknown in most human lives. But touching this wisdom is not enough. After years of inner practice many of us find awakening within us an urge to express our new understanding in the world around us. How do we know when and where to serve? There is no preset answer—the heart will tell us when we listen.

Even for those of us who are involved in teaching meditation full-time, other parts of our practice call. Some of us have been drawn to serve in other ways, working part-time as nurses, counselors, or aides to the dying.

A few years ago, when many thousands of Cambodian people were fleeing the violence in their homeland only to face starvation and disease in refugee camps in Thailand, some of us who had been deeply touched by living in those Buddhist countries felt, "We've got to go there," and so we went. We knew the people and even a bit of the local languages. We didn't deliberate much at the time about whether or not we should go to work in the refugee camps. It seemed as if it had to be done, and we went and did it. It was immediate and personal.

Vipassana in the West has started by placing a great emphasis on inner meditation and individual transformation. Buddhist teachings have another whole dimension to them, a way of connecting our hearts to the world of action. Their first universal guidelines teach about the basic moral precepts and the cultivation of generosity. These are the foundation for any spiritual life. Beyond this, Buddhist practice and the whole ancient Asian tradition are built upon the spirit of service. For some, service may seem to be simply an adjunct or addition to their inner meditation. But service is more than that; it is an expression of the maturity of wisdom in spiritual life. Understanding of this spirit of service and interconnectedness grows as our wisdom deepens.

For many people service and openhearted giving become the very vehicle for their liberation and are taken as their path or way of practice. A sense of interconnectedness leads to the realization that all our activity can be undertaken as service to the world around us. Following this path brings us face-to-face with selflessness and nonseparation as surely as our inner meditation does. At its best, service becomes an art of selfless giving, of acting from the heart without attachment to praise or fame or even the beneficial result of the action. To act in this way embraces both compassion in our hearts and wisdom that sees that in the end we cannot own or possess a single thing. Our service is more a spirit of acting to the best of our ability with our full being and understanding.

At its best, spiritual service is not a giving from the ego-sense of "See what I have done." It is not even a way of bettering the world through achieving desirable ends. Nor can it be a new form of attachment. It is not that these are bad. We will certainly find these kinds of mixed motivations within us when we act. But the spirit of service asks us to touch and act from a deeper place, a chord of the heart that responds to life out of connectedness and compassion, independently of results.

The sense of service and attuning our hearts to a more selfless vision can be developed and practiced like any other part of our path. Service requires us to cultivate the same quality of attention and mindfulness we have turned inward toward the world outside. It is a development of kindness and nonattachment in action. Even without knowing it, this spirit is what keeps the world alive. The insects and bees in the Amazon jungle pollinate the jungle plants, which in turn transform carbon dioxide into oxygen and replenish much of the Earth's atmosphere. Our lives depend upon those insects. The practice of service for us as humans is a process of making this interconnectedness conscious and allowing it to mindfully inform our actions.

Two thousand and five hundred years of Buddhist tradition has been supported by the understanding of this spirit of service. People have built monasteries, universities, and retreat centers, and supported monks, nuns, teachers, meditation, religious ceremonies, and an extensive variety of Buddhist social and peace practices and projects, all from the understanding of our interconnectedness in the dharma. But the path of practice goes farther than that. The way we drive, the way we use our money, the work we do, all of it can become a part of our path of service. As we live, whether as a plumber or waitress or physician or bookkeeper or beekeeper, we can learn to act with attention and caring. We can turn the actions of our life into the very heart of our practice. We become the server and the served, and the interconnection of it all is the heart of service.

One of the ways that our inner meditation can support and blossom into a life of service is through the cultivation of a strong and caring mindfulness and wakefulness. Equally important is the way that our inner practice brings us to look directly at the powerful facts of birth and death, at the cycling of life. From understanding this we can discover within us a place of great fearlessness.

There are two great forces in the world. One is the force of people who are not afraid to kill. These people run much of the world from a political and economic and military point of view. People who are not afraid to kill run many of our modern nations. It gives a lot of strength to be unafraid to kill. The other source of strength in the world—of real strength—is people who are not afraid to die. These are people who have touched the very source of their being, who have looked in such a deep way that they understand, acknowledge, and accept death, and in a way have already died. They have seen beyond the separateness of the ego's shell, and they bring to life the fearlessness and caring born of this love and truth. This is a force that can meet the force of someone who is not afraid to kill.

This is the power that Gandhi called *satyagraha*, the force of truth, and that he demonstrated in his own life. In 1947, when India was partitioned into two nations, India and Pakistan, millions of people became refugees as Muslims and Hindus moved from one country to the other. The process was accompanied by terrible rioting and bloodshed. Tens of thousands of troops were sent to West Pakistan to try to quell the violence, while

Gandhi went to what was then East Pakistan. He walked from village to village asking people to stop the bloodshed. Then he fasted. He said he would take no more food until the violence stopped, the insanity stopped, even if that meant his own death. And slowly the riots stopped. They stopped because of the power of love, because Gandhi cared about something—call it truth or life or whatever you wish—much greater than the person "Gandhi," and he was willing to commit his life in service to this. Discovering this fearlessness is the underlying spirit of our own practice, whatever form it may take. Living aligned with truth is more important than either living or dying. Understanding this is the source of incredible power and energy, manifesting through love and compassionate action.

One of the most exquisite experiences one can have traveling in India is going to the holy city of Benares by the Ganges River. Along the riverbank are ghats and temples where people have come for thousands of years to bathe as a purification, and there are also ghats where people bring corpses to be cremated. Because Benares is considered a holy city, many people go there to die. One may hear about the burning grounds and imagine that it would be terrifying or depressing to be there. But when one actually goes and is rowed down the river in a little boat up to the ghats, it is quite different than expected. The river itself is very still, and as one approaches the temple there is mostly a feeling of an ancient and yet ordinary process. There may be eight or ten fires burning as friends or relatives of the deceased stand silently watching the body as the river flows by. Every twenty minutes or so a new body is carried down to be bathed in the Ganges and then put on the fires as people chant, *"Rama nama satya hai,"* "The only truth is the name of god." The experience is not dreadful at all; instead it is peaceful and sacred and very sane. There is a recognition that life and death are part of the same process, that death is simply what happens to each body, and that there is no need to fear it.

There is a deep joy that comes when we stop denying the painful aspects of life and instead allow our hearts to open to and accept the full range of our experience: life and death, pleasure and pain, darkness and light. Even in the face of the tremendous suffering in the world there can be a joy that comes, not from rejecting pain and seeking pleasure, but rather from our ability to sit in meditation even when it is difficult, and open to the truth. The work of practice begins by allowing ourselves to face fully our own sadness, fear, anxiety, desperation—to die to our limited ideas about how things should be and to love and accept the truth of things as they are. With this as our foundation, we can see clearly the source of suffering in our lives and in the world around us; that is, the factors of greed, hatred, and ignorance that produce a false sense of separation. We can look directly at how we create and enforce separation. How do we make this world of "I want this, I want to become that, this will make me safe, this will make me powerful"? How do we create a world based on race, nationality, age, sex, ideology, religion, even on the name of God? Look at yourself and see who is "us" and who is "them." Does "us" mean mediators or educated people or Americans or white people? Who is your "us"? Whenever there is a sense of "us," then there is a sense of "other." When we can give this up, then we can give up the idea that strength comes from having more than "others" or from having the power over "others." When we give this up, we give up the delusion that love is a weakness, and we find the source of true compassion in all our actions.

The inner and outer aspects of practice are illustrated by a story about an old Zen monk in China who practiced meditation for many years. He had a good mind and became very quiet, but never really came to touch the end of "I" and "others" in himself. He never came to the source of complete stillness or peace out of which the deepest transformation comes. So he went to his master and said, "May I please have permission to go off and practice in the mountains? I've worked for years as a monk, and there is nothing else I want but to understand this: the true nature of myself, of this world." And the master, knowing that he was ripe, gave him permission to leave.

The monk left the monastery and took his bowl and few possessions and walked through various towns on his way. As he left the last village behind and was going up into the mountains, there appeared before him, coming down the trail, an old man carrying a great big bundle on his back. (This old man was actually the bodhisattva Manjushri, who the Chinese Buddhists believe appears to people at the moment that they are ripe for awakening. Manjushri is usually depicted carrying the sword of discriminating wisdom, which cuts through all attachment, illusions, and separateness.) The old man addressed the monk, asking, "Say, friend, where are you going?"

The monk told his story. "I've practiced for so many years, and all I want now is to touch that center point, to know that which is the essence of life. Tell me, old man, do you know anything of this enlightenment?"

At this point the old man simply let go of his bundle, and it dropped to the ground—and, as in all good Zen stories, the monk was enlightened. That is our aspiration, our task—to let it all go, to drop and put down our whole past and future, all of our identifications, our fears, our opinions, our whole sense of "I," "me," and "mine."

At this point in the story, the newly enlightened monk looks at the old man a bit confused about what to do next. He says, "So now what?" The old man smiles, reaches down, picks up the bundle again and walks off to town.

To put our burden down requires, first, that we acknowledge all that we are carrying: that we see our sorrow, our suffering, our attachment and pain, see how we're all in it together, accept birth and death. If we do not face it, if we are afraid of death and afraid of surrendering, if we don't want to look, then we can't release our sorrow. We will push it away here and grab it again there. Only when we have seen the nature of life directly can we put it down. And once we put it down, then, with understanding and compassion, we can pick it up again. To the extent that we let go, we can act effectively, even dramatically, in the world, without bitterness and self-righteousness.

A number of years ago the Menninger Foundation sponsored a conference at which Mad Bear, an Iroquois medicine man, spoke. After several days of meetings at which scientific papers were presented, it was his turn. He said, "For my presentation I'd like us to begin by going outside." Everyone followed him outside to an open field, and he asked us all to stand silently in a circle. We stood for a while in silence under a wide open sky, surrounded by fields of grain stretching to the horizon. Mad Bear then began to speak, offering a prayer of gratitude. He thanked the earthworms for aerating the soil so that plants can grow. He thanked the grasses that cover the earth for keeping the dust from blowing, for cushioning our steps, and for showing our eyes the greenness and beauty of their life. He thanked the wind for bringing rain, for cleaning the air, for giving us the life-breath that connects us with all beings. He spoke in this way for nearly an hour, and as we listened our mindfulness grew with each prayer. We felt the wind on our faces and the earth beneath our feet, and we saw the grass and clouds, all with a sense of connectedness, gratitude, and love.

This is the spirit of our practice: love—not the near-enemy of attachment, but something much deeper—infusing our awareness, enabling us to open to and accept the truth of each moment; and service that feels our intimate connectedness with all things and responds to the wholeness of life. Whether we are in the midst of our family life or in a remote monastery, whether we are sitting in meditation or sitting somewhere in protest, this is our practice in every moment.

J. K.

EXERCISE

## The Heart of Service

Take a quiet period of meditation to ask your heart about service. Let yourself sit and be silent for some time. When you are ready, pose the following questions inwardly to yourself. Pause after each one and give your heart time to answer, allowing a response from the deepest levels of your compassion and wisdom.

Imagine yourself five years from now as you would most like to be, having done all the things you want to have done, having contributed all the things you want to contribute in the most heartfelt way. What is your greatest source of happiness? What is the thing you've done of which you are most proud? What is the contribution you've made to the world that brings your heart the greatest satisfaction? To make this contribution to the world, what unworthiness would you have to relinquish? To make this contribution to the world, what strengths and capacities would you have to recognize in yourself and others? What would you have to do in your life today to begin this service, this contribution?

Why not begin?

# 16
## Integrating Practice

How can we develop and deepen our practice in the midst of our everyday lives? These are important questions. They require that we develop an integrated awareness of all dimensions of our being, making our body, our actions, our feelings and our relationships, our work and our play, all part of our meditation.

This book, based on talks given at several intensive meditation retreats, has focused primarily on the deepening of the inner meditative process, the hindrances one encounters, skillful means of mastering them, and the understandings and wisdom that can arise while in meditative silence. To integrate this understanding into our lives and actions is the whole second half of practice. To do it justice would require another entire book, devoted to the principles and laws of living an integrated and dharmic life. Still, we can touch on some of the basic guidelines here.

Whether we are sitting in formal meditation or living the dharma in action, practice is never a matter of learning formulas or imitating others. Of course, it is essential that we honor the fundamental principles of virtue and of training the mind. But we must also be willing to leap into the unknown in each new moment. And that requires courage and simplicity. Don Juan says that only with courage can we withstand the path of knowledge. He describes the world as mysterious, awesome, and unfathomable, and says that we must assume responsibility for being in this marvelous world. Since we will be here for only a short while, we must learn to make every act count.

To live our spiritual path fully offers us something beyond merely getting through life on automatic pilot. We can honor and fulfill, even ennoble, our life through the skill of our attention and the power of our heart. But it requires practice and the willingness to extend our awareness over and over again to new areas of our life.

Though this process is not always easy, it is very simple. It is learning to live in the ever-changing reality of the present moment. A woman who went to Asia many years ago and came back as a master of meditation put it this way as she was washing the lunch dishes: "Isn't it strange that we prefer the quicksand of somethingness to the firm ground of emptiness?" What an extraordinary thing to say! This capacity to be open to the new in each moment without seeking a false sense of security is the true source of strength and freedom in life. It allows us to receive all things, to touch all things, to learn from whatever presents itself. Every single situation of our life can be our teacher, can instruct us and give us the opportunity for growing fuller in our love and more understanding in our wisdom. This makes meditation a lifelong process of opening, growing, investigating, and discovering. If we ask ourselves what is the lesson for us in the situation at hand (however difficult), we will always find value.

Living fully means jumping into the unknown, dying to all our past and future ideals, and being present with things just as they are. This can be frightening, but it is only by such surrender to the moments of truth that we can participate fully in the mystery of our lives. It is a challenge we face again and again in our practice, in our relationships, and throughout each day. Meeting it requires courage.

We can see the need for letting go in our formal meditation practice, and it becomes even clearer as we end our sitting periods. When we get up, what can we hold on to? At the end of a period of silent retreat, almost all students know the experience of losing the quiet states that developed so slowly in meditation. We cannot hold on to them. As we enter the business of the marketplace, concentration and tranquillity usually dissolve, and even the power of our mindfulness diminishes. The greatest of our spiritual experiences becomes only a memory. When one Western student described to an Asian teacher all of the important experiences of his years of practice, the only response he got was, "Oh, something more to let go of."

Wisdom does not arm us with new knowledge or armor us with spiritual power. If anything, it leaves us more open and vulnerable, to be touched by and in touch with all the things around us. Coming out of a deep inner meditation into a busy world, we often sense this vulnerability. Those who return from long retreats face the unfamiliar and difficult task of integration while feeling this profound sensitivity. At times we get overwhelmed. This process too requires practice, in and out of retreat, in and out of sitting, going back and forth from stillness to action again and again, until the spirit of the stillness pervades the action and the aliveness fills the stillness. Yet vulnerability is not the end of wisdom. Wisdom leads us even deeper, to transparency and balance. While we are vulnerable in our openness, there is still a sense of "me" and "mine," of fear and hurt. These come from deep and subtle attachments. Although they will not vanish easily, in our practice we can become aware of them and begin to sense an even deeper level of transparency, a possibility of allowing all things to arise and pass with ease.

Naturally that aspect of life which is pain and suffering will not just disappear as we practice. In fact, it will actually become more evident through our awareness. This it true of the outward sufferings of the world, and it is even more true of ourselves. There will be times when our habits will become more fully revealed—as if we were seeing them clearly for the first time. Our fears, our greeds, the aspects of our personality that we reject, will wait for us like comfortable old clothes to be put on at the end of a retreat. It can be quite discouraging after touching a new level of peace or purity in the heart to see the power of our old habits. But this is just the place for the application of our practice. We are asked to relate with understanding instead of judgment, to see with love and awareness. There is freedom, there is justice to be discovered and to manifest, and we can learn to truly embody these. But it is a process that is learned and takes place as much out of retreat as in meditative silence. It is through encountering and facing our very habits and fears, our confusion and doubts, that we discover how to apply the simplicity and power of mindfulness and letting go in all of life.

A story about Achaan Chaa is relevant here. Soon after arriving at the monastery, a new monk became frustrated by the difficulties of practice, by the seemingly arbitrary rules of conduct, and of course by his own doubts. He went to Achaan Chaa and complained about the practice and behavior of the other monks, and even about the teacher himself. He said, "You don't seem so enlightened to me. One day you say one thing, the next day you say something entirely different. If you're enlightened, why do you contradict yourself all the time?"

After a good laugh, Achaan Chaa explained that his teaching was to help people to come to a balance of heart and mind. "It is as though I see people walking down a foggy road that I know very well," he said. "When I see someone about to fall into the ditch on the right-hand side I call out, 'Go left, go left.' And if I see someone about to fall off to the left, I yell, 'Go right, go right.' That is all I do."

Dharma practice is a matter of balance. If you become attached or confused and fall off to the side, let go of whatever you are clinging to and come back to center. Keep it very simple. With awareness every situation is an opportunity to strengthen this balance of mind. This balance is the central teaching of the Buddha. In fact, it was the very first phrase he used to describe the teachings—the Middle Way.

It is important to realize that to identify oneself as a meditator or a spiritual person or even a Buddhist can be another way to get caught or lose one's true balance. This is like carrying a raft on your head instead of using it for a vehicle to the other shore. The purpose of meditation is not to create a new spiritual identity, nor to become the most meditative person on the block, who tells other people how they should live. To practice is to let go.

One woman who returned home after meditating at the Naropa Institute Buddhist University encountered much hostility in her parents. They were fundamentalist Christians and believed she was possessed or had joined a cult. After much struggle with them and in herself, she discovered a way to work with the situation, which she shared with the teacher. She wrote, "My parents hate me when I'm a Buddhist, but they love me when I'm a buddha!" There is no need to become a Buddhist—only to discover and embody the compassion, understanding, and freedom of spirit that is the Buddha within us.

In reading the ancient texts, we find that the essential teachings of the Buddha are not complicated at all. One sutra tells of a man who, having heard about the Buddha's great wisdom, set out to seek his teaching. After a long journey, the man finally came upon the Buddha while he was collecting alms. The man asked for teaching, but the Buddha requested that he wait until the end of his alms rounds. After having come so great a distance, the man was in no mood to wait. The man persisted, and in response to his third request, the Buddha explained the essence of his teachings succinctly and simply as they stood in the street: "In the seeing, there is only the seen. In the hearing, there is only the heard. In the sensing, there is only the sensed. In the thinking, there is only the thought." That's Buddhism in a nutshell. It is both the beginning and the end of practice.

The truth is simple, but we often complicate things. All experience is just the play of elements of sight, sound, smell, taste, touch, and thought. In them is no self, no other, no separation, and no grasping. Seeing this brings freedom. Practicing with this spirit of simplicity cuts through the web of mental entanglements, allowing us to see things clearly and directly.

There are four kinds of simplicity that are of great help in this process of coming to understand and live the truths of the dharma. The first is simplicity of body. In the sitting practice this means working with awareness of the breath, sensations, posture, and movement with a gentle and allowing attitude. We need to let ourselves settle into a posture in which we can sit comfortably yet remain alert, erect, and still. In feeling any points of tension in the body, allow them to soften and relax. Let the shoulders drop, let the breath settle, and release any tightness in the neck, back, and facial muscles. While we sit, we allow ourselves to feel whatever is happening in the body, settling into it with awareness and balance of mind. We can practice bringing this same awareness to the whole range of our activities as we move throughout the day, staying grounded in our bodies. Awareness of the body is like a mirror that can instantly show us our tension and attachments and indicate where to relax and let go. A simple and basic honoring of our bodily needs for regular exercise and a healthy diet also contributes greatly to our well-being and to a wakeful, balanced spiritual life. Living attentively and simply in the body requires a balance. On one side we must learn to respect the body and be kind to ourselves, attentive to our needs. Yet we must do so without dissipating energy by indulging every whim that arises. A traditional image used to illustrate this balance is that of a well-tuned lute, its strings neither too loose nor too tight. Experiment with diet, with regular exercise, with bodily awareness to see what works best for you. And when you get off center, which may be quite often at first, don't judge yourself. Be aware that you are off center and return to balance.

A second area of simplicity in practice is simplicity of action, developed by a simple attention to the area of the heart. In form, it is the virtue of following the precepts. Even more directly, it is an attention to the heart, to extending our caring through basic kindness and nonharming toward the world around us. There is a process of learning to be aware when our heart is open or closed and nourish that which allows for the opening. Like a flower, the heart has many cycles, and we will discover how it closes at night or in times of cold. We need to love and respect these times too. Yet even with the most difficult of these cycles, the simplicity of virtue arises when we keep our actions connected with our heart.

A third simplicity is that of our lifestyle, what has been called a life of voluntary simplicity. This too can be cultivated, especially as we recognize that busyness, entanglements, and complexities are unnecessary for our happiness. In fact, for most of us, the fewer complexities and attachments we have, the more happily and contentedly we can live. This simplicity is the basis for those who find joy in the way of the monk and nun. Naturally for householders it does not mean dropping our jobs or family responsibilities. But we can look at our life, at how complexly or fancily we live, to see if some simplification would not lead to a quieter mind and a more contented heart. After all, we are just "accountants in the firm" anyway. We don't really keep or possess things: even our bodies are not ours. We are given them to use, and the more skillfully and simply we relate to them, the more contented our life becomes.

The fourth area of simplicity is inward, a simple relation to the mind. Our opinions rise and fall like the seasons. Our moods and thoughts come and go like the tide. What meditation practice can teach us is a simpler and wiser relationship to all changing states. The laws of the dharma are quite simple ones. All things are in change. How we act and think creates new habits and conditions for how we will act and think in the future. How we act now creates what reactions the world will return to us. This is the law of karma. What we sow, we will reap. The amount of our attachments will equal the amount of our sufferings. The principles are direct and simple. Achaan Chaa used to ask his disciples, "Are you suffering much today?" If they said no, he would smile and move on. If they said yes, he would respond, "Oh, you must be attached," and then smile and move on. It is like the warning light on our dashboard. When the suffering light comes on, it is wired directly to how much we are attached. There is where we can learn to let go.

To relate simply is to see what is directly in front of us. As one master told his students when he died, "Friends in the dharma, do not put any false heads above your own." (Do not get caught in spiritual grasping or ideals.) "Then moment after moment watch your step closely." That is all.

We can look at practice as a process of developing sensitivity.

The essence of moral virtue is sensitivity to our environment: honoring and living harmoniously with other beings and the world we share. Concentration is also sensitivity: focusing and tuning the mind to listen to what Kabir calls "the ringing of the anklets on the feet of an insect when it walks." Wisdom is sensitivity to the movements and ever-changing elements of our experience. Compassion and appreciation grow from the silence and sensitivity of our minds and hearts.

All things teach us if we are sensitive. In each moment the laws governing the dynamic play of elements of mind and matter are being revealed. Each moment is teaching about impermanence and emptiness. If we listen carefully, we can learn from the most subtle whispers of thought and sensation as well as the most overwhelming feelings and emotions. Every movement of the mind is a teaching.

This is true whether we are engaged in formal, intensive meditation practice or facing the challenges of our daily lives. Insight can develop in any circumstance; all situations can be used to deepen our understanding and the sense of magic and beauty in our experience.

Of course the same hindrances and barriers we encounter in sitting meditation will arise as we open to the world around us. There will be doubt and aversion, desire, laziness, and restlessness in relationships, in work, in all of the intimate ventures of our life. Our ideals and fears will all appear to be blocking our great openness. Yet, each of these obstacles is also our practice and the very key to our freedom.

Fear is a good example. At first fear appears as an inhibition to appreciating the moment. We're afraid to feel, to be with things fully. We're often frightened by difficult emotions, thoughts, and situations. When they arise we try to look away or stand back from them. When we do so, our relationship to the world of experience feels fragmented and shallow. Yet fear is equally a sign of growth. Fear tells us we are moving into new territory. Fear is the membrane between what we know and something new. It tells us we are about to open to something bigger than the world we usually experience. The difficulties and mysteries of life are inseparable. The whole process of discovery of the truth requires an opening to the whole of life, and our fear is a sign of opportunity as much as a problem. When we begin practice, we are afraid of making mistakes. Later we can discover that all greatness comes first from error. This is actually how we learn. As one meditation master put it, "Life is one continuous mistake."

Like fear, attachment to our ideas and opinions can also be a barrier to opening. One Zen tradition tells us to cultivate a "don't-know" mind, and another counsels the wisdom of "beginner's mind." All this is a cure for the times when we become stuck in our knowledge, our views, our way. At the opening of a beautiful and elegantly crafted Korean-American Zen temple, some devoted Korean ladies brought food and flowers as an offering to the Buddha. The flowers, however, were plastic and after the group left the American students snatched them off the altar and stashed them away. The Zen master told them to put the flowers back on the altar right away. He said that the problem was not the plastic in the flowers but the plastic in the students' minds. Because they were stuck in their ideas about beauty, they missed seeing the sincere love and devotion that the offering expressed.

We can get so caught up in our projects and plans to get the most out of situations that our vision becomes narrow. We don't appreciate the bigger picture that we are a part of because all our attention is focused upon our own little dramas. There is a story about a coyote who figured out how to dig up traps and turn them over. He evidently enjoyed this procedure because he did it often. One day a trapper buried a trap upside down, and when the coyote turned it over, he caught himself. He was smart enough to dig up traps, but not smart enough to leave them alone. Like him, we can become the victim of our own cleverness.

It is not necessary that our perception of life be so hindered by habits of judgment and evaluation and of liking and disliking. We can learn an appreciation and letting go of those habitual judgments and preferences that render our perception stale and lifeless. We can learn to see with freshness and sensitivity.

At times being sensitive can mean observing the details of experience, at other times it can mean opening the mind with an awareness that includes everything within it. Once when some geese flew by during a meditation retreat of Sasaki-roshi's, he remarked: "Most people want to capture these birds and cage them. They're so beautiful, they want them. You must develop a mind which sees you and the birds as the same—not just sees it but feels it. You see and hear the birds, you are one with them. There is no need to capture or hold on to anything because you are everything."

When we let go of whatever we are clinging to, we can appreciate each thing as it is. There is no scarcity of things to appreciate but only a scarcity of moments when we are capable of truly seeing because of how often we are unaware, unmindful. Beauty arises from presence of mind and simplicity. Though our minds may be complicated, beauty is not. We don't have to strive to make beauty in our lives, or look far to find it. When the mind is still, we can see a magnificence in even the most ordinary things—the vividness of a sunset, the warmth of a smile, the simplicity of serving a cup of tea. We can see new life and growth. Each thing is different from all others, each moment is unique. And we can see decay and passing. This is the natural course of things and has its own exquisite kind of clarity.

Our perception of the richness of our experience directly reflects the depth and subtlety of our awareness. If our minds are busy and self-concerned, our sensitivity will be shallow. Many Asian arts are based on this understanding. For example, in a traditional Chinese landscape painting, the artist prepares himself through months of meditation. When the artist's mind is collected, open, and one with the object, he or she lifts the brush and the landscape paints itself.

To bring this spirit of aliveness and wakefulness into our daily life is a wonderful ideal, but it must be directly supported by the ways in which we live. There are some important methods for cultivating a strong foundation of awareness in our daily lives.

The first is to sit every day. It is one of the most important things we can do in our life. It not only provides the foundation for the deepening of our own practice, but also makes a statement with our whole being. It is a time to be silent, to listen to our heart, and to reconnect with our deeper values. The world, after all, doesn't need more things added to it. It already has enough food and enough oil and energy. What is most needed is less: less greed, less fear, less hatred, less prejudice. To sit every day is to express one's conviction in the power of silence, to open our hearts to understanding, acceptance, and genuine caring. With a strong, consistent daily sitting practice we find it easier to remain centered throughout the day's activities. Without any self-conscious effort, whatever centeredness and peacefulness grows in us will transmit itself to all those with whom we interact. Our practice is really a gift of our spirit that is naturally shared with others.

Try to sit twice a day. It is helpful to find a regular time in the morning and evening. Sitting in the morning lays a foundation of balance and awareness for the whole day. Sitting in the evening is an opportunity to let go of whatever has been accumulated during the course of the day and to let the mind and body become settled, quiet, and refreshed. If circumstances permit, sit two hours a day. If the demands of your time make this too difficult, then sit two half-hours or one hour. Find a regimen that works in the context of your life and stick to it.

For our daily practice to become consistent and for its strengths to become available to us, we cannot be idealistic about how sittings will be. Sometimes in the mornings we may be sleepy or busy anticipating the day ahead. Often in the evenings our body will be jangling and vibrating with the business of the day, and our thoughts will seem unending. If we expect peaceful and concentrated daily sittings, we won't stick with the practice for long in the face of such discouragement. Daily sitting is not like the focused practice of intensive retreat. It is a time for the stilling of the body and a balancing of the mind.

Often the times we feel most unconcentrated and scattered are the times we need the most to mediate. If the body buzzes and the mind is full of thoughts, sit anyway, just make space for it to settle and discharge and try not to judge. If it gets calmer, then go back to the breath and body sensations. If we spend a whole hour unable to concentrate, fine. Just sit and take what comes. Then we will find true relation to our body, hearts, and minds.

At times we find it easy to sit every day. At other times we find that we begin to squeeze sitting into the other business of life, and eventually squeeze it out. Make the resolve not to let a day go by without sitting. If it is time to go to bed and we haven't yet sat that day, we can sit at the foot of the bed or on the floor next to it for at least a few minutes. Sometimes three minutes is enough to get back in touch with that place of balance, to come back to being centered. It can be an important reminder.

It can be helpful to create a special place in our home for sitting. This can be a room or even just a corner of your bedroom. Place there your cushion or chair or bench or whatever you sit on. If you wish, have a candle, maybe some incense, a Buddha image—whatever seems most appropriate. Perhaps you will want to keep a few of your favorite dharma books there and read them regularly to remind you of the meaning and power of practice.

Work with the walking practice, both as a formal meditation and as a way of making all actions throughout the day into meditation. Doing even a short period of walking meditation before sitting is a good way to collect yourself and get settled. And throughout the day, make the time spent walking from one place to another a time of meditation, of being balanced and present. So much of the time we are lost in our thoughts, completely unaware of our experience in the present moment. We could well be rid of ninety percent of our thoughts and still have plenty left for the useful purposes of thought. Let go of the rest. When you walk, just walk. Just be with your experience. When you get to where you are going, there will be plenty of time to plan and organize and do what you have to do.

Work with eating as a regular part of the meditation. Be aware of the diet you eat and of the way you usually take your food. Try on occasion to eat in silence, slowly and mindfully. Just to eat one apple with care and attention can be a powerful reminder of our life and practice, a way of coming back to center.

The spirit of this attention is to be present and learn from what we do, from all of the actions of body and mind. To do this is not a process of judging right and wrong. Clear seeing is aided by a sense of humor. Once the Korean Zen master Soen-sa-nim was eating breakfast and reading the morning paper at his center in Providence, Rhode Island. This upset a student who had many times heard him instruct in Zen, "When you walk, just walk" and "When you eat, just eat." How could the master say that and then go ahead and eat and read? So the student asked him about it. Soen-sa-nim looked up, smiled, and replied, "When you eat and read, just eat and read!" Our practice is to be where we actually are with love and attention.

In sustaining a life of mindfulness, it is extremely helpful to connect with other people who share the same values and orientation. Once the disciple Ananda spoke to the Buddha, saying, "It seems to me that half of the holy life is association with good and noble friends."

The Buddha replied, "Not so, Ananda. The whole of the holy life is association with good and noble friends, with noble practices, and with noble ways of living."

The support and encouragement we give one another in practice is extremely important and powerful. It's difficult to practice alone, particularly in a culture such as ours, which continually bombards us with messages saying, "Live for the future." "Do this and get that and become this and have that, and you will be happy." One of the blessings of joining a traditional community of monks and nuns is the sense of support such a sangha can give. As laypeople we can find that support invaluable as well. Connecting with other people involved in spiritual practice renews our inspiration and energy. It can help keep practice alive for us in times when our motivation has waned. It can provide a way for us to support and inspire others, which itself is very strengthening to our practice.

Sit with others. If there is no sitting group meeting together regularly in your area, then start one and list it in the vipassana newspapers. If there aren't other people doing insight meditation, then sit with other Buddhist groups in your area, or sit at the local silent Quaker meetings. Joining together with anyone who understands the value of taking time to turn inward, to quiet the mind and develop awareness, is very, very helpful.

In the same way, taking periods of silence and retreat regularly throughout the year is important for the renewal and deepening of practice. Regular meditation retreats are an obvious support. So too are personal retreats alone at home or at a retreat center. Similarly days of retreat and rest in nature, hiking in the mountains or along the ocean, times of silence and listening, are all nurturing to practice. It is not by accident that many of the world's greatest monasteries and spiritual centers are in forests and remote places of beauty. Silence time can renew our spirits and reconnect us with the simplicity of practice.

Just as we will discover opening and closing cycles of the heart, and up and down cycles in our meditation, there are also greater cycles of silence and service over the years of our practice. Sometimes all that we need is a quiet space in which to meditate and listen. Other cycles pull us to family life, world service, community relations—a mindful life in the world. When we work with developing a silent inner meditation, only some of what we cultivate in one area carries over to the other. Just as we must actively choose to develop consciousness in a very focused way in sitting or a panoramic way in walking, we must also choose to develop mindfulness in driving or in our relationships. In this way, we can build upon the strengths of our initial meditation practice developed in silent retreats. We can bring the power of mindfulness into all the areas of our life.

It also helps to periodically survey our lives and see what

areas need more attention and consciousness. These include our work, our whole physical bodies, our diet and exercise, our intimate relationships, or our service and capacity for generosity. Wherever we are stuck or fearful or attached can become another place for our practice and growth. But we have to be willing to earnestly develop and apply the power of mindfulness and the learnings from sitting, and to purposefully bring them into all the other dimensions of our life. Naturally, some effects from the insights in our sittings and the general strengthening of equanimity and balance will carry over to all our activities. Still, even very advanced yogis, especially here in the West, have seen the need for a periodic review of their lives and the development of careful attention to areas that have been disconnected from the practice of mindfulness and the heart.

To do this also helps heal the false split between spiritual life and worldly life. Every single activity can teach us the universal laws of the dharma. We can learn as much about attachment and patience in our family as we can by observing our breath or body sensations. The universal freedom and compassion discovered by the Buddha is not far away, to be found in some distant monastery or after years of practice. It is here and now in every moment, in any activity. Where mindfulness leads us is just here, the eternal and ever-changing present.

Another aspect of practice that can also help us to open more fully in our lives is the development of generosity. Think about what areas in your family, community, or global life you would like to support more fully. Begin to practice more giving there. While at some point generosity becomes the natural expression of a connected and loving heart, in our practice it, too, can be cultivated. We can actively look for opportunities to give of our time, energy, money and goods, love, and our service to others. Through practice and attention we will begin to notice occasions when we hold back or fear to relate and give—and consciously begin to cultivate a more generous response. Slowly, the whole spirit and joy of giving, from tentative to brotherly to royal giving, will grow in us, and this opening will affect all the other realms of our practice as well.

Another strong support for our daily practice is to resolutely undertake the five basic training precepts, to cultivate a life of conscious conduct. Following these precepts is a powerful way to bring mindfulness into our life. It can help to take them formally by reciting them with a teacher or reciting them out loud from a book.

Traditionally, one takes the precepts by saying, "I undertake the training precept of refraining from killing," and so on for each one. We resolve to follow and use them as guidelines to train ourselves. Then they can be taken again when we are aware of having broken one. To review them in detail, go back to the first chapter of this book. Each precept is a direct way to avoid harming ourselves and other beings. Each precept also reminds us of an area of life in which we can develop sensitivity and compassion. The strength of the precepts is very great. If even one-half of the first precept were kept worldwide—the precept to refrain from killing or from lying, for instance—it could transform our planet.

Work carefully with each of the five precepts: not killing, not stealing, refraining from sexual misconduct, not speaking falsely, not using intoxicants heedlessly. Learning to work with the precepts is the groundwork for genuine spiritual practice. If we are causing harm to others, if we are being dishonest or irresponsible, we become stuck, and it is impossible to go any further in our practice. More skillfully, we can use the precepts to train ourselves, to awaken ourselves and make our relationships more open and harmonious. When we are about to break them, the precepts are like warning lights and alarms signaling us to take a careful look at the mind state behind the action in which we are involved. If we look closely, we can usually discover where we became caught or confused and how we can let go and be free. Use the precepts. They are incomparable tools for changing ourselves and the world around us.

People often wonder about how best to share their inspiration and practice with others. Of course, it is wonderful to speak with others about the dharma, but we need to be sensitive to the circumstances and careful to speak appropriately. There is no need to proselytize or preach, or even to mention Buddhism at all. Rather, be open to each situation. If you speak of practice at all, let it be to those who truly wish to know. Better to be a buddha than a Buddhist, and let the teachings come more from the heart and deeds than the mouth. Remember, we communicate not only with words, but with every aspect of our being. People learn more from what we are than from what we say.

Some students once asked a renowned Tibetan Buddhist master how they could train their children to live a spiritual life. This lama reminded them that their children have their own karma, and parents cannot force them to be a certain way. He told the parents that if they took care of their own practice, the children would learn from the kindness and clarity manifested in their example. We can say, "You should love everyone," but if we then treat the people who serve us at the gas station or supermarket as though they were part of the machinery, that unspoken message is clearly communicated. Through practice our intentions, or inspirations, our words, and our deeds can all come together. We can cultivate loving-kindness and mindfulness until they become the way we live our life. Then, when the baby cries or the knees hurt in sitting or we are stuck in traffic or someone dies, it will all become part of the dharma for us.

When the wonderful old Tibetan master Kalu Rinpoche came to the United States, he visited the Boston Aquarium. As he walked through, he would stop at each new tank of colorful fishes to observe and admire them. Then, as he left each tank, he would touch the glass softly and say the mantra "Om Mani Padme Hum." When asked why he did that, he replied, "I touch the glass to get the attention of the beings inside, and then I bless each one, that they too might be liberated." What a wonderful way to greet each being who comes into our life. To silently touch them with the heart of kindness and wish that they too might be liberated.

Our growth as individuals is a long journey, and integrating our retreat experiences into our daily lives is one of the most compelling, sensitive, and important aspects of this journey.

We can get support from retreats and meditation practices. We can get guidance through a relationship with a teacher. Yet in the end we must discover our own path, moment after moment. We must become our own guides and our own teachers. Through our honest inquiry and wholehearted attention, the dharma will be found right here within us.

Before one Western Buddhist monk returned to America, he spoke to an old English monk who had many times gone back and forth between Europe and his monastery in Asia. The first monk had been wondering how to integrate practice in a Western context, and so he asked for some advice. The old man said, "I have just one thing to tell you. If, as you are approaching the bus stop, you see that the bus is about to leave without you, don't panic. There will be another bus."

There can be no hurry to be in the moment. There is no rush to reassume our true nature. It takes moment-to-moment patience to integrate our practice and thus transform our lives. It takes moment-to-moment patience to cultivate and nourish the heart and the mind, to nurture the blossoming of our own true nature.

Awareness, sensitivity, courage, wisdom—they are not qualities that can be forced on anyone, nor are they remote ideals to be attained someday. They can only be awakened, and once awakened within us, they spring forth spontaneously in our words and deeds, awakening the same in all whom they touch. Their communicative and transforming power is irresistible because they are the deepest truth of our being.

J. K.

### EXERCISES

## Strengthening Mindfulness

1. *Daily sitting log.* Here is a way to strengthen daily practice and to see its cycles more clearly. For one month or two,

keep a small notebook at the place where you sit. Each day note down how long you sit. Then note down in one sentence the general qualities of the sitting such as "sleepy" or "restless and disturbed" or "calm and light" or "filled with many plans" or "easily centered on the breath," or whatever you notice. Then in another sentence or two note the general qualities of your day such as "happy" or "relaxed and spacious" or "overworked and tense" or "frustrated and anxious." At the end of a month or two, review your notes and be aware of the cycles in your daily sitting practice and how they may reflect and be connected to your daily life. Particularly become aware of areas where you may be stuck and those which call for greater mindfulness and acceptance.

2. *Reminders to pay attention: developing the habit of wakefulness.* This exercise lasts one month. At the beginning of each week choose a simple regular activity of your life that you usually do unconsciously, on automatic pilot. Resolve to make that particular activity a reminder, a place to wake up your mindfulness. For example, you might choose making tea, shaving, bathing, or perhaps the simple act of getting into the car. Resolve to pause for a couple of seconds before each time you begin the activity. Then do it with a gentle and full attention, as if it were the heart of a meditation retreat for you. As you go through the week, try to bring a careful mindfulness to that act each time it arises in your life. Even the simplest acts can be a powerful reminder and bring a sense of presence and grace. If you choose the opening of doors throughout the day, you can open each door as if the Buddha himself were to pass through with you. If you choose the act of making tea or coffee, you can do it as if it were a gracious Japanese tea ceremony. At the end of the week add another activity, until by the end of the month you have included four new areas of your life into daily mindfulness. Then, if you wish, continue this exercise for a

second and third month, bringing the power of attention into more and more of each day.

3. *Choosing a life of voluntary simplicity.* Do this exercise after a day or more of meditative sitting or after a day or more spent removed from civilization in nature. Sit and allow yourself to become calm and silent. Then, in a simple way, review your current life. Bring to mind each of several major areas, including your schedule, your finances and work, your relationships or family life, your home, your leisure activities, your possessions, your goals, and your spiritual life. As each area comes to mind, ask yourself the question: What would it be like to greatly simplify this area of my life? Continue to sit quietly and reflect, letting the images or answers arise for each area about which you ask. Then, after reflecting in this way, again bring to mind each area and ask a second question: If it became simpler, would I be happy?

The purpose of spiritual life is to discover freedom, to live in harmony with the world around us and our own true nature. To do so brings happiness and contentment. If any aspect of your life shows a need for simplification and if the way for this simplification shows itself to you, keep it in mind and begin the process of mindful change.

# GLOSSARY

abhidharma (Skt), abhidhamma (Pali): The Buddhist psychology, a detailed and systematic analysis of the mind and body. It is the third great division of the Pali canon.

access concentration: A level of concentration in which the mind stays rhythmically on the object. This level is in the neighborhood of full absorption (jhana) concentration and provides access to it. It is also the basis for deeper stages of insight.

anatta: Selflessness; insubstantiality. One of the three characteristics of all conditioned existence.

arhant: One who is fully liberated, having eradicated all mental defilements.

bodhi tree: The tree under which the Bodhisattva (Siddhartha Gotama) attained full enlightenment.

bodhisattava: A being striving for buddhahood; Siddhartha Gotama prior to his enlightenment under the bodhi tree.

brahma realm: The highest realm of existence, attained through the development of jhana (absorption) concentration.

dependent origination: One of the fundamental laws of Buddhist teaching; it describes in twelve links how ignorance conditions old age, disease, and death.

deva: A celestial being.

dharma (Skt), dhamma (Pali): Ultimate Truth; Reality; the Buddha's teachings revealing these truths, all mental and physical elements.

Eightfold Path: The Fourth Noble Truth of the Buddha's teaching; a description of the path that leads to liberation: right understanding, right aim, right speech, right action, right livelihood, right effort, right mindfulness, and right concentration.

Four Noble Truths: The basic teaching of the Buddha, explaining the truth of suffering, the causes of suffering, the end of suffering, and the path that leads to the end of suffering.

jhana: Meditative absorption, usually divided into eight stages of increasing concentration.

karma (Skt), kamma (Pali): The volition behind action, which has the power to produce favorable or unfavorable results, according to an impersonal, universal moral law.

karuna: Compassion.

Mara: The personification of forces antagonistic to enlightenment.

metta: Loving-kindness.

Middle Way: A description of the Buddha's teaching as being midway between the extremes of self-mortification and self-indulgence.

mudita: Sympathetic joy; happiness in the happiness of others.

nirvana (Skt), nibbana (Pali): The cessation of suffering; the unconditioned.

parami: "Perfections"; virtues necessary for the realization of enlightenment.

saddha (Pali): Faith; confidence.

samadhi: Concentration.

samsara: Beginningless round of rebirths.

sangha: Community of monks and nuns; community of ariyas (noble ones), those who have attained to one of the stages of enlightenment.

santati: Illusion of continuity.

skandha: Aggregate. What we call a "being" is a grouping of five aggregates: material elements, feeling, perception, volitions, and consciousness.

sutra (Skt), sutta (Pali): A discourse of the Buddha.

vipassana: Insight meditation; insight into the true nature of phenomena.

yogi: Someone who practices meditation.

# INDEX

abhidharma, and existence, 191–192; and Sariputra, 106; and skandhas, 153–154

acceptance, and arriving, 58, 63–67; and hindrances to meditation, 54; and karma, 154–156; and service, 210–214; and suffering, 125–134

Achaan Chaa: and dharma practice, 218, 221; and existence, 181; and sleepiness, 52–53

action, activity, and compassion, 131–134, 172–176; and dharma practice, 220, 229–234; and restraint, 112–122; and service, 199–214. *See also* karma

Ananda, 227

anger. *See* aversion

Angulimala, 155

apathy, indifference. *See* aversion

arhant, Mogallana and Sariputra, 105–106

arousing qualities, and enlightenment, 75–86; *see also* effort, energy; investigation; rapture; resistance to opening

attention, 13; *see also* mind, concentration of

Augustine, Saint, 81

aversion, and hindrance to meditation, 38–44, 45–47; and suffering, 125–128

awakening, 6. *See also* mindfulness

awareness, 215–234. *See also* body, experience, feelings, mental phenomena, mindfulness, truth

balance, and arriving, 63–64; and being, 86–87; and dharma practice, 216–234; and equanimity, 201; and hindrances to meditation, 44–56; and meditation, 22–24, 39–40; and mindfulness, 77–80; and restraint, 112–122; and spiritual faculties, 169–170

beauty, 224

Benoit, 188

bodhisattva, 202

body, and arriving, 57–61; awareness of, 6; and dharma practice, 187–198, 219–220; and enlightenment, 75–96; and mindfulness, 161–162; and opening, 18–20, and selflessness, 64–65; and suffering, 123–134

boredom. *See* aversion

breath, and arriving, 58–59; and meditation practice, 13, 21, 28, 30–37; and opening, 65

Buddha, def. 3, 83, 94; and Ananda, 227; and balance, 218; and change, 118, 149; and compassion, 132; and existence, 139, 190; and generosity, 10, 148; and hindrances, 38, 39–40;